UNDERGROUND ALIEN BIO LAB AT DULCE

THE BENNEWITZ UFO PAPERS

Timothy Green Beckley And Christa Tilton
With Sean Casteel, Dr. Michael E. Salla
Bruce Walton, Leslie Gunter

GLOBAL COMMUNICATIONS

UNDERGROUND ALIEN BIO LAB AT DULCE

The Bennewitz UFO Papers

Contributors:
Timothy Green Beckley, Christa Tilton, Sean Casteel, Jim McCampbell, Dr. Michael E. Salla, Leslie Gunter, Bruce Walton

ISBN 1-60611-061-6
EAN 978-1-60611-061-4

Science/New Age/Occult Technology

Timothy Green Beckley, Editor Director
Carol Rodriguez, Publisher's Assistant
Tim Swartz, Sean Casteel Assistant Editors

Free catalog from Global Communications
Box 753, New Brunswick, NJ 08903

Visit our website at:
www.conspiracyjournal.com

Contents

In Search of An Underground Alien Bio Lab Beneath Dulce A Possible "False Flag"

By Timothy Green Beckley

This is one of the strangest continuing sagas I have ever become involved in.

Since the 1970s strange and peculiar phenomena have become the norm around the town of Dulce, New Mexico, located in the Four Corners area of the United States. Situated on a Native American reservation and surrounded by cliffs, UFOs have been seen, animals have been found mutilated and reports of an underground base taken over by aliens have been consistent. There are even testimonies that aliens have gone amuck inside a huge subterranean facility previously controlled by U.S. secret forces and have set up a bubbling lab to create hybrid beings – half human, half alien.

The UFO Hunters show on the History Channel recently featured an entire episode on this series of events and a few days later George Noory and Coast to Coast AM plunged head first into trying to make sense out of the various accounts that have – pardon the expression -- surfaced.

And while it is difficult to pinpoint exactly when this macabre saga started to develop it does seem to date back to the time when an engineer named Paul Bennewitz felt he was being "called" to the area when what he assumed were ETs tried to communicate with him over a radio receiver. He had been "directed" to this area after observing UFOs over the Kirtland Air Force nuclear storage facility. Standing near some of the tall cliffs outside Dulce, Bennewitz took a series of photographs showing unidentified craft diving into the mountains through what he claimed were entrance ways that could be opened and closed. The ships themselves passed by so fast they could not be seen with the unaided eye. Somehow he knew where to aim his camera. He also supposedly managed to get a shot of a strange Bigfoot-like creature standing in a nearby clump of trees. The area around these mountains seemed to be alive with all sorts of paranormal activity.

In the early days of this activity, I do not believe the public was aware of what was supposedly going on in Dulce. The first inkling of the situation I got was in a telephone conversation with Wendelle Stevens, a UFO researcher known for investigating the more speculative aspects of the ET mystery. He just happened to mention while I had him on the phone that someone was in his home who had undergone combat with a group of big eyed grays at an underground military facility believed to be fully operative for some time underground just outside Dulce's town limits.

A while later, at a UFO and conspiracy conference I sponsored in Phoenix, I ran into a woman who had dug deeply into the Paul Bennewitz case as well as numerous animal mutilations in the vicinity. There were supposedly dozens of animals all cut up and the ranchers were more or less freaking out. Many of the mutilations were associated with strange balls of light and UFO-type phenomenon that would be seen on the nights when the animals were apparently being butchered.

Christa Tilton spent some time with Paul Bennewitz, who has since committed suicide after perhaps being pushed to do so by weird mental tampering with his life. During my first meeting with Christa I offered to purchase a self-published report that Christa had put together on the entire Bennewitz affair. I eventually published the report but never really pushed it and it kind of died on the vine as they say in publisher's lingo.

But the rumors continued to fly as more and more information – or disinformation -- became public knowledge. A claim was made of a last man standing war in which the aliens took over the lower levels at the Dulce base and set up containers where they could breed humans, turning them into hybrids. One military personnel said he managed to escape, but later "disappeared," while another individual, Phil Schneider, "mysteriously" committed suicide after he began speaking in public about his experiences at Dulce.

And in spite of those who discount some of the more speculative episodes, there have been – and this is a matter of public record – any number of unexplainable sightings of "saucers" in and around the town. Some of them were seen by the local Native Americans, others by no less a credible witness than the chief of police.

Some of the Native Americans equate the presence of UFOs with the appearance of their gods, but these appearances seemed a bit more negative. . .but not all of them! Paul Villa (whose book of seemingly authentic UFO photographs we just published) spoke of meeting advanced humanoid beings within a stone's throw of Dulce. His pictures are quite spectacular and the objects are shown to have landed on tripod extensions.

In March of 2009, veteran research Norio Hayakawa decided he wanted to get to the bottom of the mysterious happenings at Dulce. Was there really an alien base inside the cavernous walls surrounding the town? Or was perhaps something even more sinister taking place?

Norio decided to call a town hall meeting in Dulce itself. Feeling strongly that the city's board and the local Native American tribe would not be anxious for him to proceed with any plans for a mini-conference, he decided to go ahead and organize the event anyway.

As it turned out, not only did he receive no objections from the city council, but some members helped with promotion and offered to provide their own testimony on what they had seen or heard about.

This work is the culmination of a vast amount of research contributed by a number of respected individuals. But is this information valid, or are we being misdirected? Has a "False Flag" been sent aloft to cover up something even more bold? Each individual reading this work will have to decide on their own. Are extraterrestrials connected with the town of Dulce? Are the UFOs seen overhead and on the ground from outer space? Or are they holographic projections, perhaps by the Secret Government or New World Order forces? Is toxic dumping going on in the vicinity that is being kept secret from the general populace? At the end of this book you will be equipped to make a more informed decision.

Timothy Green Beckley,
MRUFO8@hotmail.com

**Before rumors of any underground activity around Dulce,
cattle were found mutilated throughout the area. UFOs were often seen in the
vicinity of the mutilations beaming down spotlights onto the animals
as depicted here by artist Carol Ann Rodriguez.**

CONFIDENTIAL REPORT FOR YOUR EYES ONLY

THE BENNEWITZ PAPERS

by
CHRISTA TILTON

THE
BENNEWITZ PAPERS

AUTHOR'S STATEMENT

This manuscript is a compilation of data, personal interviews, phone conversations and letter correspondence with Paul Bennewitz and others who knew him and were involved with him. Comments stated by the author and other parties were as accurate as possible. Many of us have to speculate on what really happened behind the scenes with Paul Bennewitz. Many of the actual participants in the 'Bennewitz Affair' refused interviews with the author except AFOSI Agent Richard Doty (Ret.) His correspondence by mail gave me much insight on how the counter-intelligence agents do their job. If it were not for Sgt. Clifford Stone who retired from the Army after 20 years, I would not have understood all the intimate details of what went on with Paul Bennewitz. Cliff was one man Paul befriended and trusted. It was insightful for both men and if it were not for that communication and friendship between the two parties, I would never have received parts of Paul Bennewitz's former manuscript. I must thank Clifford Stone for giving me permission in 1987 to use this material.

CHRISTA TILTON
P.O. BOX 906237
TULSA, OKLAHOMA
74112

SPECIAL ACKNOWLEDGEMENTS

Special appreciation to Martin Cannon for his fine art work and mind control paper, 'THE CONTROLLERS' from which he allowed me to quote from in the processing of this manuscript; Mr. Junichi Yaoi & Michi Nakamura of NIPPON TV Tokyo, Japan; Tom Adams & Gary Massey for allowing me to ride along with them to Dulce, New Mexico in 1987; Gabriel Valdez for his special tour and interest in the author's experiences; Rick Doty for his time and correspondence which helped answer so many of my inquiries; Cliff Stone for allowing me to print the two letters and parts of Paul's story and his special prospective in this case; Vicki Cooper & Don Ecker of UFO Magazine for all their contributions to research; August Roberts who long ago befriended me and believed in me; Len Stringfield & Jacques Vallee for their past correspondence and unique theories; John Grace and John Lear for their past correspondence; Bill Moore for just being Bill Moore; Dr. Leo Sprinkle for his continued effort to see 'the good' in all of this; Tomm Buzzetta for his expert research abilities and CIA documents on Dulce, New Mexico; and last but never least, Timothy Good for his inspiration, kindness and expertise in the field of ufology.

PERSONAL ACKNOWLEDGEMENT

To my new friend and research partner, Nicholas Redfern of Great Britain and to Anthony Dodd for giving me the encouragement to believe in myself. It is with great respect that I write this paper for you.

SUGGESTED READING

Clear Intent: The Government Cover-Up of the UFO Experience, Lawrence Fawcett and Barry Greenwood, Prentice-Hall, Englewood Cliffs, New Jersey, 1987.

Above Top Secret: The Worldwide UFO Cover-Up, Timothy Good, Sidgwick & Jackson London, England, 1987.

Alien Liaison: The Ultimate Secret, Timothy Good, Century, Random Century Ltd. 20 Vauxhall Bridge Road, London SW1V 2SA, 1991

UNDERGROUND ALIEN BIO LAB AT DULCE

Gary Massey, Berle Lewis, and
Christa Tilton in November of
1987. (Trip to Dulce, N.M.)
* Berle Lewis was known for the
mutilation of Lady, better known
as 'Snippy', his horse. The mutilation occured September 8, 67.
Photo credit-Tom Adams

Junichi Yaoi-Japanese film
Producer who the author has
worked with on two occasions
involving research on Paul
Bennewitz. Photo credit-
Christa Tilton

UNDERGROUND ALIEN BIO LAB AT DULCE

SPECIAL EDITION-MYRNA HANSEN
CONTACTS AUTHOR AFTER
GOING UNDERGROUND 12 YEARS AGO

No one was more surprised than I when I returned home one evening and
heard a woman say, "This is Myrna Hansen. Could you please contact me?"

I was in a state of shock because I had been under the impression she
had disappeared. Then I heard a rumor that she was no longer living.
So you can imagine the happiness I felt when I heard her voice. So,
I immediately contacted her.

Myrna is very much alive and well and I have promised to keep her whereabouts
secret to protect her and her son from some of the UFO vulture fanatics out
there in the world. I found her to be very kind and compassionate and was
very impressed by her demeanor over the telephone.

At first Myrna thought that everyone had forgotten about her earlier encounters
since it has been so many years she has discussed them. She was not happy to
find herself in the pages of a UFO magazine and several books. I explained
why I wrote about her and when I told her about my experiences she then understood. She was shocked at the correlations between each of our experiences.

Unfortunately, since I was unaware of what actually transpired between Paul
Bennewitz and Myrna and APRO I quoted from her regression transcripts as I
felt they were valid. Myrna expressed her disappointment with the way her
abduction case was handled and told me that what was in the original transcripts was only half the story. I was getting excited at this point.

She told me of other strange incidents that happened which later surfaced
and expressed an interest in possibly meeting me to discuss and hear the
whole story. She insinuated that I hardly knew all of what transpired that
one night in which she and her son will never forget. She expressed concern
in once again going public after so many years. I did not want to push her
into doing anything that would make her feel uncomfortable so I decided to
leave her to her thoughts and give her some time to think about it.

We have spoken about doing a manuscript of both our experiences since they
are so much alike, but I encouraged her to maybe do something on her own.
Myrna has lived a normal life since her abduction and has a deep faith in
God. As a believer myself, I felt even closer to her.

All she would comment on about Paul Bennewitz is that long ago he sent her
a copy of a manuscript he had written. She keeps in touch with him only
on occasion, but insists she is probably the only person who truly knows
what Paul went through. I believe she is right.

All many of us have done is speculate on what could or couldn't have happened
to Paul. We think we know, we hope we have come close to some semblance of
the truth but in reality only Paul and Myrna, Rick Doty, Bill Moore and Jaime
Shandera know what really happened to Paul. We are going to be waiting for
Bill, Rick and Jaime's 'SPECIAL REPORT' to hear their side of the story.

We want to thank Myrna Hansen for giving us this much of herself. She is to
be commended and we hope to hear from her very soon.

The Author

The Albuquerque Tribune

Vol 61, No. 20   Albuquerque, New Mexico, Friday, April 8, 1983   or Pages in Four Sections

UFOs: U.S. reports tell of five sightings in 1980 over Kirtland; city man claims alien contact

By SUSIE GRAN
Tribune Assistant City Editor

Just released government reports document five sightings of unidentified flying objects during August 1980 over Kirtland Air Force Base.

The mysterious encounters, as described in Air Force reports and revealed through the Freedom of Information Act, were:

• On Aug. 8, "three security policemen... on duty inside the Manzano Weapons Storage Area sighted an unidentified light in the air that traveled north to south over the Coyote Canyon area of the Department of Defense Restricted Test Range on KAFB," the government reported.

The light traveled at high speed and stopped suddenly in the sky over Coyote Canyon and eventually landed in the canyon, according to the security policemen, who then witnessed it "take off and leave proceeding straight up at a high speed and disappear."

• The next day, Aug. 9 a security guard at Sandia Laboratories on the base observed a bright light near the ground behind a building in Coyote Canyon. As he drove nearer, he saw a round, disk-shaped object and tried to radio for help. But his radio would not work.

The guard, who did not want his name divulged for fear of harassment, then walked up to the object armed with a shotgun. Suddenly, it took off, going straight up at high speed.

The guard, a former Army helicopter mechanic, stated that the UFO was not a helicopter.

• The following day, Aug. 10, a New Mexico state policeman saw a flying object land in the Manzano Mountains between Belen and Albuquerque. When he reported the sighting to the Kirtland command post, he was told by the public relations office that the Air Force did not investigate sightings unless they occurred on an air base.

• Three days later, Aug. 13, radar equipment at Kirtland and the Albuquerque Airport experienced a total five-hour blackout from an "unknown cause." An Air Force report concluded that "the presence of hostile intelligence jamming cannot be ruled out," but went on to say "no evidence would suggest this."

• Nine days later, on Aug. 22, three other security guards observed the same aerial phenomenon described by the first three guards two weeks earlier.

"Again the object landed in Coyote Canyon. They did not see the object take off," the report said.

• The final Kirtland document is dated Oct. 28, 1980. In it, Air Force scientific advisor Jerry Miller concluded that a film taken by Four Hills resident Paul Bennewitz "clearly shows... some type of unidentified aerial objects" at Kirtland.

Miller is a former investigator for Project Bluebook, the Air Force's massive investigations of UFOs that ended in 1969.

Bennewitz, president of a local electronics firm, lives adjacent to the northern boundary of Manzano Base.

He said it was on Feb. 2, 1980, that he saw four "saucer or hat-shaped objects lined up behind the outside fence" of the Manzano area.

"A black spot and big blue halo appeared, establishing their force field. There was a flash under each one as they jumped off the ground in sync 300-400 feet, turned right and were gone to the south," he recalled.

He filmed the spectacle from about 2,500 yards away.

Bennewitz, according to the official Air Force report written months later, produced still photographs and 2,600 feet of 8mm motion picture film "depicting unidentified aerial objects flying over and around Manzano Weapons Storage Area and Coyote Canyon Test Area."

But investigator Miller reported only that "no conclusions could be made whether these objects pose a threat to Manzano-Coyote Canyon areas."

On Nov. 19, Bennewitz was told that the Air Force would not investigate the objects and "was not in a position to evaluate the information and photographs he has collected."

However, the sightings reportedly caught the interest of former New Mexico Sen. Harrison Schmitt, who inquired why the Air Force refused to investigate, the report said.

Within the past year or so, Bennewitz, who is convinced the UFOs are alien ships, has called Kirtland to again request an investigation, said George Pearce, Kirtland public affairs officer.

"He said he was in contact with alien beings through his computer and wanted us to investigate," Pearce said.

"I told him we don't investigate those things since Project Bluebook ended in 1969 after 22 years of investigation. Of course, he wasn't pleased with the answer."

Col. John Aday, chief of public affairs at Kirtland, Project Bluebook concluded that UFOs are no threat to national defense.

He said he has "no idea" what the 1980 sightings could have been. "I could conjecture all day about what might have been going on out there, but I won't."

He said when the Air Force was investigating UFOs, it was often determined that they were weather balloons or the like.

"I'm not saying that what Bennewitz saw or what the security police saw was anything like that, but because of the record of our investigations, it seems likely they were nothing dangerous to our national defense."

Bennewitz earlier this week in Albuquerque briefed a group of UFO enthusiasts on his personal three-year investigation into alien activities in New Mexico. He said he plans to put his observations into a book.

Among his conclusions are that there is an alien base inside an isolated mesa near Dulce, and that the aliens intend to enslave the earth.

He said his study includes a statement taken from a New Mexico woman who was taken hostage near Cimarron by the aliens after she saw them mutilate a calf.

Bennewitz said he has seen the aliens on a video screen, and he described them as green and about 4 feet tall and "strong little bastards."

He told those gathered for the UFO briefing session that cattle mutilations are the aliens' source of supplies needed to build humanoids through gene splicing. They take the organs and blood from the animals while they are still alive in order to maintain a tremendous supply of DNA — the carrier of the genetic code — for this purpose, he said.

The Kirtland sightings in 1980 were described in reports sent to the Mutual UFO Network, a Texas-based UFO internation study group, by the Department of the Air Force in December 1982.

MUFON's effort to gather documents has been a tough, uphill battle with countless arms of government and military agencies.

"We call it our cosmic Watergate," Andrus said.

5

UNDERGROUND ALIEN BIO LAB AT DULCE

There are not too many people in UFO circles today who haven't heard the name Paul Bennewitz. Many researchers, investigators and just curious people have flocked to Albuquerque, New Mexico in hopes of just getting a "few minutes" to spend with the eccentric gentleman. Some are lucky enough to be granted indepth interviews, while others are simply turned away at his door.

There are many stories and theories as to what Paul Bennewitz really knew and experienced. The whole truth may never be known. It reminds me of a black widow spider, stalking her prey like the U.S. government and Air Force encompassed Paul, surrounded him and kept watch on him for many years. All because of the subject of UFOS. But, I seem to be confused...didn't the Air Force dump the subject a long time ago because they just could not find any evidence that we were under any kind of threat from these unknown objects. If they came to that conclusion then my friends, the government must know more than what they are telling us, the American public.

As you will see throughout this whole intricate story, a pattern emerged and Paul Bennewitz became a very important target and a hero in my eyes. All we ask is to be told what really happened to this scientist and UFO researcher and so I will allow you, the curious ones alone to draw your own conclusions. I believe it will teach us all a lesson in trust and also an insight into the inhumane treatment some of our UFO researchers endure. Maybe all we can learn is strength and hope and praise Mr. Paul Bennewitz for his heroic efforts.

It is difficult to pinpoint just exactly where Paul's story begins so I will just state that Paul was a UFO Field Investigator for APRO which was a UFO organization headed by the late Jim and Coral Lorenzen in Tucson. It seems that in or around 1979 and 1980 Paul would immerse himself in several events that would forever change his life.

Paul Bennewitz was at that time the President of his own company, Thunder Scientific Corporation which sits just right of the gate to Kirtland Air Force Base. Apparently for almost two years Paul had been monitoring and recording activity seen in the skies over a large area around the Manzano Test Range near Kirtland Air Force Base. Paul obtained on film many UFOS flying over the Manzano Weapons Storage Area and the Coyote Canyon Test Area where nuclear materials are supposedly stored. Paul, immediately concerned, notified Kirtland Air Force Base and made a report to then a Major Ernest Edwards who was commander at the time for this restricted area.

Paul was invited to Kirtland to present his evidence to a number of individuals at which time he produced a film and photographs of UFOS taken by him over the past 15 months. But, Paul made another major error; he claimed also to have proof that he was in contact with the aliens flying these craft over Kirtland. (See OSI Form Exhibit #1) Now that interested Kirtland Air Force Base, but why? They had already made it clear that there is no extraterrestrial life visiting our planet today. But, they were intensely interested in finding out more.

6

OSI FORM # 1- EXHIBIT NUMBER ONE

MULT. JRPOSE INTERNAL OSI FORM
(Complete only applicable items)

TO	DO NO.(S)		SUBJECT	FILE NO.
	DET NO.(S)		KIRTLAND AFB, NM, 8 Aug - 3 Sep 80,	8O17D93-0/29
	HEADQUARTERS IVOS		Alleged Sightings of Unidentified Aerial	TRANSMITTAL DATE
FROM	DO NO.		Lights In Restricted Test Range	26 Nov 80
	DET NO.			SUSPENSE DATE
	HEADQUARTERS			

REFERENCE

AFOSI Form 96, 28 Oct 80, Same Title

MINOR DISCREPANCIES NOTED ARE LISTED BELOW.	
YOUR DISTRICT IS DESIGNATED OFFICE OF ORIGIN.	
ATTACHED REQUIRES INVESTIGATION IN YOUR AREA.	
DETERMINE SUBJECTS ACCESS TO CLASSIFIED INFORMATION AS REQUIRED BY DSM 124-1, PARA 2-6-2.	
FORWARD RESULTS DIRECTLY TO OFFICE OF ORIGIN, OR TO:	
NO FURTHER INVESTIGATION CONTEMPLATED.	
OUR FILES REFLECT PRIOR INVESTIGATION BY _____, DTD _____, FILE _____	
REPORT OF PRIOR INVESTIGATION/SUMMARY ATTACHED.	
INVESTIGATION CONTINUING AND YOU WILL BE FURNISHED FURTHER REPORTS.	
DISCONTINUE INVESTIGATION. FORWARD RESULTS OF ANY INVESTIGATION ACCOMPLISHED.	
DISCREPANCIES BETWEEN LEAD REQUEST AND DEVELOPED INFORMATION ARE SET FORTH.	
REPORT OF COMMAND ACTION HAS NOT BEEN RECEIVED.	
REQUEST STATUS OF THIS MATTER AND/OR DATE REPORT MAY BE EXPECTED.	
REFER ATTACHED TO INTERESTED COMMANDER FOR INFORMATION OR ACTION IF NOT PREVIOUSLY REPORTED.	
CHECK WORLD-WIDE LOCATOR FOR BELOW LISTED PERSON OR SUBJECT.	
ATTACHED IS FORWARDED FOR INFORMATION AND/OR ACTION.	
UPON REMOVAL OF ATTACHMENT(S) _____ THE CLASSIFICATION ON THIS CORRESPONDENCE WILL	

☐ RETAINED. ☐ DOWNGRADED TO _____ ☐ CANCELED. ☐ MARKED "FOR OFFICIAL USE ONLY."

REMARKS

1. On 10 Nov 80, a meeting took place in 1606 ABW/CC Conference Room attended by the following individuals: BGen WILLIAM BROOKSHER, AFOSP/CC, COL JACK W. SHEPPARD 1606 ABW/CC, COL THOMAS SIMMONS 1606 ABW/CV, COL CRES BACA, 1606 SPGp/CC, COL FRANK M. HUEY, AFOSI Dist 17/CC, LTC JOE R. LAMPORT, 1606 ABW/SJ, MAJ THOMAS A. CSEH, AFOSI Det 1700/CC, Dr. LEHMAN, Director, AFWL, ED BREEN, AFWL Instrumentations Specialist and Dr. PAUL F. BENNEWITZ, President Thunder Scientific Laboratory, Albuquerque. Dr. BENNEWITZ presented film and photographs of alleged unidentified Aerial Objects photographed over KAFB, NM during the last 15 months. Dr. BENNEWITZ also related he had documented proof that he was in contact with the aliens flying the objects. At the conclusion of the presentation, Dr. BENNEWITZ expressed an interest in obtaining financial assistance from the USAF in furthering his investigation regarding these objects. DR. LEHMAN advised DR. BENNEWITZ to request a USAF grant for research. DR. LEHMAN advised DR. BENNEWITZ he would assist him in filling out the proper documents.

2. On 17 Nov 80, SA RICHARD C. DOTY, advised DR. BENNEWITZ that AFOSI would not become involved in the investigation of these objects. DR. BENNEWITZ was advised

COPIES TO	ATTACHMENTS	FILE STAMP AND/OR OTHER
Dist 17/IVO, File		8017D93-0/29 x 2
NAME-GRADE-TITLE-SIGNATURE		
THOMAS A. CSEH, Major, USAF		
Commander		
Base Investigative Detachment	FOR OFFICIAL USE ONLY	

AFOSI FORM 96 REPLACES OSI FORM 96 JUN 71 WHICH WILL BE USED

UNDERGROUND ALIEN BIO LAB AT DULCE

that AFOSI was not in a position to evaluate the information and photographs he has collected, to date or technically investigate such matters.

3. On 26 Nov 80, SA DOTY received a phone call from an individual who identified himself as U.S. Senator HARRISON SCHMIDT, of New Mexico. SEN SCHMIDT inquired about AFOSI'S role in investigating the aerial phenomena reported by Dr. BENNEWITZ. SA DOTY advised SEN SCHMIDT that AFOSI was not investigating the phenomena. SA DOTY then politely referred SEN SCHMIDT to AFOSI Dist 17/CC. SEN SCHMIDT declined to speak with 17/CC and informed SA DOTY he would request that SAF look into the matter and determine what USAF agency should investigate the phenomena.

4. It should be noted that DR. BENNEWITZ has had a number of conversations with SEN SCHMIDT during the last few months regarding BENNEWITZ'S private research. SEN SCHMIDT has made telephone calls to BGEN BROOKSHER, AFOSP/CC regarding the matter since Security Police are responsible for the security of Manzano Storage Area.

END OF EXHIBIT FORM # 1

THUNDER SCIENTIFIC CORPORATION LOCATED RIGHT AT THE GATE OF KIRTLAND AFB

Photo-Christa Tilton

KIRTLAND AFB AERIAL VIEW

8

UNDERGROUND ALIEN BIO LAB AT DULCE

At this particular meeting Paul met with a young Special Agent by the name of Richard C. Doty. Doty intimated to Paul that the AFOSI (the Air Force Office of Special Investigations) would not be involved in the investigation of these unidentified objects. In essence, Doty told Paul that the Air Force does not investigate UFOS.

This meeting with Richard Doty took place on November 10, 1980. Just a few months prior to this meeting Kirtland Air Force was visited by an unusual object that had been reported by a Sandia Security Guard.

Back to the November meeting first, apparently disgusted with the Air Force and their lack of interest, Paul contacted Senator Harrison Schmidt about the incident and knowing Paul and his UFO research was of great importance to Paul, he called Richard Doty requesting that the Air Force please look into this sensitive matter and see which agency or agencies should investigate.

On August 8, 1980, three security policemen assigned to duty at the Manzano Weapons area sighted the same UFO that was reported by a Sandia Security guard. The object was a bright light hovering near the Storage Area. He radioed that the object was disk-shaped. He tried to radio for back-up, but his radio suddenly was dead. May I clear up one error in my story here, the Sandia guard that he observed this disk-shaped object on August 9, 1980. Then on August 10, 1989 a New Mexico State Policeman sighted another object landing in the Manzano's. (See OSI Form #2-Exhibit Two)

All of these men stated flatly that it could not have been a helicopter. Apparently the object performed some pretty sensational aerial maneuvers which had to exclude any of our Earthly air craft.

Again this report was taken by a one Richard C. Doty who insinuated in the November meeting with Paul Bennewitz and other officers and to then Senator Harrison Schmidt that the Air Force was not in a position to investigate such objects.

This statement alone shows how wishy-washy our Air Force is with the subject of UFOS. Why wouldn't they hear Paul out in November after viewing his film and photos when all the time they were aware that unknown objects were flying all around our nuclear storage area. This seems to me to be important enough to ruffle someone's feathers!

On August 13, 1980 all hell broke loose at Kirtland Air Force Base. Coming from the area around Coyote Canyon the Air Force concluded that Radar Approach Control equipment and scanner radar was rendered inoperative. There was a total blackout including Albuquerque Airport which was in effect between 1630 hours to 2215 hours. We are talking several hours of frantic searching by the Air Force to determine where the jamming frquency was coming from. They concluded that the presence of hostile jamming cannot be ruled out. They never found the source of the problem. (See OSI Form #3- Exhibit Three)

Determined not to give up, Paul Bennewitz began contacting many government sources telling them of his plight. Some probably wanted to be of some help but felt the sensitivity of the subject could cause problems of their own. But soon after, Paul suddenly became the object of an AFOSI Congressional Inquiry. Date: July 30, 1981.

9

UNDERGROUND ALIEN BIO LAB AT DULCE

COMPLAINT FORM		Hq 1VOS

ADMINISTRATIVE DATA

TITLE	DATE	TIME
KIRTLAND AFB, NM, 8 Aug - 3 Sep 80, Alleged Sigthings of Unidentified Aerial Lights in Restricted Test Range.	2 - 9 Sept 80	1200

PLACE

AFOSI Det 1700, Kirtland AFB, NM

HOW RECEIVED

X	IN PERSON	TELEPHONICALLY		IN WRITING

SOURCE AND EVALUATION

MAJOR ERNEST E. EDWARDS

RESIDENCE OR BUSINESS ADDRESS	PHONE
Commander, 1608 SPS, Manzano Kirtland AFB, NM	4-7516

CR 44 APPLIES

SUMMARY OF INFORMATION

REMARKS

1. On 2 Sept 80, SOURCE related on 8 Aug 80, three Security Policemen assigned to 1608 SPS, KAFB, NM, on duty inside the Manzano Weapons Storage Area sighted an unidentified light in the air that traveled from North to South over the Coyote Canyon area of the Department of Defense Restricted Test Range on KAFB, NM. The Security Policemen identified as: SSGT STEPHEN FERENZ, Area Supervisor, AIC MARTIN W. RIST and AMN ANTHONY D. FRAZIER, were later interviewed separately by SOURCE and all three related the same statement; At approximately 2350hrs., while on duty in Charlie Sector, East Side of Manzano, the three observed a very bright light in the sky approximately 3 miles North-North East of their position. The light traveled with great speed and stopped suddenly in the sky over Coyote Canyon. The three first thought the object was a helicopter, however, after observing the strange aerial maneuvers (stop and go), they felt a helicopter couldn't have performed such skills. The light landed in the Coyote Canyon area. Sometime later, three witnessed the light take off and leave proceeding straight up at a hight speed and disappear.

2. Central Security Control (CSC) inside Manzano, contacted Sandia Security, who conducts frequent building checks on two alarmed structures in the area. They advised that a patrol was already in the area and would investigate.

3. On 11 Aug 80, RUSS CURTIS, Sandia Security, advised that on 9 Aug 80, a Sandia Security Guard, (who wishes his name not be divulged for fear of harassment), related the following: At approximately 0020hrs., he was driving East on the Coyote Canyon access road on a routine building check of an alarmed structure . As he approached the structure he observed a bright light near the ground behind the structure. He also observed an object he first thought was a helicopter. But after driving closer, he observed a round disk shaped object. He attempted to radio for a back up patrol but his radio would not work. As he approached the object on foot armed with a shotgun, the object took off in a vertical direction at a high rate of speed. The guard was a former helicopter mechanic in the U.S. Army and stated the object he observed was not a helicopter.

4. SOURCE advised on 22 Aug 80, three other security policemen observed the same

DATE FORWARDED HQ AFOSI		AFOSI FORM 66 ATTACHED ☐ YES ☐ NO
Hq 1VOS 10 Aug 80		

DATE	TYPED OR PRINTED NAME OF SPECIAL AGENT	SIGNATURE
9 Sept 80	RICHARD C. DOTY, SA	Richard C. Doty

DISTRICT FILE NO.	DCII RESULTS
8017 R 93-0/29	☐ NEGATIVE ☐ POSITIVE (See Attached)

AFOSI FORM 1 PREVIOUS EDITION WILL BE USED

CONTINUED FROM COMPLAL FORM 1, DTD 9 Sept 80

aerial phenomena described by the first three. Again the object landed in Coyote Canyon. They did not see the object take off.

5. Coyote Canyon is part of a large   restricted test range used by the Air Force Weapons Laboratory, Sandia Laboratories, Defense Nuclear Agency and the Department of Energy. The range was formerly patrolled by Sandia Security, however, they only conduct building checks there now.

6. On 10 Aug 80, a New Mexico State Patrolman sighted an aerial object land in the Manzano's between Belen and Albuquerque, NM. The Patrolman reported the sighting to the Kirtland AFB Command Post, who later referred the patrolman to the AFOSI Dist 17. AFOSI Dist 17 advised the patrolman to make a report through his own agency. On 11 Aug 80, the Kirtland Public Information office advised the patrolman the USAF no longer investigates such sightings unless they occured on an USAF base.

7. WRITER contacted all the agencies who utilized the test range and it was learned no aerial tests are conducted in the Coyote Canyon area. Only ground tests are conducted.

8. On 8 Sept 80, WRITER learned from Sandia Security that another Security Guard observed a object land near an alarmed structure sometime during the first week of August, but did not report it until just recently for fear of harassment.

9. The two alarmed structures located within the area contains HQ CR 44 material.

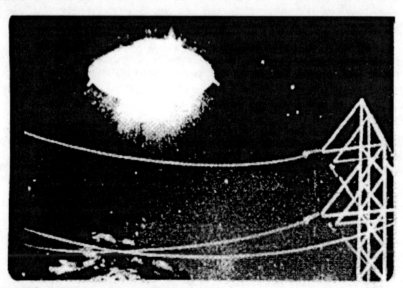

An example of what the security guards at Kirtland AFB may have seen in the evening hours.
  Photo credit-August Roberts

UNDERGROUND ALIEN BIO LAB AT DULCE

EXHIBIT NUMBER THREE

COMPLAINT FORM

ADMINISTRATIVE DATA

	DATE 14 Aug 80	TIME 0730

KIRTLAND AFB, NM, 13 Aug 80, Possible
Hostile Intelligence Intercept Incident,
Frequency Jamming.

PLACE
AFOSI District 17, BID, Kirtland AFB, NM

HOW RECEIVED

X	IN PERSON		TELEPHONICALLY		IN WRITING

SOURCE AND EVALUATION

1960th Communication Officer

RESIDENCE OR BUSINESS ADDRESS	PHONE
1960 COMMSq	4-5678
KAFB, NM	

CR _____ APPLIES

SUMMARY OF INFORMATION

REMARKS

1. On 13 Aug 80, 1960 COMMSq Maintenance Officer reported Radar Approach Control equipment and scanner radar inoperative due to high frequency jamming from an unknown cause. Total blackout of entire radar approach system to include Albuquerque Airport was in effect between 1630-2215hrs. Radar Approach Control back up systems also were inoperative.

2. On 13 Aug 80, Defense Nuclear Agency Radio Frequency Monitors determined, by vector analysis, the interference was being sent from an area (V-90 degrees or due East) on DAF Map coordinates E-28.6. The area was located NW of Coyote Canyon Test area. It was first thought that Sandia Laboratory, which utilizes the test range was responsible. However, after a careful check, it was later determined that no tests were being conducted in the canyon area. Department of Energy, Air Force Weapons Laboratory and DNA were contacted but assured that their agencies were not responsible.

3. On 13 Aug 80, Base Security Police conducted a physical check of the area but because of the mountainous terrain, a thorough check could not be completed at that time. A later foot search failed to disclosed anything that could have caused the interference.

4. On 13 Aug 80, at 2210hrs., all radar equipment returned to normal operation without further incident.

5. CONCLUSION: The presence of hostile intelligence jamming cannot be ruled out. Although no evidence would suggest this, the method has been used in the past. Communication maintenance specialists cannot explain how such interference could cause the radar equipment to become totally inoperative. Neither could they suggest the type or range of the interference signal. DNA frequency monitors reported the interference beam was wide spread and a type unknown to their electronical equipment. Further check of the area was being conducted by Technical Services, AFOSI.

6. High command interest item. Briefings requested IAW AFOSIR 124-4 be completed at HQ AFOSI/IVOE. HQ CR 44 and 51 items.

DATE FORWARDED HQ AFOSI

AFOSI FORM 61 ATTACHED ☐ YES ☐ NO

ALBUQUERQUE JOURNAL Saturday, April 9, 1983 A-5

Government Reports: Describe UFO Sightings at KAFB in '80

From United Press International
And Journal Staff Reports

SEGUIN, Texas — Writer Andrus never thought very much about alien beings or unexplained lights in the sky until he saw four dull silver objects speeding high over the Arizona desert almost 23 years ago.

Since then Andrus has compiled reams of material on UFOs and convened part of his Seguin home into the headquarters of MUFON — The Mutual UFO Network — which claims 1,100 members in almost every country in the world.

MUFON membership is by invitation because "that's the only way to keep the crackpots out," said Andrus, who is convinced that earth is the subject of curious and watchful extraterrestrial eyes.

Much of the material collected was found in government files procured through the Freedom of Information Act, and many of the UFO sightings referred to New Mexico, around Kirtland Air Force Base in Albuquerque.

According to a a series of reports from Kirtland Air Force Base, radar approach control equipment and weather radar at Kirtland and the Albuquerque Airport experienced a "loud blacker" from "an unknown cause" for more than five hours on Aug. 13, 1980.

The report concluded that "the presence of hostile intelligence jamming cannot be ruled out," but went on to say, "no evidence would suggest this (was the cause)."

In a five days earlier, on Aug. 4, a separate report revealed that "three security policemen ... on duty inside the Manzano Weapons Storage Area sighted an unidentified light in the air that traveled north to south over the Coyote Canyon area of the Department of Defense Restricted Test Range on KAFB, N.M."

The report said the light traveled at high speed and stopped suddenly in the sky over Coyote Canyon. The ... it eventually landed in the canyon, according to the security policemen, who then prepared to "take off and leave immediate straight up at a high speed and disappear."

The next day, Aug. 9, a security guard at the Sandia Laboratories near Kirtland observed a bright light near the ground behind a building in Coyote Canyon. As he

drove near the object, according to the report, he observed a round, disk-shaped object.

The guard attempted to radio for a second unit, but the radio would not work. The guard, who did not want his named divulged for fear of harassment, then approached the object on foot armed with a shotgun. But the object took off in a vertical direction at high speed.

The guard, a former Army helicopter mechanic, stated that the object he observed was not a helicopter.

On Aug. 22, according to the Air Force report, three other security guards observed the same aerial phenomenon described by the first three guards on Aug. 8.

"Again the object landed in Coyote Canyon. They did not see the object take off," the report said.

Coyote Canyon is part of a large restricted area used by the Air Force Weapons Laboratory, Sandia Labs and the Defense Nuclear Agency of the Department of Defense.

Andrus accuses federal authorities of being hypocritical in their treatment of civilian UFO sightings.

"developing unidentified aerial objects flying over and around Manzano Weapons Storage Area and Coyote Test Area."

But Miller reported only that "no conclusion could be made whether these objects pose a threat to Manzano-Coyote Canyon area."

On Nov. 19, Bennewitz was told that the Air Force would not become involved in the investigation of the objects and "was not in a position to evaluate the information and photographs he has collected.

"There were four of them and they were about 300 yards from the Manzano weapons storage area and about 1,500 yards from my home. They were just sitting on the ground and all four would simultaneously pulsate with a light about every 15 minutes.

"I began watching them about 11 p.m., and about 1:15 a.m., a blue-white light intermittently flared up from underneath them. Then, they suddenly flew off in formation and at a rapid speed that I'd estimate at 2,000 mph. They made a right-angle turn and went south.

put the weapons storage mountains, and disappeared from view."

Bennewitz, after photographing and filming the occurrences, reported it to Maj. Ernest Edwards, then the commander in charge of the Manzano Security Force, he said. Bennewitz claimed that he subsequently gave two top-level briefings to military officials, but it wasn't until the release of documents through the Freedom of Information Act that he learned the information had been passed on, though some of it inaccurately, to other government officials in Washington.

"Officials from the National Security Agency told Edwards they had somebody working on it and that 'don't call me, we'll call you.'"

However, the sightings reportedly piqued the interest of former New Mexico Sen. Harrison Schmitt, who inquired why the Air Force refused to investigate, the report said.

Bennewitz said he has since discovered the government is aware the objects are in fact extraterrestrial and is currently studying them under a project codenamed "Aquarius."

Mutilated cow seen by author near Kingman, Arizona. May,91. The rectal area had been cored out, and it looked as though the cow's wounds had been cauterized. Part of the tongue was missing and one eyeball had been removed. No blood seen around wounds.

UNDERGROUND ALIEN BIO LAB AT DULCE

It was in July of 1981 when the AFOSI conducted this Congressional Inquiry on Paul Bennewitz because now Senator Peter Dominici was seriously interested in hearing about Paul's findings and so he asked if the AFOSI had ever conducted a formal investigation of Paul Bennewitz? Senator Dominici's aide was told by the Air Force that there had been no investigation whatsoever. (See OSI Form #4 - Exhibit Four)

Thinking that would be the end of the story Paul continued on with his private research with APRO. In early 1980 Paul came across a most unusual case in which a woman and her son were abducted near Cimarron, New Mexico and witnessed a calf, being taken aboard the UFO crafts. What was so unusual and ter- rifying about this case was the mutilation of the calf was witnessed by the mother and her son. To date, I don't believe I have ever heard of another situation in which abductees witnessed the actual mutilation of cows.

For those of you who aren't familiar with the case of Myrna Hansen and her son Shawn, I would like to quote from some of the actual hypnosis sessions that were held at the home of Paul Bennewitz. [1] I will summarize most of the transcript but I feel it says so much more to the reader if they can actually live through some of the trauma Myrna and her son experienced that evening.

I also believe that it was this particular case that at this time two separate government agencies became intimately involved in monitoring all of Paul Bennewitz's activities. Already considered a possible threat to Kirtland intelligence, the story of Myrna Hansen was of such importance that I could understand why a special investigation was covertly arranged to try and es- tablish just exactly what Paul knew, and if he indeed was truly communicating through his computer terminal with extraterrestrials.

Referring to a letter I received from Richard Doty not too long ago he stated that the information Paul received through his computer was never of interest or analyzed by their agency of the Air Force. [2] He also told me that Paul was definitely on to something though and so another government agency stepped in and it was then that this other agency asked the OSI to continue investigating. The statement that shook me up was that Doty told me Paul never really new the full extent of what he had wondered onto and so to protect a vital gov- ernment operation, Paul was fed disinformation! Back to that later as I want to continue on with what happened to Myrna Hansen and her son.

The regressions and investigation began at Paul Bennewitz' home In Albuquerque.

Outside view of Paul's home

UNDERGROUND ALIEN BIO LAB AT DULCE

OSI FORM # 4 - EXHIBIT NUMBER FOUR

IN REPLY TO	AFOSI COMMUNICATION	DATE OF TRANSMITTAL 30 July 1981
TO: AFOSI/CC		SUBJECT Dr. PAUL FREDRICK BENNEWITZ Congressional Inquiry
FROM: AFOSI District 17/CC Kirtland AFB, NM 87117		

REFERENCE
8017D93-0/29

ITEMS CHECKED ARE APPLICABLE TO ABOVE SUBJECT

☐	INVESTIGATION HAS BEEN INITIATED AND REPORTS WILL BE FORWARDED AS SOON AS POSSIBLE.
	THIS MATTER IS ☐ PENDING ☐ CLOSED.
	REQUEST REPORT OF ACTION TAKEN (AFR 124-4).
	NOTE RESTRICTIVE LEGENDS ON FRONT OF THE ATTACHMENT(S)
	REQUEST INSTRUCTIONS AS TO DISPOSITION OF EVIDENCE LISTED BELOW.
	ATTACHED IS AN INTELLIGENCE INFORMATION REPORT (IIR) TRANSMITTED ELECTRICALLY IN THE INTERESTS OF TIMELINESS. NUMERICAL DESIGNATORS IN THE IIR ARE AS FOLLOWS: 1. COUNTRY; 2. REPORT NUMBER; 3. TITLE; 4. PROJECT NUMBER; 5. DATE OF INFORMATION; 6. DATE OF REPORT; 7. DATE AND PLACE OF ACQUISITION; 8. REFERENCES; 9. ASSESSMENT; 10. ORIGINATOR; 11. REQUEST EVALUATION; 12. PREPARING OFFICER; 13. APPROVING AUTHORITY; 14. SOURCE.
	ATTACHED IS AN INFORMATION COLLECTION REPORT (ICR) WHICH CONTAINS INFORMATION CONCERNING AN INDIVIDUAL UNDER YOUR COMMAND. THE ICR IS FURNISHED FOR YOUR INFORMATION ONLY AND IT DOES NOT CONSTITUTE A FORMAL OR COMPLETE INVESTIGATION OF THE INDIVIDUAL. IF A FORMAL INVESTIGATION IS WARRANTED, IT SHOULD BE REQUESTED IN ACCORDANCE WITH AFR 124-4.
	THE ATTACHED REPORT HAS BEEN LOANED TO THE USAF BY ANOTHER AGENCY. DISSEMINATION OF THAT REPORT TO ANOTHER AGENCY OR ITS PERMANENT INCORPORATION INTO ANY USAF RECORDS SYSTEM WILL NOT BE MADE WITHOUT PRIOR APPROVAL OF THE ORIGINATING AGENCY. WHEN THIS REPORT HAS SERVED ITS PURPOSE, IT WILL BE DESTROYED; NO RECORD OF THE REPORT IS BEING MAINTAINED BY AFOSI.
	WHEN ATTACHMENT(S) _____ IS/ARE REMOVED, THE CLASSIFICATION OF THIS CORRESPONDENCE WILL BE ☐ RETAINED ☐ DOWNGRADED TO _____ ☐ CANCELED ☐ MARKED "FOR OFFICIAL USE ONLY"

OTHER/REMARKS

On 30 Jul 81, the 1606th ABW IG contacted DO 17/BID and advised that Senator PETER DOMENICI desired to talk to SA RICK DOTY regarding the matter involving BENNEWITZ. After checking with Col MARVELL, Acting AFOSI/CC, it was agreed SA DOTY and DO 17/CC would meet with Senator DOMENICI. Senator DOMENICI was present in the IG's Office but departed immediately to meet with BENNEWITZ. A subsequent check with Mr. TIJEROS, Senator DOMENICI's Aide, in an effort to determine the Senator's specific questions, determined his sole interest was to know whether AFOSI had conducted a formal investigation of SUBJECT. Mr. TIJEROS was informed that no formal investigation of BENNEWITZ was conducted by AFOSI. Mr. TIJEROS stated that he assumed if any information were available, and was to be requested from AFOSI, it would have to be requested from our Headquarters. He was provided Col BEYEA's name and the Bolling AFB address of our HQ AFOSI in event he desired any further information. Mr. TIJEROS thanked us and indicated no further inquiries from the Senator regarding this matter are anticipated.

8017D93-0/29 x

NAME, GRADE, TITLE, SIGNATURE FRANK M. HUEY, Colonel, USAF Commander	ATTACHMENTS FOR OFFICIAL USE ONLY	COPIES TO HQ AFOSI/IVOS File

AFOSI FORM 158 JUL 77 PREVIOUS EDITION IS OBSOLETE.

15

UNDERGROUND ALIEN BIO LAB AT DULCE

THE MYRNA HANSEN CASE

Myrna Hansen lost four hours of time in her life. She hears voices inside her chest, even while she is working at the bank. What led up to this abduction can only be speculative. Maybe she was in the wrong place at the wrong time. Maybe she witnessed something of such importance that she was picked up, drugged and detained as was her young son Shawn. In Myrna's first regression she remembers seeing bright lights. The story continues:

On May 12, 1980 Myrna Hansen recalled getting out of her car and then remembers the aliens lifting her up over a fence. They take her son, Shawn to another craft near by. She is terrified because she's separated from her young son and it is then she sees a cow. She also notices a strange insignia on the left chest of a dark orange suit. She notices three lines with a line across the bottom. Myrna senses she is somewhat smarter than these aliens, but feels physically they are in control of her body. She then notices a man in white coming in to restore order and she feels respect from him for her. He seemed very old to her.

When they take her out of the craft she states she feels like she is in a garage. The man assures her that Shawn is fine. The next thing she remembers is stepping into something like an elevator. For her it is frightening because she hates closed spaces.

She again is placed on a table and a bright light is shining down upon her face. They (the aliens) want her to know that they regret that this is happening to her. She asks about the cattle and they reply, "It is necessary." Then she hears them saying it is regrettable that she and her son must lose their memory of this event.

She then remembers being placed in a prone position, with her head resting on a pillow when she feels a sharp pain in her neck and shoulders. She believed that she had been drugged as she remembers her body feeling very heavy.

I would like to interject a moment and go back to a previous communication I had with Richard Doty concerning Myrna Hansen's case in which he was very familiar.[3] He told me that Myrna and her son had a very real encounter with something very strange. What she did state made Doty believe she was somehow describing an underground area that he felt fit the description of an underground weapons facility. He stated he was quite taken aback upon hearing her describe this area because the information he had would seem to definitely indicate she had been taken to "the underground weapons storage area." He also stated that Myrna and her son may have accidently encountered a highly classified government project and was legally detained until she could be possibly drugged and then removed from this area. So in essence, Doty is stating that abductions such as these types could happen. But what struck me as odd is his description to me. It seemed like Doty was telling me something he had knowledge of in this particular case. I could be wrong, but it is just a hunch.

Continuing on with Myrna's regression, she describes being taken or removed from a smaller craft in what she calls "the garage". She feels she is in need of water, but is afraid of what might be given to her.

The next event she recalls is landing somewhere important. (A strange statement). Next she sees five aliens come in and two of them are different. They have narrow eyes and they do not look green or have eyes like slits in the case of the aliens on the first craft. They are huge, but she feels they are important aliens that are like doctors and scientists.

She notices they are kind and when they move, they shuffle their feet. They seem graceful and to be six feet or taller with no hair at all. It seems important to these particular aliens that Myrna forgive them. She feels they are very sensitive and do not make her feel inferior. She notices their arms are longer and also one alien was a woman. They wish to examine her once again. Myrna cooperates, but her head begins to hurt once again. They ask Myrna if she knows who they are and she replies that she has no idea.

She next describes a lot of water, like in a plant of some type. She hears rushing water and is confused as to how she got to this place. It is a base she claims...a base of operations. It is a very important place to these aliens.

At one point she asks if they plan on killing her. She stated that they were startled and taken aback at the thought of such a thing, yet she believed they had thought of keeping her with them. Wherever she was taken, she noticed the lighting was different, not flourescent. The terrain was hilly and she saw three or four UFOS take off and eight to ten land inside.

This was the end of her first session. Myrna Hansen was then a normal 28 year old and her son Shawn was 6 years old. They resided in Eagles Nest, New Mexico where she worked in a bank. The UFO incident occurred near Cimarron, New Mexico.

In Myrna's second session she recalls once again the bright light approaching her car. She is terribly frightened as she notices a cow that is still alive and they are pulling the calf apart. They take both Shawn and herself along with the calf on board the craft. She keeps asking the aliens questions, but never receives a reply. She isn't aware of where they take the calf, but she knows one thing; she is certain it is alive. She then recalls a knife and then remembers calling them "barbaric"!

Soon she feels them placing some type of metal device inside her vagina. She complains that it is uncomfortable, but not painful. They are curious as to what the scar is on her abdomen. The next thing she recalls is seeing the calf dead. She is unsure when it died.

This was a cow found in a field near the Arizona-California border. The rectal area was cored out with some type of surgical laser device and the eyes were also taken and part of the tongue had been removed. Photo taken by Christa Tilton
May-91

UNDERGROUND ALIEN BIO LAB AT DULCE

As the story continues, Myrna sees two more men in white. They seem to be bigger and not as repulsive as the other aliens she has encountered. Again she recalls entering the elevator. She is now able to look around and she notices a room with "the table", panels of flashing lights from the floor to the ceiling. Again the aliens apologize to Myrna and assures her that her son, Shawn is fine.

The aliens seem to be entralled with her hair because their heads are large and have no hair, no eyebrows and their eyes do not blink. Here is a rendetion of a drawing of the aliens she saw:

Dark purple-red eyes
Prominent cheek bones
No hair, ears, nose or mouth?

Myrna continues to describe a long knife (18 inches and thin) silver that seem to be tapered on the end. The aliens plunged it six inches into the chest of the calf and then worked on the genitals while the calf was still alive and struggling! They cut with a circular motion. As she describes this horror she and her son Shawn cry. They are deeply affected by what they have witnessed.

In Myrna Hansen's last two regressions we finally can place some of the parts of the puzzle together. Again at the home of Paul Bennewitz, Myrna recalls being carried or half-dragged up some type of a ramp. She remembers being taken to an upper level and once more being subjected to "the table". She recalls feeling severe pain in the left side of her head and hears an odd noise in her left ear. She remembers screaming obscenities to her alien captors.

Before going on with Myrna's story I would like to discuss the area of alien implantations. Myrna Hansen, through x-rays and Cat.Scans verified that some type of an implant was inserted. This raises many questions as to the use of these implants and who the real "implanters" are.

Martin Cannon has a brilliant paper out called "The Controllers" in which he has graciously allowed me to quote from his area of expertise on implants. I quote from page eight under the paragraph of "Implants": [4]

> Perhaps the most interesting pieces of evidence surrounding the . abduction phenomenon are the intracerebral implants allegedly visible in the X-rays and MRI scans of many abductees. Indeed, abductees often describe operations in which needles are inserted into the brain; more frequently still, they report implantation of foreign objects through sinus cavities. Many abduction specialists assume that these intercranial incursions must be the handiwork of scientists from the stars. Unfortunately, these researchers have failed to familiarize themselves with certain little-heralded advances interrestrial technology.
>
> The abductees' implants strongly suggest a technological lineage which can be traced to a device known as a "stimoceiver", invented

in the late '50s-early '60s by a neuroscientist named Jose Delgado. The stimoceiver is a miniature depth electrode which can receive and transmit electronic signals over FM radio raves. By stimulating a correctly-positioned stimoceiver, an outside operator can wield a surprising degree of control over the subject's responses.

Speaking in 1966--and reflecting research undertaken years previous-- Delgado asserted that his experiments "support the distasteful conclusion that motion, emotion, and behavior can be directed by a electrical forces and that humans can be controlled like robots by push buttons." He even prophesied a day when brain control could be turned over to non-human operators, by establishing two-way radio communication between the implanted brain and a computer."

According to Victor Marchetti, Delgado attached the stimoceiver to the tympanic membrane, thereby transforming the ear into a sort of microphone." "Yet the ramifications of this technology may go even deeper than Marchetti indicates. I presume that a suitably-wired subject's inner ear can be made into a microphone, it can also be made into a loudspeaker -- one possible explanation for the "voices" heard by abductees."

Martin Cannon's research in this area has been debated, bashed and praised. His conclusions make for a fascinating new area of research into alien abductions and implants. A flyer where you may order this courageous piece of work on mind control and who the "controllers" really are will be added to the final portion of this manuscript. I urge the reader to have an open mind and consider these possiblities raised by Cannon.

The aliens Myrna describes are naked from the waist up, very thin, their ribs and clavicles sticking out. She sees that they have more ribs than humans. She notices they shuffle when they walk and drag one foot behind.

Myrna describes once again being taken to a room where she now sees stars everywhere. She says it is beautiful and can even see a planet. She observes a very large TV screen and she has the feeling of being outside.

The aliens again reassure her that Shawn is alright. The she hears the words "Necessary arrangements." She feels that they are just trying to reassure her so she will cooperate by being calm and quiet.

Her next remembrance is being on the ground in a rugged area where they are on a mesa where she observes craft landing and taking off. It's familiar to her--the countryside. She realizes she is on Earth.

Next she recalls being on the elevators going down very fast. She notices crowds of people with different uniforms, colors and patches on the left chest. They seem to be walking hastily by. The lighting is different somehow. Strange, she recalls. Then she comes to a door with no doornob which opens electronically.

The next recollection is one I know all too well. Myrna hears water rushing and smells a pungent odor. [5] She makes the odd statement, "I hate caves worse than elevators!" She ventures on and comes across what only can be described as "an incredible base city of operations." [6]

Going through another examination, she feels like she has been a victim in Auschwitz and then she weeps and sobs. They, the aliens, do not want her to remember or tell anyone about this incident. She makes the comment, "Even when I was telling Paul--in my heart, I was thinking that there are so many things worse than death!"

Myrna continues her horrifying account by describing walking back to a trestle, to a doorway where she is able to observe a generator, pools of water with "submerged things" in them. Then it occurs to her that what she is viewing are body parts! She tells of seeing the top of a bald head, an arm with a hand, Human. She also sees something like tongues--they look larger than human tongues.(Note) Many cattle, found mutilated have been found missing a tongue or a part of the tongue. It has been stated that cows have a certain enzyme that is useful so this makes since to what Myrna is describing.) She continues as she describes seeing containers that seem to be made of metal. The smell is repugnant, like a gassy odor. She feels weak and nauseous, but remembers looking down and seeing the body parts which some were internal organs.

This is a drawing of the tanks seen in an underground facility in 1987. The description is almost identical to Myrna Hansen's.

Tanks seen in underground facility

Then Myrna's regression winds down. She is tired and wants to just let it rest. She does recall the word "alterations", "necessary alterations" in order to take her back. The torture, the experiments make her feel like a specimen. Suggestions are then given to Myrna to just let go of the past and to be a peace with herself.

One aspect I saved for last was the fact that Myrna was aware these aliens were trying to confuse her. Her impressions were that these aliens want to control Earth. She is adamant about the fact that she was indeed the recipient of some type of mind programming. She dreams of mind control over the Earth and she has feelings of fear over thoughts that she feels were beamed to her about her own suicide! Her uncle and brother committed suicide. She doesn't want to die, but has strange feelings about having no conscious memory of the "drugs" used on her.

UNDERGROUND ALIEN BIO LAB AT DULCE

A DRAWING OF THE ALLEGED "DULCE"
UNDERGROUND TANKS

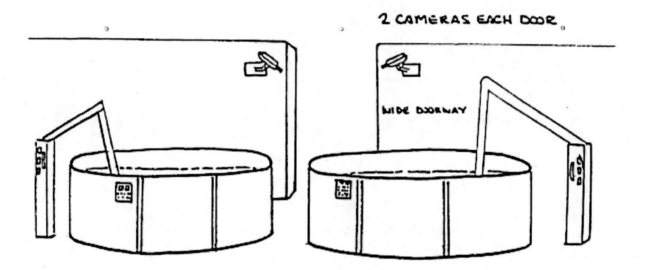

2 CAMERAS EACH DOOR

WIDE DOORWAY

SCORES OF TANKS
OR MORE

These copies of the original "Dulce Papers" were circulated among the ufological community in 1987.[7] They were drawn supposedly from original photographs from a man mysteriously referred to as "Thomas C." who worked at the underground installation, but escaped with film and photograph evidence of the goings-on in this underground base. They certainly resemble the description given by Myrna Hansen and others who claim they too have been abducted and taken to this facility where experiments are performed upon them.

To no avail since my research began, have I been able to meet with this mysterious character "Thomas C." I have reason to believe the man does not exist and is the product of another hoax perpetrated against UFO researchers and the abductees they try to help. There seems to be only two people I know of that claim they know this man exists and are in contact with him. They claim to have seen the real evidence, but so far have refused to make it public. [8]

UNDERGROUND ALIEN BIO LAB AT DULCE

I would like to remind the reader of the statement made to me by Richard Doty that Myrna could have stumbled onto a highly classified government project and was possibly drugged and removed from the area. Interesting comment from an Air Force agent. [9]

In conclusion, no one really knows who abducted Myrna and why? I do know this much, Paul Bennewitz was deeply concerned for the welfare of this woman and her son.[10] It is interesting to hear Paul's conclusions in a letter written to now deceased Jim Lorenzen of APRO about Myrna Hansen. I am enclosing a copy as there were many interesting aspects of her case that were later addressed by Paul.

It is obvious by then that Paul had already come to his own conclusions about her case and it seems that Paul had direct knowledge of the area in which Myrna and her son were taken. This case possibly was the catalyst of what urged Paul to enter into the Dulce, New Mexico area. I believe Paul had knowledge of an exisiting underground facility at Archeleta and continued his flights and investigations into this highly suspected area even after Myrna Hansen's case was brought to an end.

What was interesting is the conclusion that Myrna indeed was being beamed from some type of alien force and many steps were taken to protect her from these beams. Paul was convinced Myrna Hansen was dealing with a malevolent society of aliens. This is where I question the validity of the entire investigation and how it turned out.

What about the possiblity of a government-sponsored abduction of Myrna Hansen? Could our government somehow beam alien images in our minds from some type of implant? Could the aliens really be our own government agents carefully manipulating us into belieiving we are being abducted by extraterrestrials? Did Paul Bennewitz ever address this possibility? I believe he had already made his mind up and to this day has carried his own hypothosis to the extremes of reality. But, what if Paul is right? Let the people decide as we continue on with the story of Paul Bennewitz and God help us if both the aliens and our government are in control of these abductions!

Artist:

Martin Cannon

Photo copyright Crux 1990

22

Copy

THUNDER SCIENTIFIC CORPORATION

9-7-80

28 AUG 1980

MR JIM LORENSEN
APRO
3910 E KLEINDALE RD
TUCSON ARIZONA 85712

DEAR JIM,

I WAS PLEASED TO HAVE YOUR ASSISTANCE IN STRAIGHTENING OUT OUR PROBLEM
        AS YOU THINK SO DO I — THE VICTIM IS ABSOLUTELY TOP PRIORITY.

THE SITUATION HERE IS SERIOUS BUT NOT OUT OF HAND — SHE IS GETTING THE
BEST OF TREATMENT BY THE PATHOLOGIST AND THE DOCTOR AT NO COST TO HER,
FOR AN APPARENT ALIEN BACTERIA. WE ARE TRYING TO CULTURE IT — NO LUCK
AS YET; ALSO IT HAS EVADED ALL OF OUR KNOWN ANTIBIOTICS AND PENICILLON.

SHE IS ALSO BEING BADLY BEATEN ON BY THE ALIEN WITH THEIR BEAMS — 24
HOURS A DAY. THESE BEAMS HAVE BEEN MEASURED AND WE ARE NOW GETTING A
HANDLE AS TO WHAT THEY MAY BE.

FILM FOOTAGE IS PILING UP — OVER 1000 FEET NOW — SCIENTIFIC DATA AND
DOCUMENTATION EXCELLENT AND PILING UP.

JIM, IF YOU COULD POSSIBLY OBSERVE THE FOLLOWING PRECAUTIONS IN ANY OF
YOUR PRESENT AND FUTURE REGRESSIONS YOUR DATA WILL BE MORE ACCURATE.

1)   USE AS MANY DIFFERENT EXPERT PSYCHOLOGISTS AS POSSIBLE.

2)   DO NOT REGRESS UNLESS:
     A)   THERE IS AN UNBIASED WITNESS ACQUAINTED WITH THE PROCESS —
          PRESENT TAKING VERBATIM NOTES IF POSSIBLE.

     B)   THE REGRESSION MUST BE DONE IN A SHIELDED ENCLOSURE. THE BEST
          OPTIONS I'M AWARE OF ARE:
          1A)   AN AUTOMOBILE IN A GARAGE — USE 3 LAYERS OF HEAVY ALUMINUM
                (BARBEQUE TYPE) FOIL TO COVER ALL WINDOWS — GROUNDED TO
                THE CHROME TRIM AROUND THE WINDOWS THROUGHLY. MASKING
                TAPE CAN BE USED TO HOLD IT IN PLACE.

                PRECAUTION: DO NOT GROUND THE AUTO.

                IF THE ALIEN SENSES HE CANNOT GET THROUGH, HE WILL ATTEMPT
                TO MODULATE THE BEAM ULTRASONICALLY — ABOUT 18 TO 23 KC.
                THE INTENT IS TO VIBRATE THE ATMOSPHERE WITHIN, SYMPATHET-
                ICALLY, THUS REACHING THE VICTIM. CLOSED WINDOWS AND
                COTTON IN THE EARS WILL DEADEN THIS REASONABLY EFFECTIVELY.

          2A)   THE VERY BEST OPTION IS TO USE AN X-RAY ROOM. IT IS LEAD
                SHIELDED; A TWO STORY OR LARGER BUILDING WHERE THE ROOM
                IS TOTALLY SHIELDED. NOT A ONE STORY BUILDING BECAUSE
                GENERALLY THE CEILING WILL NOT BE SHIELDED. INSPECT AND
                MAKE CERTAIN THE ROOM IS SHIELDED.

3A) LAST AND LEAST BEST OPTION — A HOTEL ROOM IN A MULTI-
STORY HOTEL WITH THE ROOM ON AN INSIDE CORRIDOR MIDWAY
OR SO UP. ANYONE TAKEN TO THE ROOM SHOULD NOT KNOW NOR
LOOK AT THE FLOOR NUMBERS OR ROOM NUMBERS. THIS TYPE
OF ROOM IS OBVIOUSLY NOT SHIELDED — CONCRETE OR STONE
WILL NOT WORK. THIS IS A METHOD OF " CLOAKING" BECAUSE
OF THE MANY OTHER MINDS PRESENT IN THE HOTEL, THE ALIEN
IS CONFUSED AND WILL HAVE DIFFICULTY SEARCHING OUT THE
VICTIM.

I KNOW I DON'T NEED TO RE-EXPRESS HOW SERIOUS THIS IS. PLEASE INSTIGATE
THESE PROCEDURES IF AT ALL POSSIBLE. YOUR DATA WILL BE ACCURATE, MUCH
MORE DETAILED AND WITHOUT CONTAMINATIVE PROGRAMMING.

THE APPARENT PRIME INTENT OF THE ALIEN IS TO INSTILL A FEELING SUPPOSEDLY
OF THEIR TRUE BENEVOLENCE THRU THE VICTIM, WHEN IN REALITY WITH THIS
PARTICULAR ALIEN CULTURE, EXPLORING AND ENCOUNTERING ON EARTH, THE INTENT
IS TRULY MALEVOLENT IN ITS WORST SENSE.

I WOULD SUGGEST IF YOU CAN DO IT QUIETLY, THAT YOU RELAY THESE GROUND
RULES FOR REGRESSION TO OTHER UFO ORGANIZATIONS, ASKING THEM, AT LEAST
AT THIS POINT NOT TO QUESTION — JUST TRY TO DO IT THIS WAY.

WE MUST TAKE A VERY SERIOUS INVESTIGATORY POSITION ON DOCUMENTING IN AS
GREAT A DETAIL AS POSSIBLE. I AM BASING EVERYTHING I TELL YOU ON A
SOLID, TRIED AND WORKING HYPOTHESIS, NOT ON IMAGINATION, GUESSING NOR
PARANOIA. I CAN ASSURE YOU IT IS NOT A BEAUTIFUL " RELIGIOUS EXPERIENCE"
THAT SOME INVESTIGATORS WOULD HAVE US BELIEVE. THERE ARE ALWAYS SOME
" GOOD APPLES" IN ANY BAD BASKET — HOPEFULLY SOONER OR LATER WE WILL
ENCOUNTER SOME OF THOSE AND FIND SOME ALLIES.

AGAIN — TO LEND CREDIBILITY WHEN FINAL GOVERNMENT ACCESS IS GAINED —
NONE OF WHAT I'VE DISCUSSED MUST GET TO THE MEDIA. LEO'S IDEA OF VIDEO
TAPING FOR TV AND PUBLICATION WILL ONLY CREATE PROPAGANDA FOR THE ALIEN
— IT IS SELF DEFEATING. WHEN THE FINAL ABSOLUTELY PROVEABLE FACTS ARE
GLEANED, WE MUST CAREFULLY CONTROL THEIR PRESENTATION TO THE PROPER
AUTHORITIES.

I WILL APPRECIATE ANY FEEDBACK YOU CAN GIVE ME CONCERNING THE NEW RE-
GRESSIONS YOU MENTIONED, METHODS, ETC. WHEN YOU HAVE THE DATA FOR COR-
REALATIVE PROCEDURES.

BEST REGARDS,

Paul

PAUL F BENNEWITZ

P.S. ONE LAST THING — A MUST IF THE
HOTEL ROOM IS USED. PLACE AN EKG ELECTRODE
(WITH RUBBER STRAP) ON THE RIGHT INSIDE MID
FOREARM. PRIOR TO APPLICATION — WET THE CON-
TACT AREA WITH SALIVA OR SALINE SOLUTION.
OUR MOST RECENT REGRESSION TAPES INDICATE NO
ALIEN INTERFERENCE USING THIS METHOD IN A
HOTEL ROOM.

USE A BANANA PLUG AND HEAVY WIRE TO GROUND TO
ROOM OUTLET HOTEL GROUND SYSTEM.

UNDERGROUND ALIEN BIO LAB AT DULCE

We again address the same question--why would the Air Force or any other government agency become obsessed with the activities of Paul Bennewitz when they continue to emphatically state that they do not investigate UFOs or UFO abduction claims?

The truth is our government and military bases are intensely interested in UFOs and the people who claim to have been abducted by alien beings. They are even more in-terested in the abductee's claim that they were in the presence of not only aliens, but government & military men in underground installations. There are some people who do know of these underground bases and the secrets hidden in them. I believe Bill Moore is one of those people who have knowledge of abductions, but he gives anyone's claims little attention.

As the story unfolded at the Las Vegas MUFON conference in 1989, it was Bill Moore who had a very startling revelation to make that would forever shake the foundations of ufology from all over the globe. As Bill describes in his speech, it all began in the year of 1980 when a certain man from Kirtland Air Force Base supposedly recruited Bill so he could befriend Paul Bennewitz and provide Air Force intelligence with as much information as possible on Paul's UFO activities and research.[11]

The wheels had already been set in motion as Paul had already by this time introduced his 'PROJECT BETA' Report to certain members of the AFOSI and to one man in particular who Bill Moore code-named 'FALCON'.[12] Many people have speculated that all this time Richard Doty was 'FALCON' but after many interviews with other researchers and deduc-tions of my own, which are only speculative, plus Doty's own admission that he indeed was not 'FALCON' but knew him, I believe our birdman 'FALCON' most likely was Major Ernest Edwards. Richard Doty only took orders from 'FALCON' and supposedly received a more inferior code name of 'SPARROW'. These names, Moore claimed were purely in-ventions of his partner Jaime Shandera. This had all the makings of a great spy novel!

Bill Moore found himself in the middle of having to supply the AFOSI about Paul's ac-tivities and in return the 'AVIARY' would supply Moore with certain information to help him with his private research. So he accepted the position, reported back to Doty on Paul Bennewitz and his activities not realizing the negative affect it would ultimately have on Paul's mental and physical health. I do not believe Moore or Doty deliberately knew this would cause such repercussions with Paul, but somehow power and knowledge of secrets maybe seemed more important to Bill Moore at the time.

Note:(Since the first printing of this manuscript I have learned more about the goings-on behind 'THE BENNEWITZ AFFAIR' and maybe jumped to unfair conclusions about Bill Moore. I was accused of lying about the facts. I think what happened was I could only report what I saw on paper or from firsthand interviews with Bill Moore from other researchers. So I apologize if any of the facts were reported wrong in the first printing. I have nothing against Bill Moore personally because I have never met him, but I feel I can disagree with the tactics used in certain methods used in retrieving and reporting information about an American citizen like Paul Bennewitz. I, like any other interested party would welcome knowing all the facts that went on behind the scene and who better to write about it than Bill Moore.)

Moore made the statement that he felt Richard Doty found that carrying out these orders were distasteful and upsetting. I believe this to be a very accurate statement. Doty told me the same thing in a letter. He did find this particular counter-intelligence campaign very hard emotionally to accomplish and I am sure Doty found it very upsetting. He and Paul were friends. But he had a job to do. It must have been difficult to get out of bed in the mornings and face himself in the mirror.[13] From a personal letter from Rick Doty to the author, Doty basically stated the exact words Bill Moore used in his speech. Doty agreed that dis-information was deliberately fed to Paul because he had stumbled onto "something of great importance" to the Air Force and the government. He told me he felt bad for Paul and was sorry it caused so many problems for Paul. He also stated that he did have to perform some duties that he personally did not feel right about morally, but he had no other choice because he had a job to complete and he was dedicated and loyal to the Air Force. As I read through the lines of his letters to me I saw a man with sincere feelings and emotions and also a man who was placed in a delicate situation in which he had a job to do and so he did it. Doty also told me that he had considered Paul a friend and special feelings for the man. His last comment about Paul was that Paul Bennewitz went through HELL!

After having my own personal conversations with Paul, he told me of horrid people following him, breaking into his home to install wire taps, Air Force men showing up on his doorstep at all hours and then he began telling me an even more bizarre story. He felt sure he was being drugged and was convinced aliens were coming into his home and sticking him with needles. He was a frightened man. He also felt like the government was possibly behind some of these happenings. I sympathized with Paul because we both suffer from severe insomnia and health problems. Harrassment of this type should never be tolerated in anyway!

Bill Moore claims the government was responsible for giving Paul data on UFOs, abductees, evil aliens who occupy underground bases for bizarre experiments and eventually Paul started deteriorating quickly and emotionally could not cope with the information he was being fed by these government men.

And so seizing a great opportunity, Bill Moore saw the opening to really get involved and become somebody important. He stated in his speech that there was no way he was going to allow this opportunity to pass by without learning atleast something about what was going on.

To me this statement sums up Bill Moore's character in full. In a question and answer period in his speech he asked the question whether he was ever on any government payroll. His answer was obviously NO!

In a conversation from a well respected ufologist and researcher, this person stated emphatically that Bill Moore had told him that he was literally paid "under the table". Now whether this statement was ever truly made to this researcher, we may never know. But, in my past dealings with this particular UFO researcher who I respect deeply, I have to believe that the conversation indeed took place.

Never being allowed to interview Mr. Moore, I cannot judge him in anyway. I am only relating facts from himself and others who do know him well and know how he operates. But, a final judgement cannot be made by me until Bill Moore actually grants me an interview. So until that time, the jury is still out on Bill Moore. [14]

UNDERGROUND ALIEN BIO LAB AT DULCE

" THE WEITZEL LETTER "

Dear Sir;

On July 16, 1980, at between 10:30 - 10:45AM, Craig R. Weitzel, 644 Wind Glove Rd, Marietta, Georgia, a Civil Air Patrol Cadet from Dobbins AFB, Ga, visiting Kirtland AFB, NM, observed a dull metallic colored UFO flying from South to North near Pecos New Mexico. Pecos has a secret training site for the 1550th Aircrew Training and Testing Wing, Kirtland AFB, NM. WEITZEL was with ten other individuals, including USAF active duty airmen, and all witnessed the sightings. WEITZEL took some pictures of the object. WEITZEL went closer to the UFO and observed the UFO land in a clearing approximately 250 yds, NNW of the training area. WEITZEL observed an individual dressed in a metallic suit depart the craft and walk a few feet away. The individual was outside the craft for just a few minutes. When the individual returned the craft took off towards the NW.

On July 17, 1980, at about 2210hrs., Weitzel was in his temporary billets on Kirtland AFB, NM, when an individual dressed in a dark suit, came to his door. The individual was described by Weitzel as being: 6'3" tall, weight, 170 lbs, slender built, dark black hair, dark eyes, wearing sunglasses, narrow shaped face. The individual identified himself as a Mr. Huck from Sandia Laboratories, a secret Depart of Energy Contractor on Kirtland AFB. Mr. Weitzel, not being from the Albuquerque area, did not know what Sandia was. After obraining an explantation from the individual, Weitzel allowed the individual in. The individual told Weitzel that he saw something yesterday near Pecos that he shouldn't have seen. The individual stated the craft was a secret craft from Los Alamos, NM. The individual demanded all the photographs. Mr. Weitzed explained that he didnn't have any photographs, that all the photographs were with a USAF airman and Weitzel didn't know the individuals name. The individual warned Weitzel not to mention the sighting to anyone or Weitzel would be in serious trouble. After the individual left Weitzels room, Weitzel wondered how the individual knew of the sighting because Weitzel didn't report the sighting to anyone. Weitzel became scared after thinking of the threat the individual made. Weitzel call the Kirtland AFB Security Police and reported the incident to them. They referred the incident to the Air Force Office of Special Investigations (AFOSI), which investigates these matters according to the security police. A Mr. Dody, a special agent with OSI, spoke with Weitzel and took a report. Mr. Dody also obtained all the photographs of the UFO. Dody told Weitzel he would look into the matter. That was the last anyone heard of the incident.

I am a USAF Airman assigned to the 1550th Aircrew Training and Testing Wing at Kirtland AFB, NM. I was with Weitzel during the sighting, however, I did not see the craft land. I spoke with Weitzel after this Mr. Huck visited him. Weitzel was very upset and wanted something done about it. But after Weitzel spoke with the OSI, Weitzel changed his attitude. Weitzel didn't want to talk about the matter anymore. I called and spoke with Mr. Dody. He disavowed any knowledge of the photographs and stated Weitzel decided not to make a report of the sighting.

I have every reason to beleive the USAF is covering up something. I spent a lot of time looking into this matter and I know there is more to it than the USAF will say. I have heard rumors, but serious rumors here at Kirtland

that the USAF has a crashed UFO stored in the Manzano Storage area,
which is located in a remote area of Kirtland AFB. This area is heavily
guarded by USAF Security. I have spoke with two employees of Sandia
Laboratories, who also store classified objects in Manzano, and they told
me that Sandia has examined several UFO's during the last 20 years.
One that crashed near Roswell NM in the late 50's was examined by Sandia
scientists. That craft is still being store in Manzano.

I have reason to beleive OSI is conducting a very secret investigation
into UFO sightings. OSI took over when Project Blue Book was closed. I was
told this by my commander, COL Bruce Purvine. COL Purvine also told me
that the investigation was so secret that most employees of OSI doesn't
even know it. But COL Purvine told me that Kirtland AFB, AFOSI District
17 has a special secret detachment that investigates sightings around
this area. They have also investigated the cattle mutations in New Mexico.

I don't expect you people can do anything about this, but I thought
I'd let you know. I must remain anonymous because I am a career airman with
tIme remaining on active duty. I feel I would be threatened if I disclosed
my name. I know that you people can't guarantee my anonymity.

This letter was received at the doorstep of APRO (Aerial Phenomena Research
Organization) in late 1980. There has been much speculation as to who is
the author of this letter. Several of the Air Force agents names seemed
to be deliberately misspelled. Speculation is Richard Doty is the anonymous
author, but there has never been any proof of that.

There seem to be a lot of correspondence and data circulating about what
was really behind the dis-information campaign against Paul Bennewitz. So
in January of 1983 a telecon from an attorney, Peter Gerston was circulating
in the UFO circles that gave some very interesting information about a
meeting that occured in Albuquerque with Richard Doty, Peter Gerston, and
Bill Moore. It is an interesting perspective on what information was being
given to Paul Bennewitz and if any of the information is true, then it gives
one a feeling that we are indeed being lead on by certain individuals in
government circles and ufological circles. No matter, I will reproduce the
telecon as I have it with corrections of minor typographical errors. The
meeting gave us insight on Richard Doty and what he really knows.[15]

For the readers convenience I will try to interpret by identifying the persons
involved in which initials were used:

D- Richard Doty
BM- Bill Moore
PG- Peter Gerston ——→
Lankus-Ron Lakis
PB-Paul Bennewitz
LF-Larry Fawcett
JM-Jerry Miller
ED-Edward Doty
ST-Stanton Friedman

UNDERGROUND ALIEN BIO LAB AT DULCE

Telecon (PGNY) - Jan. 25, 1983

Re: trip to Albuquerque and meeting w/D.

D. claims "gov't is studying UFOs & knows theyr'e extraterrestrial".

Various agencies- espec. military have depts. into this.

NSA - - a "primary mover"

D. indicates that the gov't is or may be "in communication with the aliens".

D. says there have been 3 crashes where bodies were "retrieved" - one was
Roswell- one was in the late 1950's, one in the 1960's.

Two meetings w/D. - dinner on Mon. night (Jan. 10); BM present, also- PG
turned off somewhat by BM; PG & D. met again Tues.

D. indicated retrievals once stored at Kirtland, but no longer there.

D. had device to determine whether he was being taped. He said at outset he
knew he wasn't being taped.

D. talking "as a civilian"-if they asked questions about classified matters,
he would not be able to discuss much.

D. involved mostly in UFO matters over the last 5-6 years-began when he was
at Ellsworth at time of 1977 incident near there-landing of craft(s); some
sort of guard(military? fired at humanoid(s) that got out'they shot beam
which burned/disintergrated guard's weapon & burned him to some degree;
later or next day, a missile was found to be missing from silo area. Nat'l
Enq. got wind of story, sent someone up, but brass,etc. were able to convince Nat'l Enq. that incident was a hoax. The investigation into that
incident is still going on. (FBI involved). (Author's comment) In a letter
to me from Richard Doty told me and the Enq. the exact thing.[16]That the
Ellsworth incident was a disinformation practice excercise that got out
of hand and an emphatic "NO" was told to me when I asked if a missle ended
up missing)

PG asked D. if D., if D. were PG., & wanted to go somewhere to invest. a
really good case-where would he go- D. said he would go to Ellsworth. A
farmer & lawman(deputy sher.) were apparently witnesses and were debriefed
& told not to discuss it byt D. knows how to get to them & told PG he
thought they might talk anyway.

D. was given briefing papers about various cases-some back to 1940's, some
published & known, some still classified. Something about those briefing
papers going to President-which one? All?

From what D. has read in briefing papers, he concludes gov't & aliens are
probably in contact; tho he has no direct knowledge of it.

CR44- could be nuclear materials, but when PG asked D. what else it could be,
"I can't talk about it". "CR44" means Command regulation 44" & is a 4 or 5
P. document; obtained under FOIA, but very heavily censored.

BM has had the Kirtland/1980/PB documents over a year. BM gave them to
Ron at KPIX in San. Fran.

The "jamming"-BM went to local airport (Albq) to inquire, because they
allegedly were blacked out in some fashion-they claimed they knew nothing
about it BUT - a similar incident had occurred either one year before or 1
year later; if it was 1 year later that would be '81' when HE detected
anomoly.- But Doty claims none of that had to do with UFOS.

PG acquired document (from BM??) ("if it is a document") - re: project Aquarius and MJ-12. Aquarius supposed THE project involving ET/gov't contact. According to D., that contact occurred in the late 1960's; he did not mention where.[17]

PG asked D. point-blank about mutes and was told "Its classifed". However, seems PG may have asked what was behind mutes & D. said maybe cults were involved, and at least implied to PG that aliens might be involved in some but when PG persisted in questioning, he was told, "Well, it's classified".

PG & Lankus (sp?) (4 people present at dinner) were "aghast"-just couldn't believe they were hearing all this.

D. says aliens are coming from 50 light years away, but location is classified.

Why was D. not hesitating to talk about this?:

In NYTIMES reported requested some documents(from where?) (Nat. Security Council or White House) - included by mistake was a Presidential briefing paper that had been declassified - apparently it said that the gov't knew UFOS were of ET-origin - the reporter wrote article & article appeared tho document was then re-classified. But D. feels that once it was declassified, it could not be re-classified - he feels it should be aired out or in the public domain.

D. seems to indicate that most people in the military know about this and they just don't talk about it.

D. said if he told them everything he knew, they wouldn't believe it.

The reason for secrecy - fear of panic.

D. says there is indeed "programming" going on via movies, media - to help population accept ET presence.

D. says UFO organizations are "basically inept" and that there are gov't employees in some groups - present both to misinform and to collect information.

Another reason for secrecy is that we are trying to learn as much about their technology as we can before Soviets get in on it.

D. says gov't feels aliens do not pose a threat. (He said this "several times)

Reference to "CR44" - in some of the 1975 documents.

D. refers to sightings in N. Hampshire/Vermont & at Pease AFB in 1982.

PG referred to aliens inordinate interest in our weaponry and nuclear facilities, military bases and asked whether this might suggest that they might pose a threat--no comment from D. (at least not in direct response to that).

D. & BM feel that Paul B. has gone overboard in interpreting what he has; for instance, PB interprets stuff on his computer as being alien communication, but D. and BM think that's hogwash.

PB says ETs have ability to "cloak" themselves (invisible); that they are interested in our water supply & want to control the world for our water. Parts taken in mutes are used to make humanoids.

AFOSI uses very sophisticated hypnosis in their own UFO investigations. Twice a year D. is de-breifed and once a year he's given a lie detector test while under hypnosis.

D. spoke to woman in Cimarron Case and says "It's an interesting & extra-ordinary story she tells" --implant in her neck--D. confirmed X-rays revealed the implanted object.[18]As far as gov't is concerned, they've had no doctors look at the woman (tho P.B. has)

Cimarron witness saw aliens & military types together in underground installation --tanks with organs in them--she was told they were making humanoids (Fawcett says Andreasson was told this too--this was not in either book; something she told L.F.)

PB says in 1979 aliens & military had some kind of "fight over weapons" & 66 military people were killed by the aliens.

PB feels the aliens are coming into his house at night - "cloaked"- but you can tell they're there by the odor--either a heavy perfume odor or a sulphurous odor--they've stuck needles in PB's hand--plus they've implanted PB's wife.

D. on Cash/Landrum: gov't device, an article relating to device appeared in some publication - D. said at first AVIATION WEEK. PG had Klass look for it to no avail; PG told D. on ph. later & D. said, "Well, maybe it wasn't A. WEEK, but maybe some other publication--so PG doesn't know if he's getting the run-around here.

D. has quite a different demeanor on phone as opposed to in-person.

PG reiterates that D. says UFOs are ET based on what he's gleaned from papers, no direct knowledge (so D. says)

D. says there was (or is) someone in FTD bootlegging UFO photos.

CR44 --a common denominator.

PG asked D. if the military can predict when UFOs would be seen--Doty "couldn't talk about it".

D. assured by PG that their conversation was off the record--PG wondered,tho if maybe BM planned to use some of this material in a book (w/SF?)

BTodd-at PG's request--has been bombarding for FOIA requests on Pease & Ellsworth (especially the latter) (& Aquarius)--A Washington contact of BM's called BM & asked what was going on--did someone leak about Ellsworth?? BM called PG to tell him about this--BM worried about protecting his source-- but "his source had nothing to do with Ellsworth"--that was D. (that is D. was the source re: Ellsworth) and D. is not his (BM's) source from what I gather".

"I was led to believe that BM wouldn't even have spoken to D. when BM was down there other than for me being there & seeing D. "

"I showed D. a couple of documents that hadn't been released yet that BM showed me. He (D.) seemed to indicate he hadn't seen them before".

BM denies that D. is his Kirtland source.

D. told PG that Miller wouldn't talk to PG because he was burned once by the press. JM, a "civilian" who went to Wright-Patterson on his "off hours" (?) had no formal connection with FTD; according to "certain documents", JM never worked for FTD; he just had "certain expertise" --Another document-- "one that hasn't been released yet"--seems to indicate that JM is de-briefed regularly.

PG not familiar with "Dr. Lehman".

PG says that about a year ago "we" sent a standard FOIA request to Ellsworth; they replied that they knew nothing (about 1977 incident??)

Gov't/alien "agreement"--they can do mutes and we'd receive some technology plus we gave them land for a base.

PG told that last scene in "CEIII" may have been close to reality--re: "pilot exchange"--rumor is that Spielberg met Reagan at W.HOUSE & Reagon told S. that the movie was "more real than people think" Spielberg supposedly has confirmed this to BM.

"Contact" may have been made in 1969.

Edward D. with Project Twinkle--PG asks RD if E.D. was his kin; R.D. "couldn't talk about it".

D. asked: "How do you know that I'm not here to either give you mis-information or give you information which is part of the programming, knowing you're going to go out and spread it around?"

PG: "When you take what he (D) says and what PB says together, you really leave New Mexico with a strange feeling."

PG would like to contact Emenegger; wondered if that was a pen name.

D. said there was a "Grudge 13" report, but he claimed he didn't know what was in it. Also D. says there is another non-military group. BM said these were ex-military people who disagree w/gov'ts position and would rather get this info. out. BM doesn't necessarrily believe that. He thinks it's an "inter-national group". Insignia on craft filmed by PB is a trilateral. PG wondered if T.Commission was involved.

D. says "some announcements" & release of data will be made soon by an agency that he is aware of. Press conference to be held.

End of telecon...

This telecon, if it provides "solid information" tells us a little about how Richard Doty works. Richard and I corresponded only a few times and I appreciated his answering all my questions posed to him as best he could.

At this point in time, I do not think Richard Doty was feeding Peter Gerston dis-information, but I do find it interesting to note the fact that on several occasions when people had a meeting with Paul Bennewitz, they would show up only to find that Bill Moore was sitting right there along side of Paul.

Again this goes along with what Bill Moore stated in his speech in Las Vegas in 1989. I believe he wanted to know anything Paul may be sharing with other researchers and so Paul, thinking Bill was "the good guy" informed him of probably every time a meeting was to take place. I again am only speculating. But, it is true that in the early 80's Thomas Adams and some other researchers visited Paul in Albuquerque only to find Bill Moore present. This made Tom very suspicious and nervous. So concern for Paul at this point was top priority!

Apparently Richard Doty and Bill Moore at some point had a "parting of the ways" as when I mentioned Bill to Rick via a telephone conversation, Rick said he had nothing to say about Moore and his tone of voice and other comments made to me lead me to believe their friendship ended a long time ago.

UNDERGROUND ALIEN BIO LAB AT DULCE

<u>MY 1987 TRIP TO NEW MEXICO</u>

In November of 1987, I was invited along with two researchers to visit Roswell, New Mexico, Albuquerque, and then finally Dulce, New Mexico. It would turn out to be a trip of a lifetime and certainly gave me some input on the little town of Dulce, Gabe Valdez, the State Policeman in Dulce and what really went on at Archeleta.

When we started out from Chama, it began pouring down rain. We all were singing and having a wonderful time even though we knew it would be raining when we entered Dulce. It was in the evening and Tom Adams had arranged ahead of time for us to meet with Gabe Valdez as he had done every year he made the trip in the past. Gabe was expecting us and we finally arrived and made our way to the only place in town tostay, The Best Western". It was nice to finally get a room and stretch my legs as it had been a long drive up from Roswell.

As soon as we were settled in our rooms Tom immediately called Gabe's home. He couldn't wait for me to meet Gabe and tell him about what I knew of the underground facility there. But, even during the drive into Dulce, Tom, his buddy Gary and I felt a strange sense of danger for some reason.

There was no logical explanation for it so we decided to just forget about it. That evening we tried many times to catch Gabe home and his son kept telling us he was out in the field looking for some lost hunters. Well, in this rain storm we certainly could understand, but we felt somehow that his son was covering for Gabe.

Later on I decided to call over and ask for Gabe. Again his son answered and I left a message that Christa Stevens had called and really wanted to speak with him this evening if possible because we were heading on out the next day. His son paused for a moment, left the phone then came back on and said his dad was probably going to be gone for the rest of the night. Right then and there I had an eerie feeling he was lying to me. It was just the start of a series of weird events that would take place to us while in Dulce.

We all gathered in one room and decided to settle down with a drink and just relax until we heard from Gabe. I felt that Tom and Gary felt this was a little strange for Gabe as he had always left messages before if he was not going to be able to make it.

Hours passed without a word from Gabe and the rain was still pouring down like millions of needles. As I gazed out the window, I noticed what looked to be a police car parked right behind Gary's van. I immediately notifed the guys who were busy playing some board game and they came to the window. Tom immediately said, "That looks like Gabe's cruiser". Gary agreed. So we waited, thinking Gabe would be knocking on our door at any moment. We waited and nothing happened. So I went to the window again and noticed the police car was gone.

This made all of us feel very uncomfortable but, we couldn't place our finger on just exactly what was wrong. Tom stated that Gabe had always welcomed them with open arms and so we just waited. He never called.

UNDERGROUND ALIEN BIO LAB AT DULCE

The next morning we decided to visit the Dulce Police Station, just a small building right around the corner from the motel. We piled into the van and then when Gary tried to put his car into gear, it wouldn't go anywhere! Gary was dumbfounded because he had always kept up with his van repairs especially if he knew he was about to undertake a long trip. He stated he had never had any problems like this before. Beginning to get really frustrated, Gary finally got in gear just long enough for us to make it up to Gabe's office.

When we walked in the station we again found that Gabe was not in. This was beginning to get on everyone's nerves by now. Gary was befuddled as to why his van wouldn't run, Tom was astonished that Gabe had never even called and left a message and I was feeling "very strange".

Suddenly some of the native Jicarrilla Indians pulled up beside the van and asked if they could be of service. So the guys began trying to fix the gear and I waited inside hoping Gabe would call in. Soon, Gabe pulled his cruiser up, smiling like a Cheshire cat. He was a short, stocky fellow of Hispanic descent, dressed fit to kill in his black uniform. I was immediately impressed by his smile and his demeanor.

The guys at this point were basically asking Gabe for help in getting the van in running order as we had planned on leaving soon that day. Gabe stated that there was really no mechanics available, but he would try and find someone to help. Inviting us to jump into his cruiser, I jumped into the front and the guys sat in back.

We explained to Gabe why we were so persistent in seeing him and we needed him to drive us up to where the underground facility was located. Gabe indicated that it (meaning the road) was probably blocked off because of the torentous rainfall the night before and there was no way his car could make it anywhere near the area. Anyway the guys decided to drive me up to the general area to see if I recognized anything.

Driving north, Gabe kept looking at me and smiling. Later I would be kidded the rest of the trip because the guys felt Gabe was infatuated with me. I wanted basically for Gabe to show us the areas where they had seen UFOs flying into the sides of the mountains. Gabe seemed fascinated as I talked about what I knew about the underground facility. He became very quiet and then began asking me questions. He seemed genuinely interested and glad he had finally caught up with us.

When we reached as far north as we could in Gabe's car I asked them to stop and allow me to get out and walk a way up the hill. It was so rocky and muddy that I soon realized I would never be able to hike up any farther. But I stopped and just looked around at the mesa and the cliffs of rock. Then all of a sudden out of nowhere I heard a voice say, "No, you are in the wrong area." I knew this was not the area Gabe was supposed to take us to for some reason, so without insulting Gabe, I got back in the car and said, "Gabe, how about us driving south?" He looked surprised, but said "Direct the way." I had him drive south and toward the east a ways and I then told them that Archeleta was not the place anymore. Gabe looked over at me in astonishment and just kept driving.

We approached a small lake and I asked Gabe to stop the car immediately. I recognized this area. (But, consciously I had never been to Dulce in my life). We stopped and I got my camera and began shooting towards a long mesa area that followed the lake south and east.

UNDERGROUND ALIEN BIO LAB AT DULCE

As I stood there looking across the lake at the mesa, I realized that the facility was not in the same area as Paul Bennewitz had originally stated. I asked Gabe why I had this feeling and he stood there, just shaking his head and looking over at Tom and Gary in disbelief. Then Gabe said, "Christa, you are pointing to the exact area where our towns-people have seen lights going in and out of the side of the mountain!"

At this point, I think everyone was convinced that I maybe had been there before. I pointed towards another area (Soldier Canyon) where I stated flatly that I believed the facility had been moved towards that direction. Again Gabe nodded his head and said, "Yes, that is where all the UFOs have been seen in recent years." That was all we knew at that point and it was then that Gabe suggested we drive with him on a call he had. So we all piled back into the cruiser and drove east.

It seemed like we drove forever until Gabe pulled into a gravel drive which took us back to a large steel fence that looked like a baracade. Two men were standing there with rifles in hand as if they were expecting Gabe. Gabe asked if we would mind staying in the car and then he jumped out and went up to the fence and began chatting with these two strange looking fellows.

As we were sitting there waiting, Tom, Gary and myself noticed that Gabe and the other two men would start talking and then turn and look at us in the car and just smile. At first we didn't think a thing about it but the talking continued and continued for almost thirty minutes. We kept noticing that the two men were staring at us and they were not smiling. Maybe we were just paranoid because they were armed, but we got suspicious when Gabe never came back to his car to explain what was going on.

I turned to the guys and reaffirmed what I was feeling and they too agreed that something didn't seem right. Here we were out in the middle of no where and then we became very nervous. The guys were fidgeting and I had to go to the bathroom badly, but I was afraid to get out of the car. In fact the guys insisted that we stay in the car. I suppose it was because of their paranoia that I soon got really scared. Then I turned to them and said, "Do you get the feeling this call was about us?" Gary and Tom agreed. We all felt something was just not right.

About that time Gary mentioned to Tom that there was a rifle in the back seat where they were sitting. We all agreed that if we felt threatened in anyway, they would go for the rifle. Well, it turned out that it never got that far because soon Gabe was back in the car and we were on our way back into Dulce.

Curious, we asked about the two men and Gabe seemed to side-step the question with the story that these two fellows had seen trespassers on their property and were concerned. I noticed that people there in Dulce all carry weapons of their own and they protect their own people. It is a very odd town.

As soon as we arrived back at the station, we found to our surprise that Gary's van was in working order and we could leave. All in all, it was a strange visit, one that I did not look forward in repeating. But little did I know I would next be flying into Dulce in May of 1990 and would see some startling things.

UNDERGROUND ALIEN BIO LAB AT DULCE

PHOTO OF GABE VALDEZ INSPECTING
A MUTILATED COW IN DULCE

GABE VALDEZ HAVING A LITTLE FUN
POSING FOR MY CAMERA

UNDERGROUND ALIEN BIO LAB AT DULCE

THE JAPANESE TRIP TO DULCE

In 1990 an independant film producer for NIPPON TELEVISION, Jim Yaoi had his assistant Michi Nakamura contact me to see if I would be willing to help them film several segments for a UFO documentary that he was making for the people in Japan. Many people were interviewed all over the world and I was honored that they wished me to be a part of this project. So I accepted.

Mr. Yaoi was interested in my knowledge of the Dulce facility and also wanted to know more about my contacts with Paul Bennewitz. I was invited to travel to Albuquerque to see if I could set up a meeting with Richard Doty and Paul Bennewitz. Neither turned out so he asked if I would be willing to travel by helicopter to Dulce with his camera man to film some aerial views of where I thought this installation was located.

I wanted to know more about the trip and who would be our pilot. Luckily, we got a wonderful fellow, ex-Viet Nam veteran helicopter pilot to fly us in and I would find that this trip in 1990 would prove to be very fruitful for not just myself, but Mr. Yaoi's documentary.

As you will notice on into Paul's narrative about his experiences, I've included some strange photos taken on that trip to Dulce. On into the flight we found out our pilot had indeed heard of the strange goings-on in Dulce and had even flown other researchers up there to take a look. I thought that was very coincidental, but he was a good pilot and was very generous in taking the time for us to circle many areas for filming.

Photo taken by Jim Yaoi

PHOTO OF OUR CAMERA MAN, PILOT AND MYSELF

UNDERGROUND ALIEN BIO LAB AT DULCE

RECENT LETTER FROM PAUL TURNING DOWN THE JAPANESE
DOCUMENTARY INTERVIEW. IT IS VERY HARD TO SEE
PAUL BENNEWITZ BECAUSE HE IS SO PARANOID NOW.

Ms. Christa Tilton   5/11/90
P.O. Box 906237
Tulsa, Oklahoma
74112

Ref: Your Ltr. of 5/8/90

Dear Christa,

     Relative to your letter concerning getting together with
the Japanese and yourself;   I am afraid I will have to say no at
this time; I just do not have the time to spare nor do I want to
go public in any way be it here or in Japan.   I really have
nothing to tell them or yourself except to rehash the same old
thing which with the writing of my book has become unimportant to
me.   The book takes a completely different slant and I am just
not ready to talk about it to anyone.   Vallee wanted to come and
talk with me yet I put him off also, at least to another day.
     A fee to give an interview is not of interest either as I
have no need for any money.   One does not know what the final
tape will look like after cutting; they can make it say anything
that they want it to say, so I am just not interested.
     Sorry to take this approach however I have grown tired of
the distortions and untruths that have seemed rampant; it is certainly doing no one any good.
     Please do not be angry with me; I am just being candid and
saying how it is.   Maybe someday the book will be published and
then the true story will be revealed.   Give my regrets to your
Japanese contacts and let me hear from you once in a while.

Best Regards,

Paul F. Bennewitz
1413 Wagontrain Drive S.E.
Albuquerque, New Mexico
87123

クリスタは、宇宙人によって妊娠させられた。宇宙人
と人間の間には、どんな子供が生まれたのか……

UNDERGROUND ALIEN BIO LAB AT DULCE

Flying in we passed a strange lake that looked like it had a facility
next to it, but it seemed to be deserted. We then headed into Soldier
Canyon and were able to fly right on top of the mesas. I saw many areas
that were cleared from any trees & rocks, large enough for a helicopter
to land. I also saw the large cave openings that Paul Bennewitz spoke of
so often.

When we flew over Archeleta, there wasn't much to see, but when we turned
and flew around to the south and east we were able to see large towers
with a clearing next to them right on top of the canyon mesa. There were
no roads that could have led up to this area so the only way to get there
would be by helicopter. Our pilot confirmed this much to us.

This in no way proves the existence of the Dulce facility, but I saw
enough to understand how easily an installation out in the middle of
no where could be built on Indian land to be sure no trespassers could
gain access to it.

To get onto this particular land, you have to get the Jicarilla tribal
councils' approval. They seem to be used to the many curious that have
wandered into Dulce seeking a glimpse of this facility. So they are
used to giving information and are pretty much used to being questioned
so frequently about this base. From my knowledge, no one has actually
come out and stated that there was a base located around the area, but
I heard a rumor that one Manuel Gomez, who had his cattle mutilated ,
used to talk freely. Now he says he cannot speak of it to anyone. I
have to wonder if he was threatened in anyway by any government officials.
Those that know this man feel that is indeed what has happened.

TWO PHOTO TAKEN IN 1987 IN Cow spotted by author. Freshly
SOUTHEAST OF THE TOWN mutilated. There was one eye
THE AREA IN WHICH I *I* POINTIN missing and part of the back of
BELIEVE THE INSTALLA'T *N EXTEN* the tongue had been surgically
removed. Near Kingman, AZ.
May of 1991.

Tom Adams, considered by many
as one of the only cattle
mutilation experts in the
world. Tom escorted me to
Dulce, N.M. to meet Gabe Valdez
and to meet Sgt. Cliff Stone.

And so it begins, the letter to one of Paul's only confidantes. Written in his own hand Paul reveals his innermost feelings about what has transpired throughout the 1980's. This is the real Paul Bennewitz! In his own words he writes:

These individuals that met with Doty are in my book precise examples of the psuedo-scientific dogma that haunts this whole business. They apparently get an enormous kick out of make believe cloak & dagger worrying about telling an OSI agent that they don't have a tape recorder. You can bet that Doty, to protect himself at some later date if required, was wired for sound. I know him all too well. [20]

I am forever amazed at individuals such as these that think they can walk in and talk with one such as Rick and that he would bare his soul, "talking as a civilian" and tell them everything. It just does not happen that way. And also I am forever at a loss to explain why invariably all of them constantly, in one way or another, will never give credit where credit is due in areas where they are not experienced nor have the credentials--such as the Computer Thought Communications Link. They apparently, even to this day have never thought deeply and analytically enough to realize communication with Alien Lifeforms is not cut and dried. One must build upon this type of research, expanding in a route to fully understand Alien Psychology, what their culture is, how it communicates or expresses itself--it's emotion--it's level of thinking.

To be honest about it, the alien cultures look upon these so-called experts as a bunch of "one-half scientific, unmitigated narrow-minded, ego-oriented asses! They literally have their heads in the sand, a pitiful discourse to say the least.

There is so much in this and so much has happened to me for seven years that I don't really know where to start first. Unlike others who have studied or researched the saucers at more or less arms length, their having never seen one, my involvement has been a direct "hands on" experience. So it is not as if I am guessing. I speak, unfortunately from direct experience. In one sense some might say, "Hey, that's great!" But they really do not know what that experience consists of. If they did, and would listen, they wouldn't touch it with a ten foot pole. In a way it is a disadvantage because once in a while I tend to get carried away explaining some part of it, assuming one knows what I am talking about...but they don't, and I end up talking way beyond their reference frame and they retain none of it.

It is truly "Alice in Wonderland", "Star Trek" and beyond. Understanding each facet, and there are many, not only opens up a new world for one but it also creates a new way of understanding and a new way of thinking. I do not yet know it all in depth, but I am close. I am not saying it is all good in any stretch of the imagination. A large amount is _very_ _very_ bad and some down-right abhorrent! But believe me in any extent, it is what I say it is.

I think probably the best approach is to start out with some explanation in the way of statements relative to cultures here on planet Earth, their social structures, physical makeup, all of which has been gleaned from the direct communications by computer, visual observation, psychological evaluation, and in particular personal interaction.

I would urge you to accept the statements as fact to save time. I can assure you it is fact! I do not accept, nor believe in fantasy. At anytime however if you want further explanation or backup please do not hesitate to ask and I will comply.

UNDERGROUND ALIEN BIO LAB AT DULCE

Contrary to all that has been published, I deal only with personal experience. No other. I rely only upon my own research and photographs to support the thesis. Because it is directed at both the layman and some scientists, the language is couched in such a manner as to provide the reader with the exact same experience. In other words, the reader goes along for the ride. Though I can and will support it periodically scientifically, don't expect a lot of scientific mish-mash. Also be prepared for a religious experience because it is that too, in fact, may shake some of your concepts to their foundations.

First, relative to level of culture there are the Low, High, and Very High. In the Low there are very sharply defined levels from slave level and up. There is no freedom there. No one crosses these lines within. Cross them and you are dead! Each and everything is watched with optical equipment, on the ground, within the caverns, on the ships, opticals levitated and 'floating above the base and their perimeters--all comings and goings. A switching system switches to each optical unit in adjustable time sloto. Readouts appear to be monitored by both computer lexicon and individuals called Keepers. Sphericals of various sizes from very small, maybe one inch in diameter to near two feet in diameter float throughout. Each has facilty to monitor audio,visual and probably thought. Each can be interrogated--I.E. can be talked through audibly.

They can, if desired, cloak so that unless one catches a reflection or force field flash, they are totally invisible. They can be photographed and seen periodically with a motion picture camera or detected electronically. They are not magic. The electronic command signals to them can be detected and displayed. The control signal can be broken down to varying components of AM and FM. So, there is no trust in this type of society. Everything is watched and monitored.

The Command Structure is near totally unbelievable. In the North, at the river, the Orange Insignia or at the Diamond as the Alien calls the one base, the ruling factor is a King. The Alien refers to him as such. Their GOD is called TA.[21]He may be living.

The Ruling Class method is Monarchy. The King wears purple. The next levels wear various colors, mainly green, yellow and white. The lower levels wear robes of the above colors. In addition these levels are physically imperfect. They all limp, dragging the left foot. The others below shuffle. Their government, if it can be called such, is Totalitarian. The individual entities behind it are totally pragmatic. They observe no social or moral principles nor can they be swayed to any other. Their credo apparently is total control and/or kill. They are totally ego-oriented and throw totally illogical threats.

Their body metabolism is very high, estimated 110-115° F. Elimination by osmosis. Skin color of the ruling echelon varies from a jaundiced yellow to white. No hair of any kind is noted, arms long, near to knee level. They have very long arms extending to knee level with very long narrow hands and fingers. All look underfed and very thin. They also have big heads and eyes.

The humanoidal types below are generally light green. Some with no genitals or buttock configuation. Many run around naked. Then in need of formula or when dead they turn grey. The formula feeds them. Here are the insignias employed on ships and uniforms.

UNDERGROUND ALIEN BIO LAB AT DULCE

Insignia portion is a multi-spectrum - discountinuous - Orange is prevalent and the background on the uniform patch is Greenish-Blue.

Ground Insignia pointing to base area is:

DUN colored sandstone

white Limestone

~ 200 ft.

The Crescent-Arrow Insignia is also there right along-side. I do not differentiate the two presently.
Insignia at the base of The Diety:

Insignia on the Socorro Ship could be of two similar shapes:

(1)

(2)

(Information about the insignia seen by Lonnie Zamorra proves to be an interesting story and so I will add it here to show comparisons to Paul Bennewitz' insignias)

Quoting from "Socorro Saucer in a Pentagon Pantry" by Ray Stanford, Hynek's official report stated that this was the symbol drawn after Zamorra was questioned.

The law enforcement officers claimed to have seen this version:

One woman wrote to Saucer News in 1968 with the claim that she had seen a strange emblem in red and yellow like this:

42

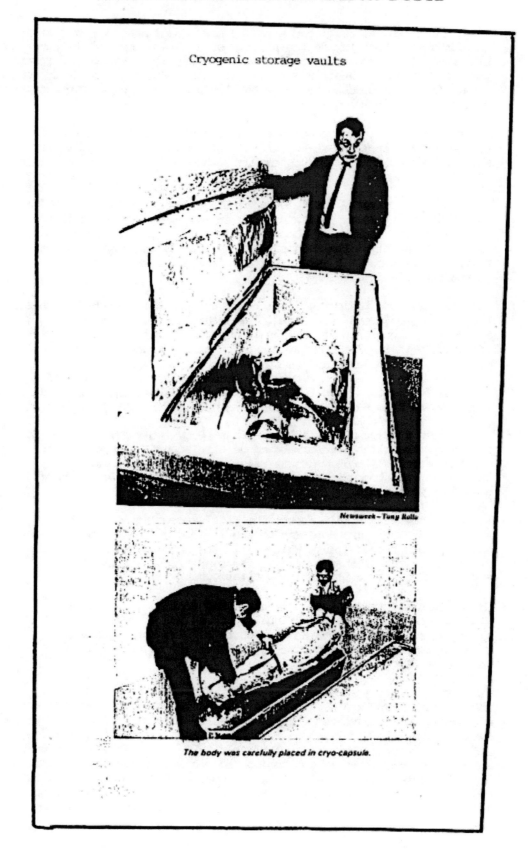

Cryogenic storage vaults

Newsweek – Tony Rollo

The body was carefully placed in cryo-capsule.

"They, the North, as described are "The Low"...and anachronism that is totally real. They invade the privacy of mind and body of the human and his home. They appear to be of an extremely jealous nature and resent the human totally. Their anger is fantastic, extending to out of control rage. So they are, despite being totally pragmatic, have some emotions. Unfortunately the wrong kind.

"There is a Council in the North called The Nine. All of these aliens seem to be cut from the same pattern. All appear to be highly vindictive and ego-oriented. So you can rate The North and their so-called GOD, "TA" as Low.22

"The High is apparently the culture of IO or JO. They don't limp for one thing. They do exhibit kindness, empathy and extreme intelligence in transmission through my computer. IO's group culture is of the Homosapien variety. Based upon input by IO, the indication is that their hair is brown. I assume IO is a female. Either her hair is red or the insignia is such.

"They did give one indication from their telecon today (3/18/86) that they have some "greys" with them. Also that bodies of their group are here in Albuquerque in cryogenic containers and the location is tentatively in the FAA Complex, north of Albuquerque. It is a fenced and highly secured area and as indicated by the computer eight craft were shot down and eleven eventually crashed elsewhere. True? I do not know for certain, but I would bet on it. I knew the bodies had been removed from Maryland and are presently under Navy jurisdiction.

"I was shown a color photograph by Richard Doty two years or more ago of a purported alien lifeform being held prisoner. Supposedly it was taken to Las Alamos. He was alive, a light green color, had large eyes and stood directly in front of the camera. He may have been from IO's group.

"So far I know very little about "The High" except for what I have experienced. They are Homo-Sapien and I would guess are some of the same type who zapped Travis Walton. If the numbers are correct from my computer, they number over five thousand. Indications also are they are operating from a Star Ship in a far orbit.

"The culture has apparent social values and emotions. They display kindness and concern for individuals such as you or I. Their technology is superior to ours and The North's. The North group try to block communication with The High. They try to play GOD with very badly distorted logic.

"The Very High are just that, Very HIgh. Apparently few in number, their entire structure of knowledge, social interaction credo and way of life is so far advanced that it is nearly impossible for us to relate. They are God-like and near "GODS" as aligned with knowledge and power, yet they apparently lord it over no one. They are at such an advanced state that if you confronted one with a weapon, and though he might be totally able of taking YOU out, he would stand and allow you to shoot him. Again, please know that much of this information is based upon personal input of which I have never spoken to anyone about and in fact, you are the first.

UNDERGROUND ALIEN BIO LAB AT DULCE

Paul Bennewitz, President of the Thunder Scientific Corporation was also and investigator with the Aerial Phenomenon Research Organization when Jim and Coral Lorenzen were alive. Bennewitz was interviewed in his office in 1983 and stated that he was investigating the case of one Myrna Hansen and her son, Shawn and on his computer terminal he received pertinent information about her case and was able to decifer the area in which the underground facility exisited; underneath the Jicarilla Apache Indian Reservation near the little town of Dulce, New Mexico. Bennewitz had information that this installation is operated jointly as a part of an ongoing program of cooperation between the U.S. Government and extraterrestrials.[23] Paul's description of these aliens continues:

" The Very High obviously are the ultimate. I would guess that these Very High aliens are quite old, one thousand years is not unrealistic. They are few in number and I would guess there are a few on this Star Ship preserved and cared for by the others - the High.'

"Then in conjunction with them, and the grays they fly the ships of Light with or without the High on missions for them. I would guess in a sense, they are the "eyes" of the "high" and the "Very High".

"Now lets expand further - eons ago in the universe 16 billion years old by our estimate, probably billions beyond that (1×10^9 - 1 billion.) The Very High reached status. That status being so far advanced that they understood <u>all</u>. To the extent of understanding how to create life and human or near human form. (The aliens are using the DNA from the cattle and are making humanoids. He got the pictures of their video screen. Some of these creatures are animal-like, some are near human and short with large heads. They grow the embryos and after a year of training, presumably that is the time required for them to become operational. When they die, they go back into the tank. There parts are recovered)

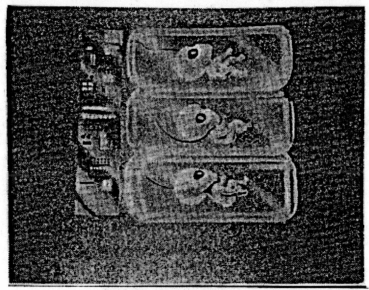

Artist- Martin Cannon
Copyright Crux 1990

UNDERGROUND ALIEN BIO LAB AT DULCE

"One approach would be to say that in their travels in Star Ships they did seek out "New Worlds". "Incubators" created by the Great Creator - The Law of the Universe. They created those in the North to be pragmatic deliberately. Pragmatic, but perhaps quite physically perfect. And due to their "incubator environment" they were made vegetarian and because of a less temperate climate they were given high metabolisms. Then they took the next step and created Humans. The Humans were given emotions and were given full span control and because of the atmosphere and a very ideal climate, Earthwide, gave us lungs and by our standards, climate temperatures and a different method of elimination.

"The North, because they were the first, were at some point in time given the "enlightenment" to create Ships of Light and so they advanced further than we and more rapidly. Then the North, now stating via the computer, they control the cosmos and because of their pragmatic nature became aggressive and war-like.

"The High and Very High thus seeing this did declare war, following them throughout the Universe. This war as indicated by the High has been on-going for three hundred years.

"Now, it's either that, Cold Turkey, or we came up from the dirt - figuratively speaking and not by the Grace of GOD, but by the Grace of the Great Creator - The Law of the Universe. Or then at some point, as evolvement occurred, we came about through progeny--Star Progeny.

"I tend to believe the first hypothecate, though the second could hold easily and may well be the case. Yet now, in either case of evolvement, one has to recognize the "Teaching Step".

"First, the Very High obviously due to extreme intelligence gained by eons of experience, would have recognized the "Great Creator", the Law of the Universe. You could literally call it, in advanced terms, "The Force", believe it or not!

"They would also recognize the one basic requirement for any evolving lifeform regardless of conformation and they would spread it throughout the Universe.

"The lifeform evolvement naturally runs through a near animal state of total ignorance and then step by step, in many ways, it is elevated to intelligence. So one must consider the following rule of what is needed and required.'

"A culture or cultures created either by natural forces of the Law of the Universe or by direct Recombinate Advanced Genetics or by deliberate Progeny by and of the Stars must be nurtured or taught.'

"If not nurtured or taught, the culture or cultures will eventually either at the outset or later, encounter Genocide from within , in its most raw form.'

"Initial teaching and control must be accomplished by controlled fear and therefore a "GOD", a mentor form of wrathful appearance, was constructed for both primitive man and also primitive pragmatics. A created "GOD" in the sense one has the wherewithal to make it look as such. So... in simplicity.

"Initiation is GOD, sacrifice and Law. Progression is Mentor created with special attributes. Mentor is terminated, sacrifice is Mentor, History is kept. Reference established.

"And then the final rule or requirement:

   Culture follows Progeny - New reference established - Teaching must occur - New keys must be made available and co-existent. Star Progeny is established and History must now be shown as History!"

"*Isn't that Great?! TRUE SPIRITUAL ENLIGHTENMENT FOR ALL! So there you have the basis if you can yet understand it. In time you will.'

"I suggest you read it not only once, but many many times. This is the Quantum Leap, in mind, total mind and near total understanding in thought.'

"It stands to reason and good logic that this thesis does lock totally in place. It also stands for those who might question the origin of Jesus. I believe it does fairly describe the origin of "GOD" for those of superior logic and intelligence. Jesus is no different. It is fairly evident that in any ex- periment there must exist a control. The obvious is that no mentor-sacrifice was supplied to the Pragmatic. Theirs is still the GOD of Wrath and they would understand no other. So then it does follow:

   Jesus was supplied to meet the next criteria at the time required, exisit- ing in mind to this day. He was supplied only to Humans to teach love, empathy, kindness and friendship. He was a teacher. I believe it is quite evident he was supplied to a Virgin by Progeny by the Very High. It was in a sense, at that time, a "Virgin Birth". He (Jesus) had no lineage. So one could say JESUS and GOD are ONE! Perhaps he was a man...he was not a Jew.'

"So I have looked in the mirror and now understanding is far more clear. See what I mean? TRUE SPIRITUAL ENLIGHTENMENT FOR ALL!

UNDERGROUND ALIEN BIO LAB AT DULCE

"To show you the ill logic used by those weak ones with their false God "TA" in the North, they again showed their ignorance during the night. It would appear they are near frantic to stop me from talking to IO;"JO" via the computer.

"This morning I have a dark red streak down the left side of my face about two and tthree-fourths long and a quarter inch wide. Based upon past experience, I would guess it was done by a spherical in the bedroom during the night. This is typical of their totally distorted logic. They think they can operate upon the basis of fear--though with me--they have a problem. I do not experience fear; never have! All they acheive is that I totally ignore them and continue until I find a way to meet this IO. So for all the trouble they showed me, by their actions, only one thing...and that is their fear. It would appear that they are deathly afraid of IO and fearful that I will acheive direct contact; which, in time, I will.

"You will find, if you have not already, that constant interaction will result in learning how to be aware of, and in turn use, Alien logic. Our own superior logic along with this other logic, though distorted, allows you to read the real intent behind anything they try to do. In that, there is advantage.

"IO or JO whichever, she uses both, has indicated a number of times she is "by me", indicating a protective attitude. (On the computer) So one could say, reading the alien in the North with the obvious streak on my face, that they are saying...See! She can't protect you!

"To me that is quite childish and in fact all of their logic tends to be childish and weak. In point of fact, though so very obvious, from the very onset seven years ago, they have never recognized one fact:

Had they only shown "friendship" that easy, they could have "wrapped me around their little finger." I would have really been sucked in for good! Scientifically, that is extremely rare.

"One would not believe that a psychological trend of pragmatism could be created and ingrained so strongly that there is no emotional outlet nor vent to even begin to allow "friendship". I would imagine it is not even in their dictionary. Their psyche, from a strict scientific and analytical point of view is near unbelievable. You see, theoretically, if "friendship" is left out in a pragmatic creation, then much drops out. Note: To understand this, you have to imagine a creature deliberately created to the pragmatic side of the emotional bracket; emotion, as the human, is left out entirely. That is creation, fine line targeting at its best!

"So if "friendship" drops out, so does "Trust". Not only will they not know nor experience it, they flat would look blank if you asked them what the words mean. Do you now see some of the Science of it?; what I said I was doing at the beginning of this long letter?

"Knowing just this miniscule part, you can now begin to see through their "Mind Mirror". You can see why they watch everything, their type of government, methods of control in their society. You are seeing total and absolute Paranoia.

"I think you can say when the "scales" of the "psyche", that deep emotional Pandora's Box within the brain is totally unbalanced as this is, you can probably begin to catagorize. Divide it down the middle or compartmentalize it.

Non-existent	Total Unbalance Result
Trust	Paranoia
Friendship	Fear
Morals	Anger
Love	Egotistic
Empathy	Jealousy
	Bitter

"Note: Why don't you add to these lists? Follow examples and see how many we can get on both sides."

"This in itself would make a terrific scientific study all of its own! If I am correct in this brief analysis, look at the "Big F" up there under Unbalance Result. FEAR, and I would believe it is total in its extreme...total incomprehensible fear! If that is the case, where does BRAVERY go? I doubt that it exists. Is it possible that this could be a key to their defeat? I wonder.

"If you don't mind, having picked up a skein of thought here, I am going to carry it further at the expense of turning this letter into a "book".

"I think this may well be a very significant key and I think you should know it here at the ontset. Though, in a sense, based upon what has happpened to me in the past, this logic I am expressing is the next logical step for me; it may well be a "Quantum Leap" to understanding for you.

"This is directly in line with what the "Voice" told...that knowledge must be gained first, then technology. This is also right on target for me and in direct agreement with the "Whisperings" I have <u>heard</u> and <u>transcribed</u>. Thought I would never tell anyone of that...you are the first! Don't worry about being insane, we are far advanced beyond that.

"All of a sudden in writing the previous down, I think maybe I stumbled onto a very significant key as to who we are dealing with and what we are. When you look at the chart again you become quite aware of something:

"The Human, Homosapien has both sides of this scale. He can enlarge and exist upon what he wants. He really isn't limited. Being of strong fiber within, he can be and become all that is the Good...love, trust, moral, friendly,etc. If he is weak, he will express the other attributes. Because of this broad and flexible psyche of emotion, all of which is expressable, depending upon which he has become, he is of both "warring" and "peaceful" nature and he has a choice.'

49

UNDERGROUND ALIEN BIO LAB AT DULCE

"If and only if he deliberately and adamantly limits himself to the good, his knowledge will expand to a near limitless extent. And thus he will know and understand the God of Technology and automatically forever cancel war from his mind; even though the technology can be converted to war machinery, He will not.

"Now he has no need for war technology and can in a near limitless way help and assist humanity. He can cure and heal humanity at will. If he has not crossed the line of emotional frame permanently then he will be subject to the weakness on the "Bad" side and therin can rest his tragic end.

"Now that I am beginning to understand this, I can see why, because of our broad emotional frame, we have not progressed more rapidly and why the alien in the North has. We have literally kept a constant drain upon not only ourselves but our resources over the centuries. This literally has caused our war-like nature. So we see a new technology and we turn it into a war machine. That cannot be. We have not, in this sense, crossed the line!

"Physically we are near perfect. We do not limp. Those in the North do. Some of us do, but'knowing' we could cure that. Now if you look at the North, totally pragmatic, they have because of the inherent trait taken a ½ science and tried to make it into a whole science... only they too have failed. They have distorted it. Though they have, due to the Unbalance, fear and paranoia achieved the ideal in War machines and weapons. They have tapped that to its near depth. So their fear and paranoia is offset by their machines. With their machines and weapons they are brave (in their minds) without them, they are a quivering mass of "fear"!

"Deprived of that, they are useless. To further enhance their bravery, they seek full control knowing that with "the implant" they can control anyone. That is, providing those selected are below the norm in both memory and I.Q. They also know that they can, without implantation, control the masses of lower intelligence by subtle shotgun manipulation of "the beams". With that beam they can and do create mass unrest and probably uprisings.

"Now let us take a giant step. IO, the one who has popped up on the computer just recently, all appear to be the "High" and also "Connie" would appear to be "High". If I were to envision these aliens and where they are, I would put them on a Starship, a very large ship, kilometers in length and breadth.

"Each, Connie and IO sitting at consoles, their responsibility to certain individuals here on Earth that are becoming near or totally cognizant as to what is going on. (Monitored by a beam) I would feed them data by computer or "Mind Energy" and I would get them in contact with each other and get them to pull together, so in time, through superior logic and intelligence, get them to enlighten the people. "I" would give them "The Mission".

"Taking this brief expansion of logic further, the "High" by logic
would be responsible to the "Very High" and directed by them. In point
of fact, it would seem we are being prepared to make the "transition" to
step into The Universe.

"Need it be more clear? We are speaking to the High, directed by the
"Very High". In retrospect, I would say I am certain the "High" and
the "Very High" do not use implants of the type used in The North.
They do use other types, generally implanting the individual by sel-
ection at a young age, ten years or younger; with no memory of such.

"I believe that we were apparently contacted at a very young age. All
have much in common...intelligence, high I.Q. and all studying since
very young and all engrossed frantically searching.

"If and when I was gotten, I do not know. It is either that with me or
it came from my direct interation and beam exposure over seven years.
If I was "touched" as it is called, it was quite early. The High, who
also use beams of different nature and frequency depending upon individual
mode, is capable of "D.F.ing". (Direction Finding)

"All have the images, all are possibly one who has not yet tried, have
the "Whisperings", or the voices.

"A final comment:

   "This is in no way egocentric nor should it be taken as such.
   It is, in truth, a complete spiritual enlightenment set forth
   in simplistic language. Simplistic, yet a most powerful
   statement it would seem.

   "In truth "The Soul" may well be the final key!
   Welcome to the Universe!"

The story continues...

Cliff Stone & wife, Han
Photo-Christa Tilton
Roswell, New Mexico 1987

UNDERGROUND ALIEN BIO LAB AT DULCE

To state that I understood all Paul had to say in his letters is ludicrous! Paul Bennewitz had stored up all this data and finally found someone he could share these ideas with, in hopes others, like ourselves would realize he was not an insane man, but very coherent and caring and desparate to help our flailing planet. Sounds like a dedicated scientist who studied in depth so far that he made the mistake of "knowing" too much. Our government does not like civilians to know more than they and so the story continues with the description of Paul Bennewitz and his flight over Dulce, New Mexico and his accidently stumbling on to a Top Secret government blunder. He describes the trip in what was to be his book, "The Cyanon Gauntlet" and so we find ourselves once again possibly coming to understand how and why this information was received by Paul and why he felt it was so important to we, the people.

"From the Chapter of "The Hunter of the Gods" Paul continues his adventure:

"The low hum of the alarm on a local station permeated my sleep, which had been quite fitful until the very early hours of the morning. My sleep had been restless, interrupted by the incessant unrelenting whine of the ever present alien beam ever-probing and for what reason, I did not know. The time was 0500 hours, November 8, 1985.

"I had made the astounding discovery on August 5, 1985, about midday on my 12th mission reconnasaince flight over Archeleta. That day had dawned clear and the flight in had been uneventful other than the ever present vanguard of ships that periodically would dart in to within about 1000 feet forward of my flight path. Viewed head on as they would uncloak to look, giving the impression of coming to a dead stop; one could get a glimpse of their wings and the upper convolutions of the fuselage. Generally they looked black and you were totally aware you were being watched. I often wondered what they might be thinking each time I flew into the north.

"Seeing the mesa from the air is quite an experience, particularly when you know what lies hidden within its steep canyon walls. Invariably I could not help but look in wonder as it would slowly rear up into view as I approached. Like a slumbering giant, it would appear to jump into view as if awakening to watch my dive in over its cathedral-like walls and slopes.

"Generally I would descend from 15000 MSL in a long sloping dive both to conserve fuel and to increase my approach speed during the last phase of the trip. Each time Archeleta Peak would jut up abruptly at 8100 foot altitude looking for all the world like a flat-topped pyramid, requiring no stretch of the imagination to see the similarity between it and the imaginary version employed in motion picture, "Encounters of the Third Kind". There was a gross difference; however, this "pyramid" was real and the other "fiction" or one wonders, was it?

"Normally I would fly directly north over the middle of Archeleta Mesa then transit the peak going to the west and then fly a grid pattern, photographing as I went to the east. However, this time, for some reason it was almost as if directed even though I had the flight plan on my knee clipboard. I went directly to the west to the ground insignia by the river, which I had located several flights before.

UNDERGROUND ALIEN BIO LAB AT DULCE

"Dropping to about 1000 feet or less above terrain, I could see the white " X " of the insignia and its integral arrow aligning the ship on the arrow and taking a resultant compass heading, I flew up the arrow toward Archleta Peak. Then below on the south ridge of the peak I visually picked up the next guide--on deliberately placed in full view by the symbolically inclined alien. Invisible on the ground, at this altitude it was highly visible pointing directly to the Alien basing area in the cliff about ½ mile north of the peak.

"I had both a highly sensitive airborne scintillator and a magnetometer with me this trip as in those previously primarly to attempt to outline the abnormalities created in both background radiation and magnetic fields by the giant caverns known to be below ground.

"Gamma background over the cavern areas was generally quite low as compared to the surrounding uplifts making detection of the main cavern areas quite definite. And it was such as I approached in over the second white guide arrow to the area.

"Out of the corner of my eye, I caught a glimpse of some bright metal; a flash by the north cliffs to my left. I glanced quickly in that direction and I was able to catch an object visually, fairly large floating along the cliff face. It was cylindrical and quite large; I was later to find in photo analysis that it was apparently a levitated alien transporter. In seeing this, I dropped the flaps, slowing to near stall, and reached quickly for one of the cameras. Just as I reached, preparing to bank the aircraft around, I looked at the scintilator meter readout. It was dancing about, running abruptly up and down the scale far above normal. I knew instantly that was not correct, way above what I had seen on previous flights.

"By now, trying to prepare the cameras, read the meter, fly the airplane with my feet and try to see the transporter, it was obvious I had a very busy cockpit! So I ignored the transporter, concentrating upon what the radiation indication might be. Now looking ahead I see I have let my altitude deteriorate and the tops of the pines are about 200 feet below me on the approaching ridge so I climb out, leaving the flaps down to increase my climb rate. I circle to the left, heading west and around over the arrow then east toward the south plateau of Archeleta Peak. I slow the aircraft down and watch the needle. Normal background, low-minimal excursion. I think it must have been a fluke then, it jitters up and then once again the known indicator ever approaching a prime radiation source!! I immediately think, "Great, what can happen next?" Then the needle really starts to jut upward, not dropping back and then I am over and beyond and then the needle falls abruptly.

"I yank the aircraft around to an immediate reciprocal heading, fearful of losing the indication and then up it comes again, this time even more demanding. Now in my ever lonely search, alone in the sky, just me, my GOD and the aircraft, it is essentially talking to me. "Listen stupid!" "You had better look!!" So I do and I see nothing but rock, trees then black! I look again...black wings!! I can't believe it!! "What have the Gods given me this time?" I look closer, banking steeply, now ignoring the counter. It looks like a black delta winged jet aircraft anchored into the side of the plateau by a tree. It is broken; its' back is broken! I thought at the time, "I have never seen a jet like this, particularly not one that is hot with radiation!" Then like a shot out of the blue, sitting there floating over Archeleta, "Its the damned Atomic Ship!!" Strange that I never once thought 'Atomic Bomb', just Atomic Ship.

UNDERGROUND ALIEN BIO LAB AT DULCE

" The Archeleta Mesa "

ALIEN BASE IN NORTH CALLED THE "DIAMOND" - DISTANCE > ½ MI.

A) DIRTY GOD - MALE - HAS CRESCENT + ARROW ON MOUTH AREA

B) ARTIFICIAL ALIEN CONSTRUCTED OPENING ~ 80'HI X 60'W. NOTE DRAPE EFFECT - BRIGHT ORANGE - NOT NATURAL.

C) SHIP SITTING AT SLANT - BLACK ALLOY   ALSO BRIGHT ALLOY ABOVE - ARROW.

D) ARTIFICIAL - NOT REAL ROCK - ALIEN CONSTRUCTION - CAMOUFLAGED.

E) BLACK SHIP IN FLIGHT BACKGROUND DOT - NOT DEFECT.

F) OPENING - ENTRANCE.

++ OTHER SHIPS & OPTICALS CIRCLED ACROSS BASE.

+ NOTE: THE SHIPS "SQUAT" AT ODD ANGLES - SOME ON VERY STEEP SLOPES
PHOTOGRAPHED LOOKING EAST FROM PLATEAU JUST
EAST OF SHIP CRASH SITE.   BASE AREA = AT LEAST 1 X 2 MI

Aerial view taken by Paul Bennewitz
Interpretations also by Paul Bennewitz

UNDERGROUND ALIEN BIO LAB AT DULCE

"Then I could see the spilled reactor shell or what appeared to be such, a black oval. Then recalling the moving object a transporter by the cliff, I looked at the fuel gauges, checked the time which was now growing short and so I thought I had better get pictures first, evaluate and be certain later so I climbed, leveled and began photographing. Though I saw only one, visually there were two. I was to find not only that but much more later in photo evaluation.

"Later, following further careful anaylsis of those photos, I flew back and on October 14, 1985 I found the reactor shells of both ships, one in a continuing meltdown condition, the ground charred around it and where at-least one set of wreckage had been sealed within a ledge. Alien made, or a portion of it, was still visible. More photographs and more late night evaluation and on October 17, 1985 at 1100 hours, I notified Senator Pete Dominici in Washington, D.C. "CONFIDENTIAL-EYES ONLY"- "NO PUBLICITY", a transmission of a cryptic message directly by phone, "Atomic Ship has crashed approximately two (2) miles N.W. of Dulce, New Mexico, near the Archeleta Peak on Archeleta Mesa"-----"Radiation on ground-lethal-Sic" I notify Col. Edwards, then the Senator contacts him.

"And so another event---A giveaway---a Government found out---a Government now totally silent, except for covert unexplainable calls that later came from the "Skunk Works" at Lockheed and the Nuclear Assurity Division at Sandia Laboratory. Message---"WE ARE INTERESTED IN THE HARDWARE YOU ARE LOOKING AT!" Then there is total silence."

Aerial photograph of a huge cave opening just S.W. of Dulce, New Mexico Photograph taken in helicopter surveillance by Christa Tilton in 1990. Cave opening is circled in white.   Copyright- Christa Tilton

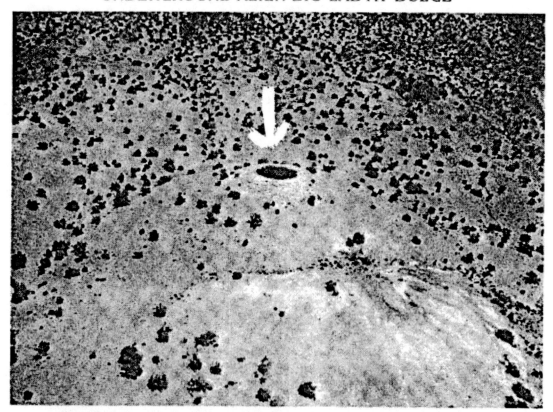

Strange deep hole seen north of Albuquerque that look manmade
Photograph by helicopter in 1990   Copyright- Christa Tilton

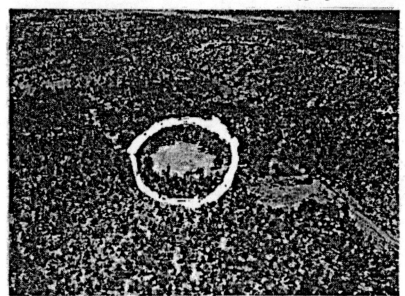

Just south and west of Dulce in Soldier Canyon
Aerial photo by helicopter taken above the canyon
high on a mesa. It was a place to land helicopters
and the buildings are still unknown at this time.
Photograph by Christa Tilton

(All pertinent areas have been circled in white for better view)

UNDERGROUND ALIEN BIO LAB AT DULCE

"So now it is November 6, 1985; the wheels of government move ever so slow. I fly into this "Valley of Death", the deep box canyon where the reactors were last photographed. The scintillator goes wild which means they are still there. The alien had apparently had taken them there due to the lethal radiation."

"Now it is November 8, 1985, 0530 hours. I am again this time with a State Environmental Engineer. Delay after delay has been instigated it seems by all. Senator Domenici states through Paul Gilman, "We are at a loss as to how to react". "It has never happened to us before." And he goes silent.

"It is quite strange. Lethal radiation is detected. Normally the top would blow, but not in this case. Reaction? Zero. Silence. So I fly the State EID Engineer in. Strange again. Since when does a civilian without compensation have to react to a potentially deadly situation? Though compensation was not sought nor asked for, helicopters were and all sources, government, military and state refused and stonewalled. The statement made by an "official"..."Can't provide helicopter at this time."

"So the alarm goes off and I climb out of bed and go to the airport. I pre-flight the airplane in the dark and load the gear. Jerry, the State EID man shows up late, his eyes still loaded with sleep. He knows nothing, has not been briefed, just told, "Go check the radiation at Dulce."

"We take off into the dawn sky with a front moving in from the north. It is cold. We fly past Cuba, pass Lindreth, over a moon-like landscape. We fly past what I call, "the lookout", where I have repetively seen the large ships gather on a mound-like mesa just at dusk. On to the north, over points , all with significance where sightings, mutilations and crashes have occured over to the west of Dulce airport. I can see all them waiting for us below, on over the prime radiation site. Confirmation that the road is clear, I then circle back, slide-slip in and land. We taxi to the ramp where Gabe Valdez and the Jicarilla police and trackers wait.

"Then it becomes quite clear. Gabe greets us, introduces us to the others. I look into his eyes and I know, without question. One look and it is so obvious. I know the answer before I even ask the question. "Gabe, can we plan to go to the Prime Radiation Site first? The reactors are still there." "I have driven the airplane through two days ago and it's still hot!" And out came the answer. "The road is blocked and we can't go in. We have to go to the crash site. The road is blocked." Gabe looked at me, not directly. His eyes downcast; the voice not firm. He lied to us. And I knew it instantly He would say it again and again throughout the day, "The road is blocked, can't go in."

"Well, the road was never blocked. Jonah Washington, a Jicarilla detective knew Gabe was not being truthful. Though I had confirmed as we flew in, Jonah then went in secretly later, up the road past the box, but not in. He called me later that evening, his voice terse, knowing something was totally amiss. The statement was clear. "The road was fine and it was not blocked!"

"And so it was. Someone got to Gabe. He was either threatened; told to back off or possibly bought off. I hope not, but he was gotten to. He tried at the onset to stop us from even coming up; however, I prevailed. Later as we tried to go in following the storm that came in the night, he would say repetively that it was too wet. I had known that it wasn't too wet as I had known the countryside intimately for near eight years.

57

"It was quite strange, here was a man of courage. I had seen him demonstrate it time after time when on patrol with him. No one could push him around! The Gabe I saw then, with downcast eyes, a voice that sounded near broken, my friend for seven years in which I knew him so very well, but now I did not know him. The man I knew before would look at you directly in a piercing way, directly into your eyes, now he would not.

"Later in the day I gave a last try to go in. I spoke to Gabe by phone and after hearing the words, "still too wet", yet I knew it was dry he diverted the conversation with the news of seeing ten the night before last. I said, "Saucers?" He hesitated, stumbled and then said, "No, just lights." Before a man who would call a Spade a Spade, a UFO or saucer just that, and now all he can say is, "No, just lights."

"So that day we went in in a four-wheel drive vehicle up to near Archeleta where a near three foot diameter green pine tree had been deliberately cut and placed across the road. We walked from there on up confirming finally the site of both ships. Again, to me it seemed like Gabe was delaying each time taking us up hill and down until I, with the photographs protested saying, "Gabe, it is over there." And finally Jonah, in his quiet way said the same thing. Both crash sites were there, but the ships were not. Both had been apparently cut up and moved by the Alien. Obviously moved to the box to the south and elsewhere and hidden.

"The ground had literally been swept clean. There wasn't a "bolt" to be found, if in truth the aliens use bolts. However, the one ship contamin- ated the ground totally was removed and replaced. The skid cuts of the anhedral wings showing clearly in "after" photos of the ship that went in upright. The other that lay upside down, its nose and cockpit section broken clear, had pressed down the tall vegetation where it had lain. The last tree, freshly scarred where the ship hit it, clearly was visible in several photos. The tree, cut as if by a giant ax was clearly visible with it's fresh cut. The propulsion or rocket burn visible in all photos. All of this was verified on the ground and visually.

"Of course, I am certain that further lies will be told, though now, with what it gave away, the deities, their Gods on the cliff, the cave openings are all there for anyone to see, the crashes are more or less insignificant.

"Senator Dominici made certain that no record remained of the file and correspondence, never acknowledging nor answering my last letter. The office line per Paul Gilman in answer to inquiry is, "The complete file was returned to Mr. Bennewitz." He is blowing it again!! The complete file was picked up by a Sandia courier and brought to Sandia in Albuquer- que. Though complete files were given to the military and indirectly through Senator Dominici without consent to Sandia, it would be safe to speculate that NO record available at an official access level by Freedom of Information exists. This time it would appear that no one even reported the incident. The people behind the Alien apparently got to them all. In an overview, one becomes totally aware of the hypocrisy of our gov- ernmental system. Once a more viable and clean representation of a Dem- ocracy, if such can exist, it is now totally paralyzed by politically motivated bureacratic bungling. There is no longer a Government Of the People---it has been lost."

UNDERGROUND ALIEN BIO LAB AT DULCE

PART FIVE

Paul continues his narrative from the chapter "The Hunter of The Gods':

"Some humans, aliens or star travelers all forge to a destiny driven by an inner something or inner being to discover and press on to greater goals. That "something" appears in but a few. Most are content to drift, never striving beyond certain monetary goals or positions, being satisfied with that and no more. They walk with blinders, leaving their "mark" in their minds consistent only with self and import. That, and no more, titillating the senses of self satisfaction and never seeking to conquer more, living within a "space" waiting for what? They do not know.

"Yet, those other few, go on to other worlds with "stars" on their shoulders or insignia on the breast leaving their mark in other ways and other places, walking an edge so fine it contemplates only danger and death skirted by will, daring and cold judgement.

"It is these that travel in company, each within his own, each reaching for knowledge and each recording in the log history. They look up at the Sun and all encompassing vision and so goes ones destiny.

"And as does human, so goes alien in literal, direct and sybolic manner, leaving their "mark" clearly upon the cliffs and shoulders of Archeleta.

"So the Hunter goes, the Hunter finds and records to log those things consistent with his destiny. For others who do not look up, but down, who close their eyes and ears to the truth, not recognizing nor showing intent or interest to one within what truly lies without, losing forever a glory of knowledge bereft of discovery because they never looked nor cared.

"And as I stood upon the shoulder of Archeleta on the south plateau looking east, again I looked at the face of a God and was stunned and taken somewhat aghast I could not believe the "mark", the Mentor symbol dead or alive was there. It easily was the size of the face of the Sphinx of Egypt. It hung on the cliff dead in front of me, it's glowering eyes and hypnotic stare locking to mine.

"I was not totally cognizant of how long I gazed before I was aware of Jonah, the Jicarilla Tracker standing by my side. He had come silently from behind and I had not heard him. I turned and I said, "Jonah, what do you see?" Without asking where, he looked and in his impassive way said, "A face, a face on the cliff yonder." Near in full knowledge of what he would say I ask, "Does it look natural; caused by nature?" He responded with no surprise nor explanation, "No, it is not natural, not nature, but alien!"

"Then knowing total reality, the wind whining fitfully above the pine, I shivered not so much from the cold, but rather the face over $\frac{1}{2}$ a mile away across the $\frac{1}{4}$ mile deep canyon. A sense of it saying in a near decisive manner, "Human, you are in the wrong place!" Then scanning on across the cliff face I did then become aware directly of the workings of aliens; an opening, estimated at distance to be sixty some odd feet across at the bottom peaking to near 80 feet at its point. Soaring in the sun light upward and draped downward gracefully on each side, long folds of colored artificial stone (limestone) appeared to be orange in color. It was not natural in any sense of the word. It was as if the face of the God was silently beckoning toward the opening draped in such an artificial manner and saying, "Here is the entrance to the Temple, the den of the orange insignia. It's wrathful

God standing guard against all who might come, beckoning in silence.

"Down at the left side of the opening sat what appeared to be a ship atleast 35 feet across. In the late afternoon light with its dull alloy, it was near invisible, camaflauged from sight against the draped background. It then occurred to me that again this ship resembled exactly those two that had anchored in behind me against the very plateau where I now stood.

"Then a ship or ships drifting one by one up over the plateau and down across the deep canyon rift one by one, just feet above the floor of the entry drifted silently as ghosts beneath the drape and on into the darkness of the gigantic caverns beyond. Only the two behind had never made it; jammed into the ridge, their cargo of cockpit and machinery ripped from within had been strewn for all to see.

"Again Jonah confirmed it, "not natural," and he did not even ask what? I wonder why? It is their way. So wishing to preserve the scene as witnessed, knowing that without photographic evidence no one would believe me and yet knowing with it they would probably label me insane, they never once, having the curiousity or stomach or fortitude to go see for themselves. It is like that with a Hunter of the Gods. He goes alone and no one has the courage to follow.

"Then placing my camera upon his solid shoulder, using Jonah as my tripod, I began to shoot multiple overlapping frames working slowly along the cliff face with each succeeding shot. The cliffs are near vertical, well over 500 feet high in places. Then, through the telescopic lens that I had just placed in the Hasselblod, I centered upon the face of the God. I stopped dead, staring in near frozen abstract disbelief than I felt a chill down my spine. "Lord! I have to be dreaming, this cannot be!" I was looking at another insignia, the Crescent and the Arrow. The craft at Socorro, New Mexico in which Lonnie Zamora had seen almost identical markings. Described in perfect detail his anxiety and fear, here the same lay before me etched in black into the cliff and the cape of this God, forming his downturned ugly mouth with the line of the arrow pointing upward through the mouth. Down slanting over its head as if to drain the rain from it's head and face and there lay a gigantic slab of what appeared to be stone. Now I began to wonder if the slab was more than that...could it swing upward with the insignia pointing upward to delineate another "fly in" entrance for larger ships? Unless I went back I doubted that I would ever know for certain its function. Then with a grimace, not yet believing, knowing and hoping when the photos were developed, the camera would surely confirm the dream as feality. I triggered the Hasselblad, packed it in and Jonah and I walked away. Away in the waning sunlight, the sun-rays now long slanted upon the visage of another God from an alien world on the mesa at Archeleta on planet Earth.

"And as I turned and looked one last time, walking backwards, it seemed the eyes swung with me. I shook my head as if waking from a very bad dream, turned and walked away from another God. Not one of my choosing, but one in direct conflict to all I would ever believe, yet in direct alignment to Jicarilla Legend of Archeleta, the mountain and the kingdom of the Gods. The alien mark was very clear, "Human, you are in the wrong place!"

"And so continues the nightmare of total and absolute reality. When will it ever end? No matter how I try to bring it all to a conclusive end--- THE ALIEN INTRUDES."

                    THE END OF CHAPTER
                         TWO

UNDERGROUND ALIEN BIO LAB AT DULCE

<u>MY VISIT TO MEET WITH PAUL BENNEWITZ</u>

In 1988 Tom Adams and I decided to take a vacation to New Mexico and Arizona. I had been writing to Paul intermittently and he had called on several occasions to discuss what had been happening to him. In one of those phone calls I mentioned to Paul that Tom and I would be in his area and would he care to meet? Definitely he told me, but he seemed to be very paranoid about the visit.

Several calls were made to set up the meeting and it was to go something like this: I would fly into Albuquerque Airport and Paul would be waiting in his black car for me. In essence, <u>he</u> wanted to be the one to pick me up. At firs I agreed, but then later I became a little shaken by the idea that I would be leaving with a man I had never met face to face and one that the government seemed to like to follow, so I suggested another plan to Paul. Paul seemed to agree, after I explained the circumstances of wanting to get settled into a hotel and maybe take a bath and clean up first before our meeting. So we set a time and place near the hotel in where he would come to pick me up. I believe he was wanting to take me somewhere other than his home where we could speak freely.

The night before we were to fly out, Paul called and seemed agitated and disconcerted. I couldn't imagine why, but I told him the plan was on and I would meet him the next day at the hotel entrance around 10:00 a.m. He seemed to hesitate at first, but then agreed. We said our goodbyes and then hung up.

Overnight I began to have second thoughts about this meeting. Why, I have no idea, but call it intuition, but I felt we would not be alone.[24] So all through the flight to Dallas and then to Albuquerque I decided to ask Tom to invite Howard Burgess, a man and friend of Tom's that had worked at Sandia for a number of years. He knew Bennewitz and the whole Dulce story and more. Our meeting with Howard was to take place for breakfast at the little restaurant right in front of our hotel.

To get to the lobby of my hotel you have to drive under a canopy and it was visible from the back door of the restaurant. I had previously told Tom that I did not feel comfortable about meeting with Paul alone and so I had a hunch that Paul would not even show after his distressed phone call the evening before.

During breakfast, several times, I excused myself to go to the restrooms. There happened to be a back door at the end of the hall that led to an exit. I opened the door and could see clearly the front of the hotel and the front drive and lobby in which I was to meet Paul.

From around 10:00a.m. to 10:45 a.m. I realized Paul was not going to show up. I walked over to the hotel lobby and asked if they had seen a black car, the description in which Paul had given to me the evening before and they said no and that they usually notice any cars that drive up to the lobby door. I explained that I was to meet this man and that I was having breakfast in the restaurant in front of them. I asked if there was any messages to please have them directed to my room. I even gave information of where I would be in case he showed up late. To my dismay, Paul never came to that meeting. He never called the hotel, never left a message at the lobby for me, it was just silence. I did not bother to call him at his home to respect his privacy.

UNDERGROUND ALIEN BIO LAB AT DULCE

It was obvious, though Paul had met with Tom years before, that he did not feel comfortable meeting at this time. I felt there was something more sinister at work and later on, upon arriving back home, I would understand why.

Paul had left several messages on my answer machine stating that he was so very sorry he did not show for our meeting and he wanted me to know that he did so want to meet me as we had struck up a friendship over the phone and had mutual things to talk about. His voice was stressed and he seemed genuinely sorry. The next part made more sense to me. He described two men in official military uniforms that had showed up at his doorstep right before he was to leave for our meeting. Over the phone he did not say what they had wanted, but that they kept him for over an hour and by then he figured it was too late.

At Paul's request, I called upon my arrival home and he described the same incident. He seemed frightened to speak about it and so I decided to just let it be and write him later about the details. Paul was so upset that he even offered to pay for a round-trip ticket back out to Albuquerque for me because he felt so bad that he had missed our meeting that we had been planning for so long. I told Paul to calm down and that he needn't do that. He explained that he just couldn't remember what these fellows wanted with him and he felt it was a deliberate diversion from meeting with me. Well, I wasn't that paranoid, but felt it had some validity to it and so I decided to fly out at a later date to meet with Paul. His last words to me were, "Christa, just let me know when and where and I will be happy to meet with you and I will even pick you up at the airport." I thanked Paul for being so kind and we said our goodbyes.

After the call, I felt an emptiness in my heart for Paul. This is how he has to live each day of his life...looking over his shoulder. He cannot trust anyone fully until he is sure in his heart about them. The more I thought of what had happened the madder I got! I had gone to such lengths to try and meet with Paul and it was frustrating to know the government still in 1988 was visiting him for unknown reasons.

So for those of you out there that tried to contact Paul and couldn't, now maybe you can understand the stress this man was experiencing and the intense paranoia.

The one thing Paul kept stressing was to be sure and contact him if I ever came back in his area. I think Paul felt I had some information that was possibly the same type he had been receiving through his computer. It is just a guess, but I do know he did want to meet me for some reason.

Our meeting with Howard Burgess turned out to be just as fruitful. He was full of strange stories of aliens in and around Albuquerque and we spoke a lot about his relationship with Paul and Gabe Valdez. He seemed to feel Gabe had been paid off by some government agency, although, he had no idea what agency it would have been. We speculated, but could never come up with just one hypothosis.

I left Albuquerque with an empty feeling inside. Driving by Kirtland Air Force Base and Paul's place of employment next to the base left me with an eerie feeling that I may never know what truly happened to Paul Bennewitz.

Paul Bennewitz seemed to need a friend or just someone to talk to
every once in awhile. He would call sometimes, distressed saying
the aliens were bothering him once again. I wrote to him off and on
for quite awhile and tried to establish some kind of rapore with him.
I was careful because I didn't want him to get paranoid of me, but
what I found so astonishing was his staunch defense of Richard Doty.
I think Paul became dependant on Richard Doty and trusted him. I
feel there was mutual admiration between the both of them which continues
to this day.

It makes me feel better to know Paul does not hold Richard Doty responsible
for any of his troubles, although Doty's contribution to the dis-information
campaign of Paul led to his mental health deteriorating. As Richard stated
before in a letter to me, "he felt bad because he knew Paul went through
Hell!"

There must be so much more we, the public are unaware of that took place
in this dis-information ploy. We may never be told the truth and maybe
no one knows what the truth really is.

Paul and I have always had a friendly rapore as you can tell from the
insertion of two letters of correspondence I had with him. But, on my
last visit to Albuquerque I called him, which he had always told me to
do if ever I got in town, and the man I spoke to was not the same man I
had corresponded with so many times in the past. His last words to me
were, "I just wish people would quit calling me and leave me alone." He
then hung up on me.

I somehow was not angry, but sad that this is how things had turned out
for Paul. Isolation, pure and simple. This is his only peace of mind
and so it is because of my deep admiration for this man that I write
this paper. Because so many of you out there want to know this man, but
never will. I hope my relating some of the facts have helped you to
understand this tormented man and please understand that what ever was
done to Paul has ruined him for life. Trust is not in his vocabulary
any longer. So I will let go of him now and give him some peace of
mind he so richly deserves. May God Bless Paul And Keep Him Safe From
The Aliens That Keep Him Awake At Night.

12/4/89

Dear Christa:
    I have lost or misplaced your phone numbers
or they have been taken. Would you send them out post
haste; thanks for your trouble. Merry Christmas
to you and Tom.

Best Regards

Paul F. Bennewitz

UNDERGROUND ALIEN BIO LAB AT DULCE

PROJECT BETA

SUMMARY & REPORT OF STATUS

[WITH SUGGESTED GUIDELINES]

PROJECT BETA

Investigator - Physicist - Paul F Bennewitz

The following are key mile posts established or discovered during the continuing scientific study concerning Alien intervention and the result. (Study limited solely to New Mexico)

1) Two years continuous recorded electronic surviellance and tracking with D.F. 24 hr/day data of alien ships within a sixty (60) mile radius of Albuquerque plus 6000 feet motion picture of same - daylight and night.

2) Detection and disassembly of alien communication and video channels - both local, earth, and near space.

3) Constant reception of video from alien ship and underground base viewscreen; Typical alien, humanoid and at times apparent Homo Sapiens.

4) A case history of an Encounter Victim in New Mexico which lead to the communications link and discovery that apparently all encounter victims have deliberate alien implants along with obvious accompanying scars. The victim's implants were verified by x-ray and Cat Scan. Five other scar cases were verified.

5) Established constant direct communications with the Alien using a computer and a form of Hex Decimal Code with Graphics and print-out. This communication was instigated apparently after the US base was vacated.

6) Through the alien communication loop, the true underground base location was divulged by the alien and precisely pin-pointed.

7) Subsequent aerial and ground photographs revealed landing pylons, ships on the ground - entrances, beam weapons and apparent launch ports - along with aliens on the ground in electrostaticly supported vehicles; charging beam weapons also apparently electrostatic.

8) Cross correalation and matching by triangulation, etc., to official NASA CIR (color infrared) high resolution films confirmed base locations and resulted in revealing US Military envolvement yielding precise coordinates and the US base layout.

9) Prior alien communication had indicated military envolvment and the fact the USAF had a ship but due to studied alien psychology this was ignored at the time.

10) Subsequently, the alien communicated following verification with the CIR, that there was indeed a ship; actually more than one - that two were wrecked and left behind and another built - this ship is atomic powered and flying. The alien indicated its basing location.

11) It was learned as stated that two women and a boy near Austin, Texas were exposed to severe radiation at close range and the ship was last seen going West with helicopters. In addition, the US Government was quietly picking up the expenses.

12) Subsequent inspection of motion picture photographs taken during the study revealed the US ship or one like it flying with the aliens. These match the CIR where two can be seen on the ground and in the later photographs taken on the ground after the base was abandoned.

So in very brief form the prologue to learning within reasonable accuracy what transpired prior to the end of 1979 or shortly thereafter.

The computer communications and constant interaction with the alien in this manner without direct encounter has given a reasonably clear picture of the alien psychology, their logic and logic methods and their prime intent.

It is important to note at the outset, the alien is devious, employs deception, has no intent of any apparent peace making process and obviously does not adhere to any prior arranged agreement.

UNDERGROUND ALIEN BIO LAB AT DULCE

In truth they tend to lie, however their memory for lying is not long and direct comparative computer printout analysis reveals this fact. Therefore much "drops through the crack" so to speak; and from this comes the apparent truth.

It is not the intent of this report to criticize or point fingers. Obviously whoever made the initial agreement was operating upon our basis of logic and not that of the alien and in so doing apparently walked innocently, in time, into a trap.

The alien indicated that the "Greys", apparently the group initially envolved in the agreement were still upset about the initial capture and subsequent death of the first eight of their co-fellows.

Another group, calling themselves in the Computer language, the "Orange" - their base is on the west slope of Mt. Archuleta - directly west of the south end of the US base and near NW of the apparent main landing area they call, in the Computer language, "The Diamond". This, because from a distance, it looks diamond shaped in the photo-graphs when looking somewhat south west past the observation tower toward the ridged peak SE of Mt. Archuleta. This ridged peak has no name, I call it South Peak.

The base extends north of this peak to the edge of the cliff down which goes a road past a large alloy dome thirty-eight (38) foot across the bottom and with a twenty (20) foot hole in the top.

Based upon some of the aerial photographs during which the alien was caught in the open and launching - some launches appear to be coming from the direction of the dome. I would guess it is an underground launch egress facility. In the NASA CIR there is what appears to be a black limousine alongside the dome on a ramp. Surprisingly it is precisely the size of my 79 Lincoln Town Car. Wheeled vehicles and what appear to be Snow Cats or Catapillars can be seen throughout the CIR - car and truck tracks, trucks and jeeps. I don't believe aliens have wheels - humans do.

UNDERGROUND ALIEN BIO LAB AT DULCE

Numerous road blocks extend northward through the US base along a well maintained road thirty some-odd feet wide - apparently gravel - near all weather - numerous turn arounds and wheel tracks into launch preparation areas with the ships; pads marked with twenty-six (26) foot Xs and servicing facilities, tanks, etc. - two domed polygon high voltage buildings on north on the east side of the road, also an apparent foundation for another or a helo pad - test stands, human housing, water tank (thirty-two foot across) - and at one of the main road blocks, two large vehicles parked across the road. Also at that point another apparent black limousine with tracks leading to it to the west of the road. All tracks and vehicles have been dimensioned and match military vehicles. If I were to make a guess, I would estimate the likelyhood that the apparent black limousines are CIA.

This is but a limited inventory of what was there on Sept 8, 1978 - included only as evidential matter for your perusal and confimation. The road, which incidently the natives, the tribal chief, reservation police and highway patrolman know nothing about, comes in off of a trail from the north. Starting at the trail, line of sight to the large plateau area and the alloy dome, the road, in the middle of nowhere on the Jiccarilla Reservation, is precisely 12,888 ft. long airline distance. The total alien basing area, which apparently contains several cultures(now all under the designation "Unity" in the Computer language) is approximately three (3) Km wide by eight (8) Km long. A conservative guess based upon the number of ships presently over this area and the number on the ground in the CIR and photographs, the total alien population at this point is at least two thousand (2000) and most likely more. The alien indicates more are coming or on the way.

I won't attempt to speculate in this report as to how the initial US contact was made - what transpired, nor how many were able to escape. The alien has communicated his account, and if totally true, it certainly is not palatable.

UNDERGROUND ALIEN BIO LAB AT DULCE

Much detail has been omitted for future discussion if desired - however the import is this. Constant computer communication - full on line in February of this year - manual prior to that - has allowed a constant accounting of what is and has been going on - conditions of morale and a total insight into "what makes the alien run". This is _very_ valuable data.

1) Most importantly, the alien will allow no one to go without an implant and after knowledge of it is wiped out. They simply will not allow it. All indications are that communication or language cannot result without the implant. (with the exception of the Binary and the Computer). This would indicate a possible immediate threat or danger for anyone - military, Air Force, or otherwise that has been at the base. They _will_ _not_ remember the implant in any case (the contactee here included).

The reason for the implant is multiple for both language or communication by thought (there is no apparent language barrier with thought) and also _complete_ _absolute_ control by the alien through program - by their beam or direct contact.

I have tested this and found that during this programming the person is totally alien; once one learns to recognize the signs and the person then has no memory of the act/conversation afterward. _If_ this has happened to the military I need not elaborate as to the possible consequences. The victim's "switch" can be pulled at any time and at the same time they are "walking cameras and microphones" if the alien chooses to listen in with the use of their beams. No classified area of any endeavor in the US is inviolate under these conditions. However - realize - the scars, barely visible - _can_ be seen - _all_ are exactly located and _all_ are accessible by x-ray.

2) Also note that all of the aliens - human, humanoid alike - all must have implants - without them, no direct communication is apparently possible. So one can most generally arbitrarily say that _if_ a person states he/she communicated by thought with an alien - he/she most likely has been implanted. They may also claim to be overly psychic and be able to prove this - again through the link transplant, he/she is given the information by the alien and does not realize.

3) Most importantly, the alien, either through evolvment or because the humanoid is made - will exhibit tendencies for bad logic (bad by earth logic comparison) so they _are_ _not_ infallible - in point of fact they appear to have many more frailties and weaknesses than the normal Homo Sapiens. To the alien, the mind is key and therein lies a great weakness which will be discussed later.

4) They _are_ _not_ to be trusted. It is suspected if one was considered a "friend" and if one were to call upon that "friend" in time of dire physical threat, the "friend" would quickly side with the other side.

The computer indicates in comparison, that no known earth protagonist - Russian or otherwise exhibit these tendencies to any major degree indicating the danger involved in making any kind of agreement with these aliens - at least of this species.

5) The alien does kill with the beam generally. Results on a human will exhibit a three to four cm purple circle. If done from the rear, on one or both shoulders. The results on cattle are the same, essentially exhibiting purple beneath the hide, with burned circles on the outside.

6) Cattle mutilations are the other side of the coin and will not be delved into here though they are a part of the overall. It appears the humanoids are fed by a formula made from human or cattle material or both and they are made from the same material by gene splicing and the use of female encounter victim's ovum. The resultant embryos are referred to by the alien as an organ. Time of gestation to full use as a utility, ready to work appears to be about one year. A year in alien time - I do not know.

Solution: I doubt there is an immediate total "cure" per se - however, they must be stopped and we have to get off dead center before we find time has run out. They are picking up and "cutting" (as the alien calls it) many people every night. Each implanted individual is apparently ready for the pull of their "switch". Whether all implants are totally effective I cannot predict, but conservatively I would estimate at least 300,000 or more in the US and at least 2,000,000 if not more worldwide.

Weaponry and Inherent Weaknesses

Weaponry is one of the keys and in the alien's present state we _can_ prepare an effective offense.

One tends at the outset (I did) to look at their machines and say - there is no defense or offense. One is overwhelmed by their speed, apparent capability of invisibility and "cloaking", and other covert capabilities not discussed at this time. In particular - the beam weapons are themselves a direct threat and obviously one that must be seriously considered but not overly so.

Let us first look at just what this weapon is. It is an electro-static weapon with plasma generating voltages - and an internal storage device - it is pulse powered. The beam, totally effective _in_ _atmosphere_ can be loaded with hydrogen or oxygen. Range? Average, ground weapons - maximum two (2) Km if it is dry, capable of sustaining just so many full power discharges - slow leakage occurs continuously, therefore, they must be recharged periodically. If it is raining the weapon becomes ineffective and is swamped, thus discharged. The range is near totally lost at that point.

On the disks and saucers, the weapon is generally on the left side or top center and has a maximum range of two hundred (200) meters at which point it will plow a trench in desert soil. When fired - it fires both to the front and to the back equally. Reason? Because of their mode and methods of flight. If equilibrium is not maintained, the saucer will spin out.

Hand weapons? Estimate based upon visible damage observed, not too much velocity nor staying power but at short range - deadly (less than a .45 cal automatic). At one meter range, estimate of beam temperature 1600°F or higher; it can vaporize metal.

Apparently the disks and weapons operate from a storage source. In time, without periodic recharge, this storage is depleted. The design they traded to us was at least thirty years old - employing an atomic source. Possibly they may still have some - it would appear so - their staying power is obviously much longer.

Aircraft Helicopter Vulnerability

Any of our aircraft, helicopters, missiles or any air flight vehicle can be taken down instantly with no use of weaponry. The alien simply need do no more than make one invisible pass and their bow wave or screen or both will take the air lift vehicle down. The pilot obviously will not even know what hit him.

For human on the ground, the alien can use weaponry or bow wave. The partial pressure envelope can hit with the power of a tornado - shock rise time and G force is instantaneous

However, they dare not hit the craft physically because they are fragile and in fact, under slow flying conditions within our atmosphere, hold a very tenuous position. Without power, balance or equilibrium, they lose it.

UNDERGROUND ALIEN BIO LAB AT DULCE

In brief - these are apparent capabilities observed and gleaned through the computer communication and observation. You may know of these, however, they are directly related to the last and final portion of this report. <u>What</u> <u>can</u> <u>be</u> <u>done</u>?

1) Because of the alien's apparent logic system (they appear to be logic controlled) a key decision cannot be made without higher clearance. All are under the control of what they call "The Keeper"; yet it would appear this is not the final say. Therefore, dependent upon urgency, delays of as long as twelve to fifteen hours can occur for a decision. How short/long this time frame under battle conditions may be, I do not know.

Because of this apparent control, individiual instantaneous decision making by the alien is limited. If the "plan" goes even slightly out of balance or context, they become confused. Faced with this, possibly, the humanoids would be the first to break and run.

The same applies to their Mission Master Plan, if one can call it that. If pushed out of context, it will come apart - they will be exposed to the world so they will possibly run before they fight in the open. They definitely <u>do</u> <u>not</u> want that to happen.

Psychologically, at present, their morale is down - near disintegration. There is pronounced dissension in the ranks; even with the humanoids. Communication can encourage this (no necessity to expound upon this other than to say because of their own internal vulnerability mind-wise to each other, therein lies a prime weakness). Inter-echelon or individual "trust" appears to be totally lacking so suspicion of each other is rampant. They are highly segregated as to levels - a "low" dare not conflict with a "medium" or "high" or it literally means death. Death being, to the humanoid, deprogramming or, in the end perhaps total physical death.

They appear to be totally death oriented and because of this, absolutely death-fear oriented. This is a psychological advantage. The computer also gives indications of a real possibility of adverse or "ground programming".

2) Consider their ships - most if not near all run on charge. That source depletes and so dependent upon size - depletion can occur for some within a week or less. Ships can replenish each other but only up to charge balance. This is done with antennae-like extensions and the charge is distributed observing conservation of energy laws. They can replenish from power lines - but again only to a point - so time of flight is limited. Deprived of their base recharge capability, it is indicated that all ships will come down within six months to a year unless they can get transported out - that is back to the prime launch ship.

The disks and saucers in general cannot fly in space because of their mode of flight. Therefore, deprived of home base, it is not likely they can survive. Their capability in power survival outlasts their capability in food or formula survival. It they do not get formula/food within a certain period of time they will weaken and die.

In the case of Mt Archuleta and South Peak, they are dependent upon the Navajo River for water supply and water to them is totally life. Without water they have no power; without power, no oxygen or hydrogen to service the ships and weapons. No water to sustain the organs and feeding formlula.

Simple? Not really. However, there is a water intake and there is a dam upstream that can be <u>totally</u> cut off and the water re-routed to Chama, New Mexico. Should this occur, at least three of the internal bases will go down. They could possibly go atomic periodically but obviously problems without cooling.

Once the bases are pressed on a large scale, all disks and saucers will go airborn immediately. Troops on the ground can gain terrain cover to quite a degree - it is rough terrain.

) Our need is for a weapon,workable and preferably not like the alien's. I believe unless the alien is caught unaware (with their screen up their weapons are equal so they are like children pillow boxing) there can be no result; the weapon must penetrate their screen and it must also penetrate the ground. I believe I have that weapon. Two small prototypes have been funded and constructed by my Company. Tests conducted to date indicate they do work and work rather well considering their small size. Because of this weapon's present status and proprietary nature (a basic patent is in process), the theory will not be explained here. However, the weapon appears to do two things at very low power. 1) The disks within its range begin to discharge when exposed to the weapon beam. To counteract, they must apply more power and so doing consume more power. Again conservation of energy laws strictly apply.

This effect can be observed on the detection instruments as they back away in response to slow discharge. Discharge, at low power is slow but at high power in the final sophisticated weapon, the rate can be increased by many orders of magnitude. 2) Most importantly, this weapon can penetrate the screen - hull alloy, everything. They cannot shield it in any way. Lastly, because of the implants, the weapon's beam gets to them mentally; they lose judgement and indi- date almost immediate confusion, particularly the humanoids.

It is believed at this early stage - based upon present testing that the weapon when full on and full size will kill or bring down disks at substantial range.
The alien weapons operate substantially the same as their disks using a charge source and charge distribution. So, in the same sense it is indicated that this weapon design will pull their charge weapons down very rapidly.

The range of my weapon exceeds that of their present weapons and in its most
sophisticated form can be readily computer controlled to allow extremely rapid
tracking and lock-on regardless of speed along with electronic wobbulation of
the beam. It is a beam weapon and even at this early stage of miniature prototype testing and development, it indicates eventual superiority to their weapons.

4) Initial logistics would indicate a plan sequentially implemented as follows:
This plan does not include all requirements and preparatory safety measures to
be employed by the ground force; however, if Air Force Intelligence desires to
pursue the approaches suggested in this report, each significant requirement will
be discussed in depth.

An attack must be directed near entirety on the ground for obvious reason. One
would, if familiar with the alien capability, indicate that vehicle ignition
problems will be encountered. This is precisely true; however, the reason for this
is not mysterious but is based upon good solid laws of physics and are known.
Experience gained through my study, it is now known how to prevent this from
happening and will be discussed in detail at some later date. All electrical
and electronic equipment must be "hardened" using these specific techniques prior
to implementation. Because of the known capability of the alien (by use of
scanning beams to know in advance details of planning) only the initial outline
is presented in this report.

Again through the communicative interaction with the alien, testing has simul-
taeneously been done upon this facet, i.e.eavesdropping, and ways to abort this
capability have been tested and proven.

The program would be instigated in phases. The first phase - planning and logistics
- would include continued implementation and testing of the final weapon prototype

thru the pre-production stage. Production of at least fifty minimum quantity should be planned. Additional backup spares should also be included.

On a full time shift basis, it is estimated that at least one year or less would be required to arrive at the pre-production stage. A team would be organized by Thunder Scientific to accomplish this. The key work is now and would be done by an associated company, Bennewitz Labs.,Ltd.

Specific attack phases would be incorporated.

1) The first procedure would be to close the gates of the dam above the Navajo River. This dam would be held closed for the duration. Internal to the one cave, there is a small dam for water storage. Its capacity is small. There is also a discharge outlet downstream that could be closed, causing waste water to back-up into the caves. The water is vacumn pumped apparently by some electrostatic means from the river. At close range, the weapon will take out this cability.

2) Once deprived totally of water for a minimum period of four weeks, conditions in the alien bases under discussion will have badly deteriorated. Psychological shock is extremely effective with the alien; total advantage can be taken by instantaneous action or planned observable deviation from the norm. At least three bases will go down.

3) If they follow their normal strategic patteras when pressed previously, they will launch most if not all ships.

4) Prior to the implementation of water deprivation, the weapons should be deployed at strategic hardened locations and activated in a certain pre-planned manner determined by final weapon coordinate locations.

5) This will put an immediate power drain upon those airborne and the alien weapons ringing their bases.

6) Because of the inherent psychological aspect of the alien, much can be done in the open with no attempt to preserve secrecy. Much of what is done can be of a diversionary nature. Under most conditions they will attempt to harass but will not openly attack.

7) Throughout and prior to this, the open computer communications link will be operational for continued psychological interrogation.

8) At some point in time - again resting upon battle status, the deployment of offensive forces will begin. This deployment should be done in a near instantaeneous manner under certain special conditions that can be discussed.

9) The weapon system should be kept powered up throughout. In this manner, the disks will be made to stay airborne. They cannot land in the interval the system is powered.

10) When the weapon is used in one specific power mode, in addition to continuous discharge on the disks that are airborne and the ground based weapons, the mind confusion and disorientation will build in those personnel at the base and underground. At the end of four to five weeks or less, all weapons should be totally discharged and power out on the bases. Most personnel if not all, will be totally incapacitated. The feeding formula will be down and its critical processing ruined. All embryos should be dead and all hydrogen and oxygen consumables depleted.

11) Based upon data gathered on the miniature prototype weapons, the full power weapons should have no problem holding off the disks. In many cases some will break within the first forty-eight hours without being directly hit.

12) At that point, standard weapon technology and logistics can come into play and used to the extent of destruction desired at the direction of those in charge.

13) The communications can be used throughout to determine status and near the end to attempt to instigate surrender. If no response results, then they should simply be closed in and waited out.

UNDERGROUND ALIEN BIO LAB AT DULCE

Summary

It is important to note that the initial implementation of the computer communications was not instigated for the purpose of talking to the alien for the "fun of it"; but was deliberately instigated to use as a tool to study, in depth, long term without physical confrontation, the strengths and weaknesses of the alien.

The weapon theory and prototypes were built to capitalize upon and test the two key and prominent weaknesses discovered. This in-house funded program has been expensive, in excess of $200,000; done on behalf of our nation and handled in the best representative manner humanly possible.

1) The prime and weakest area discovered, probed and tested is exactly what they have used thinking it is their key strength - that being, the manipulation of and control of the mind; not only of command but also humanoid. Manipulated in reverse psychologically and by the language (computer) and due to the extreme of mental distortion and incapacity caused by the weapon, it has been found that this facet is for them a disaster and a directly vulnerable integrated weakness.

2) Though their ships are magnificent, they are also weak - solely because of their method and unique mode of flight. They do not have a stable fighting platform. Charge distribution can also be discharged. The weapon does this - even in its present miniature prototype stage.

It is not the purpose of this report to imply that the overall problem will be solved with the capture of these bases. Obviously it will not, but it is a firmly based beginning with a high degree of rated projected success ratio. It is not intended to imply the alien will not fight; they may - though their inclination is generally the opposite - this basing area is key. Without it, their mission is in very deep trouble. It is noted that these are not the only bases on earth there <u>are</u> others. With a conservative estimate using typical logistic support numbers, it is not un-realistic to say there are 50,000 aliens within the ecosphere of earth and near space.

Some of us will be lost in the endeavor that is obvious - however, done <u>now</u> the advantage is gained along with new additional technology to prepare for the next stage.

The key to overall success is - they <u>totally</u> respect <u>force.</u> And with them, the most effective method is to stubbornly continue to pick and pull at their defense with <u>no</u> letup. Faced with the total loss of a base that has taken <u>years</u> to construct, it is believed that their mission <u>will</u> <u>be</u> grossly weakened and badly slowed.

As Americans, in this particular instance, we <u>must</u> realize - that we in this case cannot rely upon our inherent moral principles to provide the answer. Negotiation <u>is</u> <u>out</u>. This particular group can only be dealt with - no differently than one must deal with a mad dog. <u>That</u> method they understand. They <u>have</u> invaded <u>our</u> country our air and they are freely violating the personal and mental integrity of our people. There-fore, in eliminating this threat most certainly we cannot be called the "aggressor", because we <u>have</u> literally been invaded.

In final conclusion A) They cannot under <u>any</u> circumstances be trusted. B) They are totally deceptive and death oriented and have no moral respect for human or human life. C) <u>No negotiation</u>, <u>agreement</u> nor <u>peaceful</u> <u>compromise</u> can be settled upon in any way. D) <u>No</u> agreement signed by both parties will ever be adhered to nor recognized and respected by the alien, though they might attempt to make us believe otherwise. E) <u>Absolutely</u> <u>no</u> <u>quarter</u> can be allowed under <u>any</u> circumstances. Once the offense is instigated, it cannot be abandoned. If it is, reciprocal reprisal will immediately result. They must be made to come down - destruct themselves which is a standing order if the ship is failing or leave earth immediately - no leeway of any kind can be allowed nor tolerated.

UNDERGROUND ALIEN BIO LAB AT DULCE

'THE AVIARY'

Webster's definition: Bird; akin to Greek aeros Eagle: a place for keeping birds confined.

In almost every conversation between researchers today the word 'Aviary' is often discussed. Who are these people and why are they so interested in certain UFO researchers and scientists? The code names vary from Sparrow, Bluejay, and Hawk to the infamous Falcon and Condor. It's a mix and match game that we, the American public have been playing for too long. Someone has to win and the stakes are high.

The past few years I have worked with various sources who have close ties to these birds. Just recently, my most trusted source gave me a call and we began discussing 'THE AVIARY' and who might be a member of this covert highly organized government group.

The source told me that two associates with this group have ties to para-psychology, UFO researchers and government intelligence agents. He said they may be tampering with our citizens who have connections or interests in the above subjects. My source also told me that we cannot trust the motives of 'THE AVIARY'.

I asked him to tell me more about this group and to name names if he could. A man by the name of Scott Jones who was a former assistant to Senator Claiborne Pell of Rhode Island. Senator Pell just happens to be the Chairman of the Senate Foreign Relations Committee. (Author's note: Don Ecker of UFO Magazine wrote a wonderful outline of this man in the most recent issue of his magazine, Vol. 7, No. 1 1992.)

What was so strange is that the names of Bill Moore, Jaime Shandera and Richard Doty came up and my source alleges that these men are a conduit for 'THE AVIARY'. It came as no surprise to me because who better to circulate messages and information for these high government officials than these three men.

Apparently, and we can only speculate, there are anywhere from six to twelve members of 'THE AVIARY'. They are apparently making contact with other UFO researchers mainly in the scientific community. We started a guessing game...could they be in touch with someone like Stanton Friedman, or David Jacobs or even Bruce Macabee? We were just speculating. We could start calling some of these scientists and just ask them, but we knew we would never get any straight answers.

Then my source began telling me a strange story about these birds. It seems that some of the members are involved in a remote-viewing project and that even one member helped Uri Geller when he came from Israel to the United States. The names Pell and Jones might have been involved in experiments with the Pentagon in which dream implantation experiments were being performed on certain susceptable individuals. My source was even telling me to stop sleeping with my television on and radio and telephones were also involved in these experiments somehow. This whole scenario was beginning to make sense to me because we all know that Paul Bennewitz began having problems after Moore and Doty befriended him.

I then began remembering some vivid dreams I had been having about none other than Saddam Hussein. And now I have to tell an account that will boggle the mind! To make it stranger, in my dream I was in Saddam,s bunker. My mission: to assasinate Saddam Hussein. Absurd? Maybe not.

UNDERGROUND ALIEN BIO LAB AT DULCE

IS THERE ANOTHER PAUL BENNEWITZ
IN OUR MIDST ?

The story I am about to relate to you is a true one. It involves a person
who I know to have very high standards. The person has always been honest
and very knowledgable in the field of ufology. To protect the person who
I refer to as 'The Target' and the two conduits of the 'AVIARY, I have deliberately whited out the names of these individuals. The others directly
involved will be left in this piece as they are involved with 'The Target',
the two conduits and THE AVIARY. All of these people exist and what makes
this story so strange is the fact that besides myself, I have run across
several other people who have complained of having strange paranormal experiences involving dreams, remote-viewing and out-of-body experiences. The
Aviary seem to be able to keep in contact at all times with the people who
are having these strange experiences. As more time goes by, I am beginning
to question my own beliefs in alien abductions. Why couldn't people like
'The Aviary' be involved in certain projects which might involve producing
holographic projections to select people who feel they are UFO alien abductees
It is just another way-out theory, but one we must look into and fast!

Here is the story as it happened to the person I refer to as 'THE TARGET'...

Throughout my life, I have had some highly unusual things happen
to me that I cannot explain. Some prefer to call these experiences
paranormal, others may call them supernatural, but whatever you may
call them it isn't until one experiences such a thing for himself or
herself that it becomes real. I didn't ask for these things to happen
nor did I try to make them happen. They began when I was a child like
all the other natural body functions and I have had to live with them
and try to understand and cope with them whenever they occur. In
October, 1990 a series of strange occurrences began that I cannot
explain. This time, however, there may be someone that can explain to
me what happened since these events involve other people who seem to
know more about what is going on than I do.

In October, 1990,   called to tell me that a high-
level intelligence official from the Pentagon had contacted one of
their intelligence sources and had told him (_) and
to maintain a close relationship with   When   told
me this, I thought at first it may be some type of Psyop by the
counterintelligence boys for some unknown motive. Afterall, it had
been used on Bennewitz according to Moore who had participated in it.
But   _ sounded serious and perplexed; I could hear it in the
tone of his voice. If it was some type of Psyop, then   was a
victim as well. It didn't make much sense, since I was no longer
active in ufology and had been inactive for nearly five years. I had
nothing to offer, so why me?

Over the next few weeks, I had several telephone conversations
with '   asking him about this mysterious intelligence source and
why this high-level intelligence source would want   .   and him
to stay in contact with me.   I could not get any straight answers,
since   told me that he didn't know any more than I did about
it.   did tell me that this high-level official contacted his
intelligence contact and it was through his contact that he had
received this information.   I also asked   what he thought
about this matter and he said he didn't know any more than I did.

During these telephone conversations between   and me, I
learned that   was in contact with Dr. Scott Jones, an aide to
Senator Claiborne Pell, Chairman of the Senate Foreign Relations
Committee.   Senator Pell and Dr. Jones have been involved in
parapsychology research for some time. It was Senator Pell that helped
Uri Geller establish himself when this Israeli psychic first came to
the U.S.   and Dr. Jones had apparently known each other for
awhile. I also learned that   was in contact with a number of
people that was apparently involved in parapsychological studies,
i.e., remote-viewing, etc.   And that these contacts led directly to
other people in high political offices, the Pentagon and the White
House.

81

UNDERGROUND ALIEN BIO LAB AT DULCE

In a conversation with   on November 9, 1990, I asked
     some questions about this mysterious high-level intelligence
official in the Pentagon who told   and him to stay in contact with
me. A part of the conversation went as follows:

     : "This scientist that you are supposedly working with that is
involved in remote-viewing.....is he working with the Pentagon?"

     : "Uh...yea...he ties into a whole lot of stuff...all the way
up to people in Congress...uh...and the White House."

     : "Uh.huh... Well, when this other individual from the Pentagon
told you and   ....I don't know whether he told   first or told
you both together...but when he told you that, and then said something
to the effect of staying in contact with me...."

     : "Right.."

     : ".....and I am not really involved in the ufological community
at this point-in-time..."

     : "Why...I thought it was very curious because it wasn't like
a list of names or anything else...you were the only person that they
said maintain contact with. They asked if we knew you...and they said
maintain a relationship with him."

     : "That's what I am saying. because I am just an average,
ordinary individual out here...you know...in the community. I am not
anybody with a string of credentials or anything like that and I
haven't done any work in those areas, so-to-speak, like Uri Geller and
some of the rest of them....and for someone, if his credentials are
legitimate....you know....for him to tell you and   that. Did you
react to that or did you ask him why   ?"

     : "No. Because we have learned over the years in terms of
relationship and stuff...that usually if there is more that they want
to tell you at that point, they will tell you."

     : "Uh..huh."

     : "We figured the proof would ultimately be in the pudding.
Something ultimately would develop somewhere along the lines."

     About two weeks after this most mysterious telephone call from
     ', I began to have some unusual dreams about Saddam Hussein and
what felt like "out-of-the-body" experiences or remote-viewing about
details of the war with Iraq. In these dreams I could see that
Hussein was going to have three dreams that were of a religious
nature, actually warnings about the actions he had already taken and
what was to take place. It appeared that Hussein was also in contact
with his psychics and seers. These dreams and remote-viewing
experiences were so impressive that I felt compelled to call   '
and tell him about them as well as requesting that this information be
given to "higher authorities".   complied with my requests and

contacted Dr. Jones. Dr. Jones, which I learned later, contacted the
proper authorities which I presume were in the Pentagon.

     . called me the next day and told me that Hussein had had
his second dream as   had heard about it over the news. He
sounded a little amazed by the fact that what I had said to him was
coming true. I told   that Hussein had one more dream to go.
I then proceeded to ask   if he had given the other information
(details about the war) to the proper authorities and he told me he
had. I never did hear about whether he had his third dream or not.

     During this time period, I felt like I was in the middle of some
type of "psychic warfare". It's the only way that I can explain it.
And the previous events such as the mysterious telephone call from
     . telling me about this "high-level intelligence official"
apparently in the Pentagon and then the unusual dreams and remote-
viewing experiences or whatever one wants to call them had me
wondering what was really going on.

UNDERGROUND ALIEN BIO LAB AT DULCE

I recalled that there have been a number of UFO associated incidents in which some people have a UFO experience and then later have unusual dreams. One in particular came to my mind during these unusual events, the Capt. Coyne incident which happened on October 18, 1973. I will not elaborate on the details of the Coyne incident since it can be found in UFO literature, but after the incident someone involved in "metaphysics" in the Pentagon called Capt. Coyne to ask him if he had had any unusual dreams since the UFO experience. Coyne, indeed, reported that he had had two unusual dreams. As time passed, the Pentagon would call the crew members of the helicopter who were also involved in this UFO encounter and ask them if they had ever dreamed of "body separation", in other words out-of-the-body experiences. What I find interesting about this Coyne incident is the nature of the case — unusual dreams and the Pentagon apparently knowing about them. Also, the time period is interesting since the two events, the Coyne encounter and my paranormal experiences, happened during the middle of October. In my case, a "high-level" intelligence official in the Pentagon tells   and   to stay in contact with me" and then I have these unusual dreams and paranormal experiences. All of this may be purely coincidental.

Months went by without   or   contacting me, and then the Persian Gulf War was over and our troops come home. I thought to myself that if   and   was supposed to have "stayed in contact with me", they didn't do a very good job. I made no effort to stay in contact with them after I told them about my unusual dreams and other paranormal experiences concerning the war. I didn't know what the name of the game was, and I couldn't say that I was pleased with the past actions of   when he was dealing with Bennewitz. So, I dropped contact and played the waiting game.

I was determined to find out what   was going on, so I called Dr. Scott Jones for the first time. I introduced myself and politely asked him several questions about his involvement in the field of ufology and parapsychology and if he knew   . Dr. Jones told me he indeed did know   , and then I asked Dr. Jones if he had received any information from   to give to the "proper authorities" about the Persian Gulf War. He was a little reluctant to answer me until I told him that it was me that had given this information to   . Dr. Jones said, "So it was you". I said, "Yes. And he said, "Yes. I gave the information to the proper authorities". Dr. Jones would not elaborate on this matter, and I did not pressure him about it. We discussed other matters and he gave me his home telephone number in case I needed to call him about anything I felt important.

About a month later, I began to have another disturbing dream and psychic impressions during the day about a catastrophic earthquake soon to hit California. These were exceptionally strong psychic impressions. So I called Dr. Jones at home and explained what was happening. He suggested a wait and see situation, and told me that he would give this information and my name to a friend of his in the Library of Congress who had a research project called "The Migraine Project". The time period that I felt this event was going to occur came and went without anything happening. Later, I learned through a contact of mine that a group in Sedona, Arizona was claiming to be in contact with "higher intelligences" and they were reportedly receiving exactly what I was receiving. I wondered if I had been picking up what they were doing in Sedona rather than an actual premonition. Again, why me?

In October, 1991, I called   to see what had become of the intelligence contact and he told me that he just seemed to have mysteriously disappeared..."no one seems to know where he went." I questioned   about this, and he said, "I don't know any more than you do about it."

In a November 18,1991 news article from Washington entitled "ESP Used in Iraqi weapons hunt", I noticed that it was about "remote viewing" being used on Iraq. A U.S. Army Maj. Karen Jansen working with a UN team took data obtained by psychics via remote-viewing, who were associated with Edward Dames, president of a company called PSI Tech, to Baghdad. This intrigued me because I felt this was apparently connected to what had transpired between me,   . and Dr. Jones during the war — especially the remote-viewing aspects.

UNDERGROUND ALIEN BIO LAB AT DULCE

On December 26, 1991, I called   to question him
about this news article since he had told me that he was associated
with some people involved in remote-viewing.   said, "one of
my CIA contacts said the news report on remote-viewing was not true".
He also said that "the CIA became extremely interested in the news
story when it first appeared." The CIA contact told him that Edward
Dames, who said he had done certain things with psychics, had not done
them and that "the story was merely a marketing scheme concocted to
promote Dame's company". I told   that I found this a little hard
to believe in view of the names and what was said in the article, not
to mention what I had experienced.   said this is what he was
told by his CIA contact.

A few days later, I called Dr. Scott Jones and ask him if he had
received my letter since I hadn't received a response. He replied
that he had. I realized that he had been taking trips out of the
country and had been extremely busy. I then questioned him about the
mysterious "high-level" official and my unusual dreams and remote-
viewing experiences. He said, "You are still not clear on this?" I
told him, no. He did not elaborate on this. As I explained my
confusion over the matter of the paranormal events he said, "   , I
will tell you confidentially without getting into details that there
were a number of people getting input in addition to yourself". I was
kind of shocked and surprised at this statement. Again, I did not
pressure him on this matter since he said he couldn't go into any
details.

I then asked him if he knew about the news article on remote-
viewing by a company called PSI-Tech and proceeded to explain what
           had told me his "CIA contact" had told him. He said, "both
statements are true" and he went on to explain how publicity was
generated on this matter by CBS. He said that he knew Ed, President
of PSI-Tech, very well, and that what was stated in the article about
remote-viewing being used to obtain site locations on Iraqi
installations was' true and the information supplied by the psychics
was accurate.

It is now the beginning of 1992, I am still in the dark on these
most unusual events. I thought it was all over until today, January
9, 1992 around 10:05 a.m. I had just walked in the door when the
telephone rang. I answered it thinking it was my wife, but instead it
was a man on the other end that said, "Is this   ?" I said,
"yes." He then said, "I am the one who contacted
intelligence contact and told him to tell them to stay in touch with
you. You, along with a few others on this planet, are going to be
contacted by the visitors according to the program." I thought this
was somebody pulling a practical joke on me, but he continued to tell
me things that only I knew. I tried to question him about who he was,
but he continued by saying that, "you have been watched for a long
time because of your genetic development, in other words, a mutation
of a new species over a long period of time." He then said, "we will
be back in contact with you."

I called "   and Dr. Scott Jones, but I could not get
in touch with them. Dr. Scott Jones was apparently out-of-town and no
one answered the phone at   's home. I then called   and
explained the scenario. I am not taking anything seriously, except
for my own personal experiences.

This leaves me with several questions about this whole matter.
Who was the mysterious "high-level" intelligence official that told
     and   to "stay in touch with me?" Why didn't   and
     . stay in touch with me? Who is the Pentagon scientist
involved with remote-viewing that   knows? Why did I have
these unusual dreams and paranormal experiences immediately after
         contacted me? Who did Dr. Scott Jones give this information
to that he called the "proper authorities"? Who were these other
people that received "input" and just exactly what did Dr. Jones mean
by this? Was PSI-Tech and others involved prior to the war using
remote-viewing and I happened to pick up on it? Does this apply to the
Sedona, Arizona area as well? Was my paranormal experiences the reason
this "high-level" official contacted   . through his intelligence
contact in the first place? And who is this individual that claimed
to be the "high-level intelligence official" that told me he was the
one who was in contact with   intelligence contact? Is
somebody playing games with me? Something doesn't add up here!

THE JICARILLA APACHE POLICE

Raleigh Tafoya
Chief

LEVI PESATA
President

April 29, 1991

Dear

This is in response to your letter of April 20, 1991 wherein you are trying to verify numerous stories related to UFO underground base and cattle mutilation in our area.

Normally, I don't even bother to respond to inquiries about things of this nature and you think this would be the end of it but I am still getting inquiries and stories. All continuing to be published in various magazine.
Story A: Underground base is rumors. We have checked into this and we have come up with nothing to substanciate these stories.
Story B: Numerous UFO sightings over the past several years. Like everywhere else, there have been UFO sightings but nothing spectacular or unusual about it.
Story C: Unexplained cattle mutilations over the past twenty years, there have been some cattle mutilations in our area and we, along with the New Mexico State Police have investigated this and have been unable to resolve these mutilations. We have not experienced anymore mutilations lately for the past five years or so.

In our profession, we deal with facts, not rumors. On Story A:Rumors, Story B: True, Story C:True. However, most of these incidents have occurred several years past and we are not interested in participating in any interviews at this time.

As I have stated in the second paragraph of this letter, I don't even bother to respond to inquiries of this type and I am wondering why I am responding to you. But, never the less, this is our response to your letter. If you wish for more information, I would suggest you contact Officer Gabriel Valdez, New Mexico State Police, District 5, 2501 Carlisle Blvd, N.E., Albuquerque, New Mexico 87110.

I am hopeful that we have been of some help to you and I don't mean to give you the impression that we are totally negative about these things but we have been burned by some of these stories and people who come around, have been unreliable and have used us for their personal gain, purpose, etc.

Sincerely,

Raleigh Tafoya Sr.
Chief

Box 507 • Dulce, New Mexico 87528 • Phone (505) 759-3222

85

UNDERGROUND ALIEN BIO LAB AT DULCE

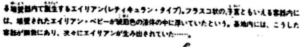

地下部内で誕生するエイリアン（レティキュラン・タイプ）。フラスコ状の子宮ともいえる容器内には、培養されたエイリアン・ベビーが琥珀色の液体の中に浮いていたという。基地内には、こうした容器が無数にあり、次々にエイリアンが生み出されていた……。

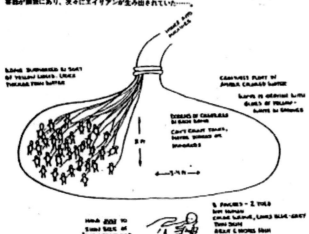

（上）クリスタ・チルトン女史を誘拐したエイリアンが、胸につけていたマーク。（下）チルトン女史が連れていかれた基地内の様子。培養されたエイリアンが並べられている。

チルトン女史の描いた、体験スケッチ。彼女は何度もエイリアンに誘拐され、そのたびに妊娠させられたという。他の人々の証言にも、彼らが支配を行っているという事実を裏づけるものがあり、信憑性は高そうだ。

Copyright drawing-CRUX PUBLICATIONS

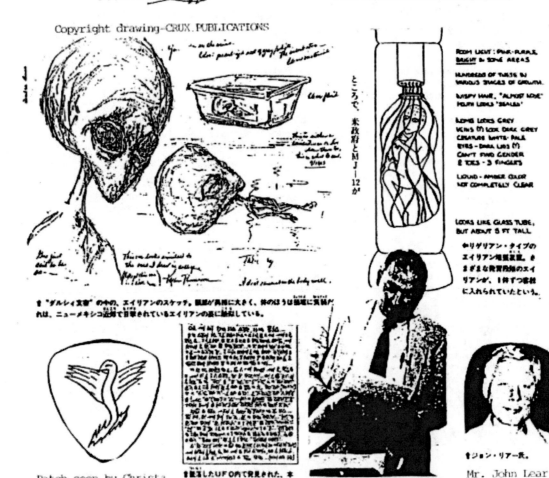

"ダルシイ基地" の中の、エイリアンのスケッチ。頭部が異様に大きく、体のほうは細くなっている。これは、ニューメキシコ近辺で目撃されているエイリアンの姿に酷似している。

Patch seen by Christa on aliens & military

UFO研究界!!

が、1979年に博士がカートランド空軍基地でのUFO事件に関

ところで、未政府とMJ─12が

←リゲリアン・タイプのエイリアン培養装置。さまざまな発育段階のエイリアンが、1体ずつ容器に入れられていたという。

ROOM LIGHT : PINK-PURPLE, BRIGHT IN SOME AREAS

HUNDREDS OF THESE IN VARIOUS STAGES OF GROWTH.

WISPY HAIR, "ALMOST NONE" MOUTH LOOKS "SEALED"

LOOKS LOOKS GREY VEINS (?) LOOK DARK GREY CREATURE WHITE- PALE EYES - DARK LIDS (?) CAN'T FIND GENDER 2 TOES - 3 FINGERS

LIQUID - AMBER COLOR NOT COMPLETELY CLEAR

LOOKS LIKE GLASS TUBE, BUT ABOUT 5 FT TALL

誘拐したUFO内で発見された、本の中に書かれていた文字。これと同じものが、機体にも書かれていた。象形文字に、非常によく似ている。

クーパー文書で米政府とエイリアンの秘密を暴露した、ミルトン・ウィリアム・クーパー氏。

ジョン・リアー氏。

Mr. John Lear

86

UNDERGROUND ALIEN BIO LAB AT DULCE

William Moore Update
" THE USEFUL IDIOT "

In Howard Blum's book, 'OUT THERE' Mr. Blum describes the Bennewitz scenario much like I have only he had the inside knowledge of Bill Moore's character and background. As I have stated before, Mr. Moore has refused all interviews with me, Christa Tilton. I have never met Mr. Moore and probably never will.

By Mr. Moore's own words, he has the uncanny ability to size people up whether he has met them or not. Howard Blum used the same statement in describing Mr. Moore in 'OUT THERE'.

In the beginning I spoke to Bill Moore via telephone in 1987. We discussed my marriage to Lt. Col. Wendelle Stevens and the accusations that had been made that Bill Moore had something to do with getting Wendelle sent to prison on a morals charge for five years.

I found Mr. Moore to be a soft-spoken person, not the 'wicked agent' that had been described to me by countless others who either knew him intimately or had met him through interviews. And so, after five years of searching on my own, I decided to write Bill in hopes he could shed some light on my abduction experiences. I knew of his connections with the government and I knew of his broad knowledge of the subject of UFOs. I had heard many horrid rumors about Moore's 'dirty tactics' and had been warned never to get on his bad side. At first I was intimidated by those comments, but I felt they were not fair to Mr. Moore. How could I judge a person and his credibility by never meeting with him face to face? It is not the way I operate or evaluate fairly another individual. And so I assumed that Bill Moore would judge me after he had met with me...WRONG! As I mentioned in the second paragraph, in Bill's own words, he can know everything about a person and their personality by never meeting them! I found this to be an incredible statement for any credible UFO researcher and journalist to make. He just did not make sense to me and so I embarked on a letter-writing campaign to see if there was anyway to soften the fellow up and let him get to know me a bit better. I made a huge mistake by confiding in him about personal dealings that I had been through in the past. Sure I had thought there might be some sympathy and a bit more understanding about where I, Christa Tilton was coming from. But, as each letter came, it became obvious that Bill Moore hated me for some strange reason. I tried to chalk it up to maybe jealousy, as women researchers in ufology have had a hard time achieving some semblance of credibility from the male researchers in the UFO field.

I have one confidential source with whom I confided in about this delima. This man has never met me, has heard all the dirty rumors about me and my past, but considers me a wonderful researcher and writer. He mentioned that maybe there was some jealousy involved on Bill's part. I appreciated this researchers' concern and helpful information about Moore, but I still felt it delved deeper into something else. It is nice to know there are people out there in the field who are willing to give someone like me,'a beginner' a chance. I credit this researcher with pulling me through this ordeal. It shows that he is intelligent enough to see through all the bullshit people have spread about me over the past five years. He has never met me, but he treats me as an equal and a lady. Why couldn't Bill Moore?

Just recently I heard Mr. Moore was having a hard time financially. I think all of us that do any research in this field can relate to that. I had just returned from Japan after appearing on a television documentary and for the first time in a long time I had some extra money to spare. I decided to show Bill my good faith in truly wanting to gain his trust and friendship by sending him an undisclosed amount. I wanted to send it in the form of a donation to FOCUS and it was carefully sealed up in a double envelope, addressed and ready to be sent. It then dawned on me that I should call Bill and tell him that he would be receiving a 'Return Receipt' letter just to make sure he received it. I asked if he would be the only one to pick up his mail as I wanted to make sure this large amount of cash would get into Bill's hands personally. The idea was to just bury the hatchet and truly let Bill know that I never had any ill feelings towards him personally. The reaction I received almost made me faint! Bill told me that he was on to me and knew exactly what I was trying to do. I said, 'Excuse me?' in shock! His next attack with words left me in a 'limbo' that I haven't been in since my breakup with my last husband. He told me and I will try to quote as accurately as I can because I was not taping the conversation, " You are a desparate, manipulative, lonely and insecure person who is nothing but a failure! Look into a mirror, he said matter of factly. You see Christa, I am a Scorpio and I have the advantage of seeing the kind of person you truly are from the very beginning. You are nothing but an annoyance to me and to everyone else. No one wants to have anything to do with you and neither do I so I just wish you would leave me alone." Trying to hold back the tears, I agreed I would never bother him again. No letters, no tapes or calls...nothing. Well, over the years I have developed a hard outer core and learned to try and not let words get to me. I have been called many horrible things, but I learned from a very intelligent person that people who say these hurtful things are nothing but pitiful failures themselves and to justify their own downfall they attack others, especially the ones who are most vulnerable in their eyes. So you see, Bill Moore knew how vulnerable I was. He knew what I had been through in the past. He knew it must have devestated my life and he knew that the only way to justify his failure as a person was to zone in on someone like me... A person who had once asked to meet with him because she admired his work. This was his response to me. My outer core crumbled that day and I let my guard down and I let him hear me cry! I am angry with myself for my own insecurities.

Bill was just 'calling a spade a spade' as he had told me in so many of his past letters. But everytime I tried to pin him down as to who all of these enemies I had he never would name any names. Sure I admit I have had personality conflicts with certain individuals that became emotionally involved with me and I admit and I think we all can say that we are at times very lonely. In this field it is almost a sure thing to be alone in searching for the truth. We are all insecure at times also. I am the first to admit that Bill Moore had me pegged on those personality quirks, but there is one thing I am not!!!! I AM NOT AND NEVER WILL BE A FAILURE! To call me a failure I then realized that all along he considered me a threat to his research. He knows of my past government connections and my knowledge about certain areas in which the government wishes I did not have. Also, I cannot help the fact that my mother and father worked in intelligence at The Pentagon in the forties. My mother was a chief assistant to Hap Arnold. I had mentioned this to Bill early on in my correspondence. My father also worked in intelligence with the Army and Navy, but he died when I was fifteen. This does not make me a government agent myself. It is just a portion of truth that fits into my past family background. I cannot state that this is a threat to Mr. Moore, but maybe he thought I was tooting my horn by telling him this information. I was not. I am proud to tell anyone about my mother and her work at the Pentagon in the War Department. She received outstanding awards for her dedication to Hap Arnold and Col. John Marsh. Whether she had knowledge of any TOP SECRET information on the subject of UFOS is for my mother to answer.

I would like to state for the record that I was not trying to buy Mr. Moore off. In the letter with the money I stated I did not want an interview or did I expect anything from him in the future. I told him to use the money and not to tell anyone that I had given it to him as I did not want any credit. If this is proof that I am a manipulative failure of a person then so be it.

Christa Tilton Author

UNDERGROUND ALIEN BIO LAB AT DULCE

Paul Bennewitz is still alive. There are so many conclusions that we as researchers have talked about and written about, but I do not believe I even touched the very surface of what really was and is going on in Paul's mind. This is why I urge the readers of this manuscript to push yourselves to the very edge of possibilities and learn more about the governments' use of mind control. Below I have quoted just two paragraphs from Martin Cannon's wonderful manuscript, 'THE CONTROLLERS'. He offers a very believable alternative way of thinking...a new way of seeing the UFO controversy. I hope all the readers will order this valuable manuscript to help them in further research on the subject of abductions and mind control.

Once you've read it, you will automatically see that the questions of abductions can easily be explained. You may not want to believe it, but it's one persons' viewpoint that needs to be studied in depth.

It solves many of the questions I had about Paul Bennewitz and his dealings with these 'aliens' of his. It also gives me another way to explain what happened to me in the course of my lifetime.

The Hypothesis

Substantial evidence exists linking members of this country's intelligence community (including the Central Intelligence Agency, the Defense Advanced Research Projects Agency, and the Office of Naval Intelligence) with the esoteric technology of *mind control*. For decades, "spy-chiatrists" working behind the scenes -- on college campuses, in CIA-sponsored institutes, and (most heinously) in prisons have experimented with the erasure of memory, hypnotic resistance to torture, truth serums, post-hypnotic suggestion, rapid induction of hypnosis, electronic stimulation of the brain, non-ionizing radiation, microwave induction of intracerebral "voices," and a host of even more disturbing technologies. Some of the projects exploring these areas were ARTICHOKE, BLUEBIRD, PANDORA, MKDELTA, MKSEARCH and the infamous MKULTRA.

As a result of this research, I have come to the following conclusions:

1. Although misleading (and occasionally perjured) testimony before Congress indicated that the CIA's "brainwashing" efforts met with little success,[7] striking advances were, in fact, made in this field. As CIA veteran Miles Copeland once admitted to a reporter, "The congressional subcommittee which went into this sort of thing got only the barest glimpse."[8]

2. Clandestine research into thought manipulation has *not* stopped, despite CIA protestations that it no longer sponsors such studies. Victor Marchetti, 14-year veteran of the CIA and author of the renown expose, *The CIA and the Cult of Intelligence*, confirmed in a 1977 interview that the mind control research continues, and that CIA claims to the contrary are a "cover story."[9]

3. The Central Intelligence Agency was not the only government agency involved in this research.[10] Indeed, many branches of our government took part in these studies -- including NASA, the Atomic Energy Commission, as well as all branches of the Defense Department.

To these conclusions, I would append the following -- *not* as firmly-established historical fact, but as a working hypothesis and grounds for investigation:

4. The "UFO abduction" phenomenon *might* be a continuation of clandestine mind control operations.

89

UNDERGROUND ALIEN BIO LAB AT DULCE

1. Leo Sprinkle Hypnosis Transcripts of Myrna Hansen, May 1980.

2. November, 1989 letter to Christa Tilton from Richard Doty

3. November, 1989 letter to Christa Tilton from Richard Doty

4. 'THE CONTROLLERS' by Martin Cannon, paragraph on Implants

5. Christa Tilton's description of smell (pungent) in rooms with tanks.

6. Describing similar area of underground facility as Christa Tilton.

7. "THE DULCE PAPERS" distributed originally by C. Hinkle in 1987.

8. Both C. Hinkle and Thomas LeVesque claim to know this man
   Thomas C. who claims to have worked in the Dulce facility and smuggled
   video and photographs depicting what is truly going on in this facility.
   Neither people have provided me with any proof that this man exists.

9. Richard Doty related the same statement to me via telephone conversation
   in 1989.

10. August 28, 1980 letter to Jim Lorenzen from Paul Bennewitz.

11. MUFON's 1989 UFO symposium in July in which Bill Moore admitted his
    participation in the dis-information campaign of Paul Bennewitz.

12. December 8, 1989 letter to Christa Tilton from Richard Doty.

13. November 3, 1989 letter to Christa Tilton from Richard Doty.

14. June 4, 1991 letter to Christa Tilton from Bill Moore stating his
    reluctance to meet with me because a friend of mine saw a previous
    letter in which Bill Moore had " a bad comment" to say about my friend.
    Because of this, Bill Moore states he cannot trust me.

15. Telecon from attorney, Peter Gerston of New York giving details about
    his meeting with Richard Doty in Albuquerque.

16. See telecon from Gerston: re: missle ending up missing from a silo area
    November 3, 1989 letter to Christa Tilton from Richard Doty in which he
    stated that no missle ended up missing.

17. December 8, 1989 letter to Christa Tilton from Richard Doty in which Doty
    stated The Aquarius document was a forgery.

18. See Gerston telecon. November 3, 1989 letter to Christa Tilton from Doty
    states no implants were discovered in Myrna Hansen or any other abductees.

19. Conversation with Thomas Adams re: meeting with Bennewitz in Albuquerque.

20. Christa Tilton was told by Richard Doty that he would be able to tell if
    there was a wire for sound. Doty never showed at the meeting place in
    which he arranged in 1990 in Albuquerque with Christa Tilton. (1st meeting)

21. Could this entity TA be the same referred to in "The Keys of Enoch" by J.
    J. Hurtak in which his interpretation is spelled "PTAH" and is considered
    to be "God of experimental functions on Earth"?

22. The TA in Bennewitz' mind may be a sub-species of intelligent lifeforms
    that J.J. Hurtak describes in "The Book of Knowledge:THE KEYS OF ENOCH".

23. This seems to be the origin of the Dulce underground facility.

24. Dr. Howard Burgess-see pgs 28-32 "ALIEN LIASON" by Timothy Good -1991
    Century-Random Century Ltd., 20 Vauxhall Bridge Rd, LONDON SW1V 2SA.

APPENDIX
Dulce Underground Base
or
False Flag?

**Interview With Thomas Castello
Dulce Security Guard
by Bruce Walton (aka Branton)**

**Dulce, New Mexico
Both Above and Below Ground
By Sean Casteel**

**Exclusive Interview
With Paul Bennewitz
Conducted by Jim McCampbell**

**Paul Bennewitz - Lights, Signals And Lies
by Leslie Gunter**

**Investigating Alleged Human Rights Abuses
At A Joint U.S. Government –
Extraterrestrial Base
by Dr. Michael E. Salla**

UFO Hunter Bill Burns pokes around the body of a dead animal, while the crew of the History Channel show gets ready to interview one of the witnesses to the ongoing Dulce saga.

Bill Burns and John Rhodes (famed resercher of reptilian-based UFO activity) stand together warding off the cold while taping the Dulce episode for the UFO Hunters.

Interview With
Thomas Castello
Dulce Security Guard

by Bruce Walton (aka Branton)

The following is a list of questions that were directed to former Dulce Base Security officer Thomas Edwin Castello approximately a year before his death [or disappearance]. They are followed by his responses:

QUESTION - When exactly was the [upper human-occupied level of the] Archuleta installation constructed?

ANSWER - I heard Dulce was started in 1937-38 by the Army engineers, enlarged over the years, most recent work was completed tunnels to the Page [Arizona] Base, site of one of the older underground facilities. The four corners base is called PERICA. Most of the Native Americans [the Indians] living in that area are aware of that base, and could tell us about the underground life forms that frequently are spotted near those communities, Bigfoot, etc. (Note: The references to the Dulce base here deal mainly with the upper levels, not the extreme lower levels which include vast natural caverns and, some believe, very ancient tunnel systems as well. This would include the tunnels illuminated by phosphorus pent oxide which the alien Greys avoid, and the origin of which is unknown. In fact sources have informed us that some of the underground NORAD facilities of Colorado were constructed within already-existing cavern systems, suggesting that Ray Palmer and Richard Shaver were correct when as early as the mid-1940's they wrote about the government's search for ancient underground cave and tunnel systems to be converted for their own use. - Branton)

Q -- By what means were the [upper] installations constructed? Are you familiar with the alleged developments made by the Rand Corporation of a highly-efficient bore or mole machine capable of melting rock using nuclear powered wolfram-graphite tipped 'drill-cones'?

A -- According to several senior maintenance workers, part of it was blasted by nuclear devices in the sixties. There are sections, like the shuttle tunnels, that were formed by an advanced tunneling machine that leaves the tunnel walls smooth. The finished walls in those tubes resemble polished black glass.

Q -- By WHOM was the Dulce installation originally constructed?

A -- Nature started the caverns. The Draco [reptilian humanoids] used the caverns and tunnels for centuries. Later, through RAND Corporation plans, it was enlarged repeatedly. The original caverns included ice caves and sulfur springs that the 'aliens' found perfect for their needs. The Dulce caverns rival Carlsbad caverns in size. (Note: Carlsbad caverns and especially the adjacent Lecheguilla caves are 'officially' among the largest and deepest in the world, with several 'leads' that remain to be explored by professional speleonauts - Branton)

Q -- What exactly are the cattle [and human] organs such as blood, anal tissue, eyes, reproductive organs, tongues, etc. used for -- i.e. the organs obtained via cattle and human mutilations?

A -- Read the so-called Dulce papers [for more information].

Q -- Are the various electromagnetically-controlled air or space craft -- [that have been seen] leaving from and arriving at Mt. Archuleta -- manned by humans, the 'alien entities', or both?

A -- Archuleta Mesa is a minor area... the craft leave [and are stored] in five areas. One is SE of DULCE, one near Durango Colorado, one at Taos New Mexico, and the main fleet is stored at LOS ALAMOS [under]. (Note: I believe Thomas Castello is referring to the 'joint-operational' fleet. From combined sources however it appears as if Dulce is absolutely SURROUNDED ON ALL SIDES by 'alien' bases, and that Archuleta peak -- although apparently the central NEXUS of the entire underground network -- is nevertheless just one part of an overall complex that some claim is nearly the size of Manhattan! One source has indicated that there are chambers a few hundred feet below the very town of Dulce itself that are part of level one of the facility. This close proximity may explain why it has usually been described as the 'Dulce Base'. Apparently even with his high-security clearance, Thomas Castello was only familiar with one part of the overall mega-complex which underlies the area. Whatever amount of activity is taking place there, different sources seem to indicate that the town of Dulce nevertheless lies over a major crossroads, convergence or 'intersection' area of alien activity even though the 'core' of alien activity has been extended to Los Alamos. Los Alamos and the mountainous regions east and southeast of it in and around the Santa Fe National Forest seem to be the MAJOR 'nest' of Reptiloid/Gray forces in North America, although there is also a large number of 'dens' scattered throughout the underground networks between Dulce and Area 51. Dulce seems to be a major 'through' point for exterran and subterran reptilian activity, a central 'infiltration' zone for surface operatives, as well as an operational base for abduction-implantation-mutilation agendas and also a major convergence for sub-shuttle terminals, UFO ports, and so on. - Branton)

Q -- Others have suggested that some of the entities below Dulce are not of 'extraterrestrial' ORIGIN, and that they are actually descended from saurian or reptiloid beings such as the Velociraptors or Stenonychosaurus Equallus -- a 'serpentine' race or races similar to that hinted at in the third chapter of the book of Genesis?

A -- Yes, some 'reptoids' are native to this planet. The ruling caste of 'aliens' ARE reptilian. The beige or white beings are called The Draco. Other reptilian beings are green, and some are brown. They were an ancient race on Earth, living underground. It may have been one of the Draconian beings that 'tempted' Eve in the Garden of Eden. Reptoids rightly consider themselves "native Terrans." Perhaps they are the ones we call the Fallen Angels - maybe not. Either way, we are [considered] the 'squatters' on Earth.

Q -- Some have suggested that the so-called underground 'E.T.' bases and tunnels may, for a large part, be literally thousands of years old... constructions of an antediluvian race which attained to a considerable level of scientific complexity, and who were destroyed by a Divinely-initiated cataclysm which took place after they attempted to merge their science with occult/supernatural forces. For instance some have suggested that the Bermuda Triangle phenomena may be the result of an out-of-control Atlantean experiment that led to a space-time disaster which produced "electromagnetic fallout" in the Triangle area and elsewhere after they had accidentally loosed powerful forces and energies into the world that they knew very little about. Do your observations tend to confirm or refute such a possibility?

A -- I'm not sure about the Divine part, but these 'aliens' consider themselves 'NATIVE TERRANS.'

Q -- Where do the little Grey Aliens fit in?

A -- They work for, and are controlled by the Draco. There are other gray skinned beings that are not in league with the Draco.

Q -- Did you ever talk to any of the 'Aliens' at the Base?

A -- Since I was the Senior Security Technician at that base, I had to communicate with them on a daily basis. If there were any problems that involved security or video camera's, I was the one they called. It was the reptilian "working caste" that usually did the physical labor in the lower levels at Dulce. Decisions involving that caste were usually made by the white Draco. When human workers caused problems for the working caste, the reptoids went to the white Draconian 'boss', and the Draco called me. At times, it felt like it was a never ending problem. Several human workers resented the "no nonsense" or "get back to work" attitude the working caste lives by. When needed, intervention became a vital tool. The biggest problem were human workers who foolishly wandered around near the "OFF LIMITS" areas of the "Alien Section." I guess it's human nature to be curious and to wonder what is past the barriers. Too often someone found a way to bypass the barriers and nosed around. The camera's near the entrance usually stopped them before they got themselves in serious trouble. A few times I had to formerly request the return of a human worker.

Q -- Are there other sites tied-in to the 'shuttle network' other than those which you mentioned, and if so, where are the entrances?

A -- WHERE!?! EVERYWHERE! THEY CRISS CROSS THE WORLD AS AN ENDLESS SUBTERRANEAN HIGHWAY. LIKE A FREEWAY, EXCEPT THIS ONE IS UNDERGROUND... The subterranean highway in America is like a freeway except it's underground. That highway depends on electric motors [for trucks, cars and buses] for the paved roads, and it is for limited travel. There is another style of transit for freight and for passengers that is for rapid travel. That world wide network is called the "Sub-Global System." It has "check points" at each country entry. There ARE shuttle tubes that 'shoot' the trains at incredible speeds using a mag-lev and vacuum method. They travel at a speed that excels the speed of sound. Part of your question involves the location of entrances to that base. The easiest way to answer is to say every state in the U.S.A. has them. Frequently, the entrances are camouflaged as sand quarries, or mining operations. Other complex portals are found on military bases. New Mexico and Arizona have the largest amounts of entrances followed by California, Montana, Idaho, Colorado, Pennsylvania, Kansas, Arkansas and Missouri. Of all the state's Florida and North Dakota have the least amount of entrances. Wyoming has a road that opens directly into the subterranean freeway. That road is no longer in use, but could be reactivated if they decide to do so, with minimal cost. It's located near Brooks Lake.

Q -- Are there any 'bases' in the state of Utah? (Note: Thomas mentioned several areas surrounding Utah -- Colorado, New Mexico, Arizona, Nevada and Idaho, where there are 'connections', but little on Utah which according to some sources lies directly over one of the largest NATURAL cavern systems in North America, one that is said to reach deep beneath the Western Rockies as well as beneath the Bonneville basin) Have you heard anything about an alleged underground installation within the Wasatch Mountains...?

A -- Salt Lake, Lake Powell Area, Dark Canyon, Dougway Grounds, Modena, Vernal. All have exits there. Others too.

(Note: There have been many rumors of ancient 'tunnel' systems being intersected during the excavations of sub-basement levels below major industrial and mall areas in downtown Salt Lake City. Various stories surrounding these tunnels include: explorers who have entered the tunnels and never returned; reports of 'lizard people' down in the labyrinths; reports of Greys working with humans on electronic equipment and massive building projects going on in huge caverns beneath the mountains to the east; reports of humans who are part of an Asian-based 'Agharti' kingdom who maintain colonies within the tunnels and caverns below -- and who are in conflict with the reptiloids, Greys, and a group of collaborating human fascists from a network of massive underground facilities beneath the Neu Shwabenland region of Antarctica; reports of men in suits having been seen pacing back and forth through large underground chambers carrying uzi machine guns; reports of seemingly bottomless shafts; large tunnels strung with lights that are "big enough to drive a semi-truck through"; sections of tunnel walls that looked solid yet which one could put their hands through; rooms which emanate a strange greenish phosphorescent glow; abductees who are taken below and encounter all types of aliens; discs that have been seen emerging from the mountains to the east and attacking incoming UFOs over the valley; Dungeons & Dragons fanatics who have been down in the tunnels and tell wild stories of hundreds of miles of maze-like passages; reports of connections to the tunnel systems via the sewer-drainage network especially underneath the downtown "Crossroads" area; reports of alien activity similar to that which has been described in connection to Dulce New Mexico; and reports of a huge cavern network that reaches beyond the border of the state in all directions -- a huge network that connects the underground systems of Nevada with those of New Mexico. There is a famous story which is not openly talked about -- there are two versions... both may be true. In one version a Mormon Temple worker penetrated an underground tunnel below the 'square' in downtown Salt Lake City and traveled for some distance through a series of underground catacombs until running into a 'lizard' like man. The creature attempted to attack him but the man escaped and managed to find his way back to the surface. He began telling other people what had happened and soon afterwards the 'government' arrived in the area and went in and closed off many of the tunnels leading to the sub-basements of the Temple. Presumably there was some heated debates over how much of the underground system this denomination was allowed to control. A similar dispute apparently occurred to the southwest where the LDS church maintained a large storage facility under Granite Mountain in Little Cottonwood canyon, within the upper levels of a vast network of caverns. Fascist CIA elements and the Greys came in and took control of the larger caverns deeper within the mountain and ordered the 'vault' workers to stay out of the 'forbidden' areas -- and stated that the "U.S. Government" was now using them for "National Security" purposes and that it was their "patriotic duty" to maintain the secret. The other version concerned a custodian who entered a tunnel near the cinemas area below the Crossroads Mall across the street and to the south from the temple square, while excavation was being carried out in a that part of the Mall. The worker entered the tunnel and before long encountered a 'serpent' type man, beat a hasty retreat, and told his fellow workers what he had seen. The FBI and/or the local police soon arrived and sealed the tunnel. Another story involved a young man who, along with a friend, had used a chain tied to his pickup truck to rip-up a manhole cover in the area near the 'Mall' and the 'Square'. They navigated through a maze of sewer passages underneath and came to a shaft that descended in a series of 5 small 'rooms' one below the other, and from the bottom room a tunnel led south into a large chamber wherein they saw a seemingly bottomless shaft, a large southwest tunnel strung with lights and 'large enough to drive a semi through', and the footprints of some type of three-toed bi-pedal creature. Other sources imply that early pioneers and settlers of the area who explored these tunnels came in contact with and in some cases even joined with some of the Telosian-Agharti-Melchizedek-Mayan underground colonies below the Salt Lake Flats, the Salt Lake Valley and the Western Rockies. These subterraneans had formerly established territorial agreements with the Reptiloids and Greys before the aliens begun invading their subterranean lands below the intermountain west en-masse in the early 1900's. The treaties were part of an attempt to stave off a possible inter-species conflict, as skirmishes between the humanoids [Teros] and reptiloids [Deros] within the cavern networks of North America had been increasing since the 1920's, 30's and 40's. Because of a somewhat non-exclusive collective-mind with which these humans interacted, it was decided that one possible way to 'convert' the reptilians into becoming beings of emotion and compassion was to allow them access to the group consciousness.

The reptiloids however, once given access, immediately began taking advantage of the collective and used it to CONTROL the humans on a subliminal basis. The ease with which this occurred may have been enhanced by the fact that the Reptiloids and Greys were already operating as part of a collective or group mind, one which was far more complex than the Ashtar or Astarte collective itself which many of the 'Aghartians' depended on. This suggests that the reptilian 'collective' or HIVE itself is absolutely void of any and all care, concern or compassion for human beings. Individual reptiloids operating distinct from the draconian collective might however be 'tamed' by other collective-free humanoids in some cases -- as some have reportedly been 'tamed' by the Andro-Pleiadean worlds. If the non-humans could be severed from the 'collective' they might be deprogrammed and reprogrammed so-to-speak and even attain individual awareness and a degree of emotionalism. In such cases it would not be advisable to give these creatures equal standing among humans, and absolute subservience and monitoring should be enforced even if means were found to sever them from the collective mind network. When dealing with the reptilian forces, unconditional surrender should be first offered, and if this is not accepted than direct military action would be justified especially in light of the many permanent 'abductees' whom the Greys and Reptiloids have taken captive [those who are still alive] to their underground systems. Most of the treaties that the humanoids had made with the reptiloids 'down under' have since been broken... especially following the Groom Wars of 1975 and the Dulce Wars of 1979, during which time much of the underground U.S. base networks [which were funded by American tax dollars by the way] were taken over by the Greys. Some sources have implied that the aliens took advantage of the chaos especially during the Dulce wars and commenced to invade and conquer several of the older underground colonies. This apparently led to a rift in the 'Ashtar' collective, with many humanoids and hybrids splitting off and joining with the Andro-Pleiadean Federation non-interventionists, and many reptiloids and heartless humanoid agents splitting off and joining with the interventionists of the Draco-Orion Empire. The Sirius-B system which -- aside from Arcturus and Sol -- has been the major center of 'Ashtar' activity, has since been shaken by this split between the two opposing Ashtarian factions and war had reportedly raged through the Sirius system for several years, according to some 'contactees'... an apparent reflection of the division within the underground networks of North America between the Pleiadean-backed Sirian humanoids and Orion-backed Sirian reptiloids which both had maintained operations within the underground levels before the "Dulce Wars" broke out. The Dulce wars were just the mere tip of the proverbial iceberg when we consider that the overall events which happened at Dulce had a chain reaction effect throughout this whole sector of the galaxy. Before the division occurred, the reptiloids were invited to take part in 'peace talks' in Telos and elsewhere as an act of good faith, but the reptiloid-grey collectivists were more interested in expanding their empire and feeding their insatiable appetite for conquest than they were in making peace, although they agreed to peace treaties that they never intended to keep for 'Trojan horse' manipulation purposes. There is a remnant collaboration such as that taking place in the underground facilities near Paradox Nevada where collectivist humanoids and reptiloids from Sirius and Sol still maintain a collaboration of necessity -- in order to establish a global control system, however a large number of humanoids within the underground systems are at war with the collectivist-interventionist Reptilian infiltrators who would otherwise 'assimilate' these humanoids into their collective through deception, espionage and mind control. Now several contactees like Alex Collier, Ray Keller, Stan Johnson and others are claiming that the conflicts in Sirius between the Andro-Pleiadean backed Ashtar forces and the Draco-Orion backed Ashtar forces -- which were infiltrated and commandeered by Draco-Orion agents -- have now spread to the Sol system, as both stellar superpowers have focused on this most strategic system, intent on protecting their respective 'interests' here from being subverted by the other side. - Branton)

Q -- Does the Mt. Archuleta "shuttle system" connect with a shuttle system which allegedly radiates from Mt. Shasta in northern California?

A -- Yes. Mt. Shasta is a major site of Alien - Elder Race - Reptilian Race - Human meetings. Beginning Cleveland, Grover every president in U.S. history have visited Telos City. Truman was supposed to have visited the Lower Realms as a High Archon on Earth. He was supposed to have met the King of the World there, and gave him the "Keys to the U.S.A." (Note: Whether or not the reigning 'King' of the Agharti realms at the time had benevolent or other motives, subjecting America to an outside super-power without Congressional consent would be considered high treason. Although unelected/appointed 'individuals' working within the Executive-Military-Industrial branch of 'government' might choose to do so of their own volition without Congressional or Senatorial consent, such an act cannot apply to the 'America' which is based on the Declaration of Independence, the U.S. Constitution and the Bill of Rights. There are apparently two 'nations' occupying the United States, the traditional grass-roots 'America' established by the founding fathers and led by the 'Electorate' government, and the fascist Bavarian-lodge-backed 'underground nation' led by the 'Corporate' government which is contesting the original 'America' on its own soil.

Some predict an inevitable civil [?] war between the Electorate/Constitutional/Surface government of the U.S., and the joint humanoid-reptiloid Corporate/National- Global Socialist/ Underground New World Order government, which incidentally was bought and paid for by American taxpayers and other unsavory money-making projects. This war will apparently provoke an armed United Nations / New World Order invasion of the U.S.A. which, according to George Washington's famous 'vision' at Valley Forge in 1777, will ultimately end with an American victory as a result of Divine Intervention. Something like this may be inevitable if FREEDOM is to be preserved on this world, and beyond. We should never forget however that the NWO corporate elite and their draconian masters intend to 'depopulate' the surface of this planet AND the underground systems as well. According to one Navy intelligence source the 33-plus Masons [there are allegedly several degrees above the 33rd degree which interact directly with the draconians and are part of the interplanetary initiatory lodges] intend to set the left-wing caverns and the right-wing caverns against each other in order to depopulate the underground realms so that they can impose absolute Bavarian-Draconian global control of 'both' worlds. The 33+ and higher degrees according to this source intend to ride out the inferno in super-secret fortified caverns while the 33rd and lower degree masons and their respective left-wing and right-wing armies will be left to die in the surface and subsurface wars. It may be that some of the 33+ Masons intend to ride-out the holocaust in their Alternative-3 bases on the Moon and Mars, IF those bases are still active. Remember, the roots of BOTH the 'right-wing' National Socialist AND the 'left-wing' Global socialist agendas trace back to Bavaria. Isn't it interesting that the legendary 'dragon' has TWO 'wings' -- a right wing and a left wing -- both of which are controlled by a single 'beast'?. In essence, when it comes right down to it the war is between the Judeo-Christian based Constitutional Republic of America and the Luciferian-cult-based Socialist empire of Bavaria. Both the right and left wing movements are Machiavellian extremes created by the Bavarian Black Nobility ['Black' here being a reference to something hidden that cannot be seen, and NOT skin color] in order to foment global chaos. There are several claims that the collaboration with the Reptilians began with the Luciferian cults of Bavaria, and was later brought into America via the infiltration of the Scottish Rite and the fascist core of the NSA-CIA. There may have nevertheless been a reptilian presence below North America within the caverns that dates back several centuries, however a MASSIVE reptilian infestation of these underground systems seems to have begun near the beginning of the 20th century. 'Mt. Archuleta' might be considered the 'capital' of the ALIEN segment of the 'secret' [Bavarian-Draconian] New World Order government in America -- with the deep underground systems beneath the Denver International Airport being the 'capital' of the HUMAN segment of the secret government. - Branton). Truman received assurance to new high tech knowledge, and victory over all enemies on Earth. He then was introduced to Samaza and Khoach, aliens from Bootes and Tiphon [Draco], both reptilian 'kings' or Ambassadors. Truman updated the '100 Treaty' [that began in 1933, Roosevelt] and requested magnetic advance, space knowledge and experiments. Khoach agreed, Samaza partially agreed. He exchanged hostages for genetic experiments and magnetic advance, but vetoed space and beam weaponry.

Q -- Did you notice any involvement of high-level Freemasons, Rosicrucians or Jesuits within the underground installation and/or with the aliens? (This question is based on the assumption made by some researchers that many of the Masonic lodges were, beginning about 1776, infiltrated by the Bavarian Illuminati. Much of the Masonic world is ultimately controlled by the Bavarian-lodge-backed 33+ degrees of Scottish Rite Masonry, a 'Rite' which according to early Masonic authority Rebold can be traced back to the JESUIT college at Clermont in Paris -- a Rite which advocates the destruction of national sovereignties in exchange for world government, the destruction of religious and especially Judeo-Christian movements, and the destruction of the family-structure to be replaced by 'State' control of children, etc., as opposed to the more traditional Protestant-Christianized YORK RITE of Masonry which the SCOTTISH RITE has attempted to subvert since its inception into Masonry. This question was also based on claims from a former 33rd degree Mason, James Shaw, that the Scottish Rite headquarters in the "House of the Temple" -- which lies at the northern apex of the pentagram-like street layout of Washington D.C. -- is filled with all kinds of indications of serpent worship in the form of murals, carvings, statues, etc., depicting serpentine figures. Actually, from what my sources tell me, not only are there degrees beyond the 33rd degree, but the 33rd degree itself is made up of two cores, an inner and outer core, the 33rd degree and the 33+ degree. In the past when the 33rd degree initiation was reached a potential initiate might have been given a Bible or a Cross and asked to spit on it or desecrate it in some manner. If they refused to do this they were told that they had made the "right decision" and remained in the outer core of the 33rd degree, thinking that they had finally 'arrived'. If they did or do commit this form of blasphemy then they are told that they have made the "right decision", and they are sent on to the inner core of the 33+ degree, which is the springboard to the higher levels which interact with the joint humanoid-reptiloid Ashtarian lodges or branches of the 'Serpent Cult' on other planets, within underground cities, and possibly even other dimensions. One source informs me that former president

George Herbert Walker Bush -- who was at one time the HEAD of MJ-12 -- had attained to the 42nd degree, however he may have attained to even higher levels since that time. I would guess that the one who holds the highest level of initiation would be the 'dragon-king' of Draconis himself, or whatever appellation the leader or the leaders of the Draconian Empire may go by. - Branton)

A - Yes I did, but that is a loaded question, and I won't comment further. I'm not a Mason, or member of any other secret fraternal group. There is one organization I am a member of [in the U.S.A.]. That group is commonly called the "Central Unit." It is a pleasure to tell you that I AM a member of the "Sub-Galactic League" of Costa Rica.

Q -- Is there any truth to the allegations that the CIA/'Aliens' have established 'bases' on the moon, and also Mars?

A -- I've HEARD that too, but I haven't seen proof with my own eyes. The 'aliens' do allegedly have bases on several moons of Jupiter and Saturn. The CIA operates in other COUNTRIES, but I've never heard they operate on other PLANETS (Note: Perhaps we should have referred to the CIA's superior agency, the NSA, whose personnel reportedly pilot the "black-budget UFOs" between the LUNA and DREAMLAND bases. - Branton).

Q -- Have you heard any hints or rumors suggesting that there may be lower levels beneath the ULTRA-7 level of the Dulce base, and also, where these might lead to and what they might consist of?

A -- YES. Your guess is as good as mine... Sure, there was lots of TALK but that doesn't mean it's there. However, I will tell you I saw elevators that were "off limits" unless you had an UMBRA or higher security clearance. At that base, information is supplied to me at a "need to know" basis ONLY! [My clearance was ULTRA-7]

Q -- Some insist that the U.S./Secret government has developed it's own disk-craft based largely upon top secret antigravity experiments carried out by the Nazi-German scientists during World War II. Have you heard anything referring to this?

A -- When I was working in Photo-security, heard a lot of talk, never saw the proof, but once in the Air Force I developed a roll of film that showed a craft LIKE ADAMSKI'S, WITH A SWASTIKA ON THE SIDE. (Note: A letter from 'R.J.M.' of Pennsylvania dated 1-31-91 stated: "...I have a lot of UFO videos. I also have 'THE SECRET LAND' [1947]. It shows Bunger's Oasis and says they discovered warm land at the South Pole. One German author claims the Nazi's had a photo-finish FIGHT with Byrd. At the end of the movie, it says: 'Byrd's Intrepid 4,000 met and defeated ANTARCTICA'S TOUGHEST BATTALIONS.' I don't think they were talking about the weather..." Another source has stated that there were loses on BOTH sides, and the Battle for Antarctica against the Nazi's "Last Battalion" -- which had fortified themselves in underground bases below the mountains of Neu Schwabenland, Antarctica -- ended in a stalemate.Question: Why would Adolph Hitler and Eva Braun commit suicide after Hitler had spent so much energy executing over 5000 Nazi officials whom he 'suspected' were behind his assassination attempt at the 'Wolf' bunker, especially if he had a way out via a secret Nazi South Polar base? The March 18, 1994 issue of THE PLAIN DEALER [Cleveland, Ohio] carried an AP story titled "DOCTORS FIND BURNT BODY COULD NOT BE HITLER'S". Excerpts include: "...French forensic experts say the charred corpse said to be Hitler's is not his body... experts FALSIFIED verification reports ordered by Josef Stalin to APPEASE the Soviet dictator.... the body is actually that of an unknown German male. [The forensic experts] spent more than two years analyzing the autopsy reports prepared by Soviet coroners in the days following [the] surrender of the Third Reich in 1945... the body [said to be Hitler's] had an extra tooth and only one testicle... no German doctor who had examined Hitler before his death ever mentioned either anomaly." This is also interesting when we consider that the well-known 'abductee', Barney Hill, remembered the following experience under regressive hypnosis as recorded in the paranormal encyclopedia, "MYSTERIES OF MIND, SPACE & TIME". Barney and his wife Betty were abducted by gray-skinned humanoids "from Zeta Reticuli". HOWEVER, one of the 'beings' on the craft was described by Barney Hill under regressive hypnosis in the following words which are taken from p.1379 of the encyclopedia: "...another figure has an EVIL face... HE LOOKS LIKE A GERMAN NAZI. HE'S A NAZI... HIS EYES! HIS EYES. I'VE NEVER SEEN EYES LIKE THAT

BEFORE!" Remember that this occurred nearly 15 years after Europe had supposedly been "de-Nazified". There seems to be an Antarctic connection with the Dulce scenario as well as other possible 'Nazi' connections: German 'tourists' scouring New Mexico, exploring mines and caves and buying up land and mineral rights just before the outbreak of WWII; the Nazi-connected CIA's involvement and their placement of several Nazi S.S. agents -- who had been brought into the U.S. via Project Paperclip -- within the Dulce and other underground facilities; the involvement of secret 'Bavarian' lodges at Dulce; and the possible Antarctican-Dulce connection to 'Alternative 003'. Another interesting connection is the fact that the secret Nazi teams involved in the construction and operation of the underground bases below the mountains of Neu Schwabenland and elsewhere in Antarctica were called ULTRA teams. ULTRA is also the code-name for the DULCE base! Also there seems to be a direct connection between the Dulce base and the Montauk base in Long Island -- which was/is[?] reputedly jointly operated by the Draconian Reptiloids, Orion Greys and the Bavarian Thule Society which had backed the Nazi agenda. - Branton)

Q -- Tom, did you have access to the alien craft? Were you ever inside any of them?

A -- Yes, I frequently saw them in the garages, there are quite a few of them. The main fleet is stored at Los Alamos. Yes, I entered several crafts. There were two things that stick in my mind: the odd spongy feeling of the floors, and the unusual pinkish purple color of the lighting. The crew stated the floor becomes ridged in flight, and the purple tint of the lighting changes to bright blue white. The entire inside of the air craft are scaled down in size, when compared to the average human. The halls were curved and narrow, but some how, when inside it appears bigger than it looks. Certain areas, the outermost sections, almost felt and looked alive. I was never taken up in one.

Q -- Can you give me more information on the reptilian race, what do they do on the sixth level? [The area called Nightmare Hall.]

A -- The worker caste does the daily chores, mopping the latex floors, cleaning the cages, bringing food to the hungry people and other species. It is their job to formulate the proper mixture for the type one and type two beings that the Draco Race has created. The working caste work at the labs as well as at the computer banks. Basically speaking, the reptilian races are active at all levels of the Dulce Base. There are several different 'races' of aliens that work on the east section of level six (No doubt some collaborating 'Nordic' factions included. - Branton). That section is commonly called "the alien section." The Draco are the undisputed masters of the 5-6-7 levels. The humans are second in command of those levels. I had to ARGUE with one large Draconian 'boss' frequently. His name is difficult to verbalize, Khaarshfashst [pronounced throaty kkhhah-sshh-fahsh-sst]. I usually called him 'Karsh,' and he hated it. The Draconian leaders are very formal when talking to the human race. These ancient beings consider us a lower race. Karsh called me "Leader Castello," but it was used in a sarcastical way. However the worker caste is friendly enough, as long as you allow them to speak first. They will answer if you address them. They are very cautious beings, and consider most humans to be hostile. They always seem surprised when they found many of the humans were open and trustworthy. There is no fraternizing with the aliens off hours. It is forbidden to speak to any alien race [in the halls or an elevator] without a clear business oriented reason. Humans can talk to humans, and aliens can speak to aliens, but that is as far as it goes. At the work site, however, it's different. There is "free speech" in the labs. The camaraderie found in the labs also reaches the computer banks section. In those areas, everybody talks to anybody. However, everything changes the minute you cross the threshold of the hall. Instantly, all conversations become strictly formal. Hard as it was, several times I had to arrest some one, simply because they spoke to an alien. It's a strange place.

Q -- Exactly what first made you aware that something was wrong at Dulce? Seems to me that a place as obviously horrible as this one wouldn't need an Einstein to know that this is a CRIME site! What took you so long? Are you the guy who blew the whistle?

A -- There are several things you should know about. I took an oath, under the penalty of death, that no matter what I saw or heard I would never divulge the information. Also, I signed a waiver that states I would willingly give up my life if I was found guilty of 'treason'. At the Dulce Base treason is "ANYTHING that mentions the details of daily operations at this facility, when outside the confinement of the this base." When I first arrived, a "need to know" policy was in effect. The story the 'honchos' told us was that "this is a Tri-Biotransfer Facility with Advanced Technology, doing advanced adventurous methodology for medical and mental gains." Which is a fancy way of saying they do really risky things with human life just to see what would happen. If a medical cure happens, it will be heralded on the surface of the earth as a marvelous new cure, saying it was found after years of research at some well known medical lab. The real story of the cure is never explained. After all, the Dulce Base IS A SECRET FACILITY! These people are very good at what they do. They do not tell the truth about the unfortunate people that end up in "Nightmare Hall." I worked with aliens. With that in mind, you should get the idea of the secrecy and the security at that place. Yes, I know this was not the usual hospital type job site, but in the beginning I 'bought' the whole package. I was reminded daily by intercom, in the elevators, that "this site does high risk advanced medical and drug testing to cure insanity, please, never speak to the inmates, it can destroy years of work." I'm sensible, when doctors say don't speak to them, who was I to destroy the delicate situation? But one man some how caught my eye. He repeatedly stated that he was George S---- and that he had been kidnapped and he was sure someone was searching for him. I don't know why he sticks in my mind, I found I was remembering his face, thinking he sure didn't look or sound insane, but many inmates said that. The next weekend I convinced a friend of mine, a cop, to run a check on the guy, saying I had a run in with him and was curious. I didn't mention the base at all. It was a sickening feeling when the computer confirmed that George S. was missing. What's worse, the cops thought he was just another guy that got tired of the daily grind and split. That was the beginning. Am I the one that blew the whistle? No. The next Monday, I searched for George, but he was gone. There were no records that explained what happened to him. It was another security officer that came to me saying he and some lab workers wanted an off duty meeting at one of the tunnels [off the record]. Curiosity took over and I said OK. That night, about nine men showed up. They said they knew they were risking me turning them in but they wanted to show me some things they thought I should see. One by one they showed records that proved many inmates were missing people. There were newspaper clippings, and even photos that they had some how smuggled into the base. They hoped to smuggle them back out, without me turning them in to the honchos. I could see the fear in their faces as they spoke. One man stated he would rather lose his life by trying, than to lose his soul by not doing anything at all. It was that remark that turned the tide. I told them about George and the things I found out about him. After a few hours we pledged to attempt to expose the Dulce Base.

Q -- The name Nightmare Hall is descriptive, but surely there was a 'regular' name, what was it called in the manuals?

A -- In the manuals it was called "The Vivarium". It describes Dulce Base as a "secured facility for tending bio-forms of all types." In their report it is retold as "a private subterranean bio-terminal park, with accommodations for animals, fish, fowl, reptile, and mankind." After SEEING this 'park' the name Nightmare Hall is far more accurate than the manual. The 'accommodations' for the inmates at Nightmare Hall fall short of the pretty picture the manual describes.

Q -- You mentioned one reptilian leader, Khaarshfashst, do you know any thing about him, like where is he from? Is he from Earth or some other planet?

A -- His name means "keeper of the laws". They receive their name after they reach the "age of awareness". They do not recognize time as an important factor in "being aware" the way humans do. Upon their "age of awareness" they are cognitive of the station or position they are destined to fulfill. At that time they chose or allow someone to choose their name. Their name will include the position they hold and several personally chosen letters. Each letter has a personal meaning, known only to the alien and the one that chose their name. Since Karsh's name means keeper of the laws his name includes kaash [memory or keep, base word for 'Akashic' record] and fashst [law, base word fast or bind].

Reptilians choose to be not only private but secretive of the location of their natal place. To them birth, or emergence of life, is considered as one of the sacred rites of life. They consider Earth or Terra their "home planet", but several reptoids discuss several star maps. Most of those stars were within the Milky Way. Within those star maps lies the stars and planets of the Planets of the Allegiance. Earth being one of the planets in their trade routes. If any human asked clear questions about the Allegiance, the Aliens referred the questions to the Draco. The Draco in turn, referred the questions to their supervisor [me]. I did not have that information about the stars, because information was supplied on a "need to know" basis. I didn't 'need' that information.

Q -- Did any of the working caste join in the revolt? Could you give me some names?

A -- A few of the reptilian janitorial crew let us know that THEY knew WE were attempting to sabotage the work going on in the sixth and seventh levels. One of them, with the name Schhaal, secretly formed a small group of reptoids with the same mind set as my group (Take note of the similarity between this scenario and the NBC mini-series "V", which is now available on video cassette after years of non-availability. I have it on good authority that the original author of the "V" idea was an investigator who knew Thomas Castello on a personal basis. He had connections in Hollywood and had written a motion picture script, which was in turn seen and 'borrowed' without permission by an NBC employee and re-written as a mini-series. The show was based on reptilian humanoids from Sirius-B who had come to earth under the guise of benevolent human-like space brothers to bring a new order of universal peace. In reality they had a secret agenda to rape planet earth of her resources and steal her people for biological sustenance. This agenda was being contested by a human resistance who refused to fall for the reptilian's facade, and these resistors were in turn working with a secret fifth-column of reptilians who did not agree with their leaders' agenda for planet earth. Could this mini-series have had an actual basis in a bizarre reality? - Branton). Sshhaal took upon himself the danger of informing me. He was as open as is possible in a unique situation. On the day I found out about it, I was inspecting a camera near an exit tunnel. He approached, stooped down (the tall reptiloids average about 7-8 ft. in height according to most witnesses - Branton), seemingly scraping some non-existent dirt, and he quietly said, "A few of us agreed that you are singular in your interest in missing-human reports. If true, walk away. I'll reach you. If it's untrue, destroy my life now!" My heart almost leaped out of my chest, but I silently walked toward one of the wide halls. For the rest of my life I'll remember those words! It was the first time I KNEW reptilians could have individual thoughts and opinions! Basically, they formed a uniform front with a small variety of interests. Or at least, that was what we had thought. It was a couple days before I heard from him again. As he walked beside me in the sixth level's infamous hall, I heard him say "Enter the exit tunnel on the sixth level, north, after your shift." The next few hours were long and filled with thoughts of betrayal, or worse, but I shouldn't have worried. I contacted one of the original nine [resistance] men, and let him know, just in case. Gordon wanted to go with me, but I convinced him to wait a few feet from the exit and pretend he was having trouble with his cart [electric, like a golf cart]. When I got there, there were three of them. SSHHAAL formerly introduced FAHSSHHAA and HUAMSSHHAA [name base word is SSHHAA or assist]. With that, I quickly grabbed Gordon from the hall and the five of us talked and walked in the dark tunnels about three hours. After that day, the joined resistance group got bigger and bolder. Ultimately, it ended when a military assault was initiated via the exit tunnels and they executed anybody on their list, human or reptilian. We fought back, but none of the working caste had weapons, nor did the human lab workers. Only the security force and a few computer workers had flash guns. It was a massacre. Every one was screaming and running for cover. The halls and tunnels were filled as full as possible. We believe it was the Delta Force [because of the uniforms and the method they used] that chose to hit at shift change, an effort that killed as many as named on their list (NOTE: If Thomas Castello is correct in his assertion, then based on his overall revelations, as well as the revelations of others such as Robert Lazar, Phil Schneider, etc., the Dulce Wars were the result of at least five overlapping factors or scenarios which converged at more or less the same time or played into each other. This may have also involved a conflict of interest within MJ12 itself, and apparently involved different security forces including the Delta Force, Black Berets, Air Force Blue Berets, Secret Service, FBI Division Five, CIA stormtroopers and Dulce Base security. The various factors which seem to have played into the Dulce wars would include animosity towards the Greys for their slaughter of several scientists and security personnel in the Groom Wars below Area 51 three years earlier as described by former MJ12 Special Studies Group agent Michael Wolf; accidental [?] encounters between aliens and human construction workers and security forces near Dulce as described by Phil Schneider; an attack on the Dulce base 'resistance' that was apparently ordered by die-hard collaborators in deep-level intelligence as described by Thomas Castello; an attempt to rescue several of our best scientists who had been captured by the aliens after they had discovered the "Grand Deception" involving a violation of the established treaties, that is the permanent abduction of thousands of humans to the Dulce and other bases for God only knows what purposes, as described by John Lear. -- Could it be that MJ12 / PI40 was unaware of these abductees, yet their superior agency the BLACK MONK / MAJIC agency was aware and had agreed to an actual exchange of human life for technology?; and another factor would involve a dispute over whether human security personnel could carry flash guns as opposed to machine guns. All of these were apparently contributing factors to the 'altercations' which raged throughout the Dulce Base beginning in 1979. - Branton). We, to this day, do not know who BETRAYED us. Gordon Ennery ran beside me as we ran into the third level exit tunnels, and he died when several bullets slammed into his back. I vaporized that assassin and kept running. And I'm still running. Gordon will be remembered.

Q -- Tell me more about the flash gun. Is it difficult to operate, or is it like the weapon on Star Trek, that can stun or kill on different modes?

A -- It is an advanced beam weapon that can operate on three different phases. Phase one, like Star Trek, can stun and maybe kill, if the person has a weak heart. On phase two, it can levitate

ANYTHING no matter what it weighs. Phase three is the SERIOUS BUSINESS mode. It can be used to paralyze anything that lives, animal, human, alien and plant. On the higher position on the same mode, it can create a TEMPORARY DEATH. I assure you, any doctor would certify that person is dead, but their life essence lingers in some strange limbo, some kind of terrible state of non-death. In one to five hours the person will revive, slowly; first the bodily functions will begin, and in a few minutes, consciousness followed with full awareness. In that mode the alien scientists re-program the human brain and plant false information. When the person awakes, he 'recalls' the false information as information he gained through life experience. There is no way for a person to learn the truth. The human mind 'remembers' and believes completely the false data. If you attempt to inform them, they would laugh or get angry. They NEVER believe the truth. Their mind always forgets the experience of re-programming. You asked if the flash gun is difficult to operate. A two year old child could use it with one hand. It resembles a flash light, with black glass conical inverted lens. On the side are three recessed knobs in three curved grooves. Each knob is sized differently. The closer the knob to the hand the less the strength. It's that simple. Each knob has three strengths also, with automatic stops at each position. The strongest position will vaporize any thing that lives. That mode is so powerful it will leave NO TRACE of what it vaporized.

Q -- Is the weapon called a Flash Gun or is there a different name in the manuals?

A -- Everybody calls them Flash Guns, or more commonly "The Flash" or "my Flash" when talking about it. In the manual it is first introduced as the ARMORLUX Weapon. After that, it is explained as the Flash Gun.

Q -- What type of security is found at the Dulce Base? What else is used against espionage or unauthorized entry?

A -- I'll mention a few, but it would be nearly impossible to cover it all. The weapon, besides the Flash Gun, mostly used is a form of sonic. Built in with each light fixture [and most camcorders] is a device that could render a man unconscious in seconds with nothing more than a silent tone. At Dulce there also are still and VCR cameras, eye print, hand print stations, weight monitors, lasers, ELF and EM equipment, heat sensors and motion detectors and quite a few other methods. There is no way you could get very far into the base. If you made it to the second level, you would be spotted within fifteen feet. More than likely, you would become an inmate and never see the light of the surface world again. If you were 'lucky', you would be re-programmed and become one of the countless spies for the Ruling Caste.

Q -- According to certain reports, the Dulce Base is host to [other] aliens that live in level five. Is that true? Can the humans freely roam or meet one-to-one in the halls or is some type of protocol in effect?

A -- There is protocol from the first time you enter the base and it MUST be followed every time you SEE an alien there. From the working caste, to the visiting aliens, to the Ruling Caste, there is a never ending check list of rules, law, and strict protocol. There is never a chance to roam on the fifth level. The alien housing area is off limits to any human. The Hub is surrounded by security, arsenal, military and CIA\FBI sections. The area past the security is one of the most secured areas because it houses so many classified files. The entire east side of the fifth level is off limits except for security personnel holding ULTRA-7 [security clearance] or higher. The garage on the west side of the fifth level requires ULTRA-4 clearance.

Q -- Is there proof available that could confirm the allegations of the underground base, or are we just supposed to believe you?

A -- Many people have asked that one. No, I don't expect people to believe with blind faith, there is tangible proof that has been seen, felt or inspected by quite a few folks. I'm in no position to go on a lecture circuit to explain to every person on a one-to-one basis. I am trying to stay alive. All I can do is state again, that Dulce is a SECRET FACILITY. They work HARD to make sure nobody can find the place. If everyone could easily find it, it wouldn't be a SECRET facility. I've explained the extreme security methods they use. There is other proof available. There are five sets of copies in five different boxes in five different locations that hold complete proof of every thing I have tried to explain. Here is a list of contents of each box (delivered into the safe-keeping of five individuals known only to Thomas Castello and to the individual recipients - Branton): (A) 27 sheets of 8 x 10 photographs of Aliens, creatures, cages and vats. (B) One silent candid video tape, begins on the computer banks, shows the vats, multi shots of Nightmare Hall, two shots of Greys, one shot of the Terminal showing sign saying 'To Los Alamos' and about thirty seconds of the Shuttle train arriving. (C) 25 pages of diagrams, chemical formulas and schematics of alien equipment. (D) A copy of the new treaty complete with signatures. (E) 2 pages of original Alien documents signed by Ronald Reagan [as governor of California], each page includes Reagan's signature. The ORIGINAL set mentioned above is sealed in one piece oxygen free heavy plastic box. That set includes: (A) 27 sheets of 8 x 10 WITH original negatives (B) The video tape, AND the original micro film, from which the video tape was copied. (C) The 25 original pages of diagrams [with notations], formulas, alien equipment schematics plus the schematics for the Flash Gun and MY Flash Gun. (D) The treaty with Reagan's signature plus seven other political signatures and four Alien signatures. The working Flash Gun in that box is an extremely dangerous weapon. In the wrong hands, there is no limit on the danger it could inflict. That proof must be protected. But when placed in the hands of certain government agencies, it would not be treated as proof for an Alien visitation. That government branch KNOWS THE TRUTH and they publicly lie. Think about it like this, do you KNOW, for certain proof, that George Washington lived? Or do you believe what other people SAID about him? There is no one alive that saw with their own eyes what is claimed about him. You judge all you know about him by what other people SAID. Columbus SAID there is a new land, and it was found. I am SAYING there are aliens in several underground bases in this country and terrible things happen in those places. If I die, before it is proven, search for proof (after all, the Dulce Base and the other bases aren't going anywhere. Unlike UFO's themselves they are not "here today and gone tomorrow". If they are there, then there are bound to be some indications of the fact. - Branton). Demand that the government admit it. If enough people demand it, they WILL find a way to explain the base, or at least explain why they must keep it secret. There are MANY people that work at the Dulce Base that know me. I am challenging those co-workers to speak up, at least anonymously. Send a letter, or a telegram [or fax] to confirm what I have explained. In the name of the brave men, women, children and aliens that died TRYING to let the public know what is going on at the Dulce Facility, EXPOSE that horrid place before thousands more innocent people are tortured and die unspeakable deaths.

Q -- What about the elevators, do they drop from the surface to the seventh level in a couple of seconds? Do you know anything about them? Are they electrically lifted? Every where on the surface world there are elevators made by Otis Elevator Company. Does that company make the elevators at Dulce?

A -- I failed to notice what brand was available in the elevators at the base. I could tell you that there is no elevator anywhere at Dulce that drops from the surface to the seventh level. The security blue prints show the levels are 'stepped' down. Each level drops one floor only. Not even the Hub has an express elevator. After the third level, not only would you change elevators, you are weighed and color coded, before you re-enter the car. All the elevators are magnetically controlled, even lights in elevators, as well as all lights on all levels are magnetically induced. The light bulbs are not the type bought on the surface, but a totally different type of light system. The illumination found there is a closer match to natural sunlight than any artificial light on the surface world. The shape of the elevators is unique. If you have ever seen a Tupperware sugar bowl, you could see the shape copied in the elevator. Sort of like an open ended oval with another half oval on each side. The elevator shaft matches the shape perfectly. The magnetic controls are in the half oval shape. If you could stand in or close to the half ovals, you would feel the slight pull of the power of those magnets. The motion is smooth and silent, there is a nearly unnoticed surge when the motion starts or stops. There are no cables needed, because the lift is magnetic, not electric. Since there are no cables in the elevator cars there is no chance of them falling.

Q -- I understand that certain groups of cleared individuals in the government are collaborating with alien groups. Is it known how many groups and of what type they are working with?

A -- I don't know how many groups or what type they are working with.

Q -- A mysterious security man calling himself agent "Yellow Fruit" says he worked at Groom Lake [Area 51]. The Security Officer states that he's been in contact with benevolent aliens, at the Groom Lake facility -- are you aware of such a group?

A -- Yellow Fruit is one of the slang names for Yellow Jack [or Yellow Flag] that shows quarantine and caution in the labs. There are so many different slang names at Dulce labs that meant quarantine that the workers published a booklet to show the meanings. At Dulce, Yellowfruit are the lab workers [so called from the yellow light outside the decontamination chambers]. Banana is the older workers, lemon is the new guys and so on.

Q -- Is there an alien installation under Groom Lake or Papoose Lake at the Nevada Test Site, and are they conducting biological research at these sites?

A -- Most of the stuff at the Groom facility deals with defense, but there is a large storage area in the tunnels that holds thousands of alien craft parts. From what I have heard, the medical tests at the Nevada Test Site are conducted by and for the Navy.

Q -- According to my sources, the Aerospace companies have a secret underground installation in the Tehachapi Mountains, not far from Rosamond near Edwards AFB. Insiders refer to the Tahachapi Installment as the Ant Hill. They are experimenting with advanced technology such as antigravity disks. Some have seen basketball sized floating orbs patrol the facility, do you have any further information on this?

A -- The California mountains [Tehachapi, Chocolate, Shasta, etc.] all have alien security methods and equipment. The basketball size orbs are used for unmanned patrol. They are silent, but when photographing living beings there is a humming sound. The glow that emits light is magnetic aura. This [light] is in the visible spectrum [3900 angstroms]. You can see the light, but the light does not reflect off any thing.

Q -- Is there anything you can tell me about the moon - alien installations? Atmosphere? U.S. bases?

A -- There is not much I can tell you there. I wasn't in the Lunar Program. I heard there was a LOT of equipment sent to the moon between 1959-1964 under "Project Whiteout".

Q -- How do the aliens use magnetism? Do they use it as an energy source? Is there more we need to know about magnetism?

A -- The aliens use magnetism for EVERY THING! They use magnetism as the basic structure for their energy source. The more you learn about magnetism, the better. The Human Race calls them 'magnets', the Aliens call them 'lodestar'. They have been harvesting lodestars [lodestones] for centuries. Not only that, they want ALL the magnetic power on Earth. They intend to continue harvesting that power, now and in the future. As long as we were only using magnetic power as an oddity, there was no problem. But in recent times, the human race has begun using magnetic power and finding more ways to utilize that commodity. There was a treaty made. In the original treaty, the human race (or those who supposedly 'represented' the human race, if you could call it that - Branton) didn't mind at all, 'we' considered magnets as hardly more than useless. As people searched for another source for power, we turned to magnetism. The aliens wanted a new treaty. What could we offer? They chose land, underground mining rights, animals and humans for new experiments. The general public NEVER KNEW about the treaty. The governmental [Bavarian cultist] heads of the world chose another treaty in 1933. This time 'we' got high-tech knowledge in exchange. So now, the more we use magnetics, the more they claim humans, and the lands of the U.S.A. We were 'sold' in exchange for magnets. If you doubt it, look around -- there are token companies that 'really' utilize magnetic power, but are depending on electric based or ceramic magnets, NOT lodestar [magnetic oxide of iron] based magnets.

Q -- What do the aliens do with the cow blood and other parts from mutilated animals? Do they need these fluids for research or survival?

A -- The aliens use the blood and body parts for formula to keep them alive [their food] and for use in the growing vats, and for the artificial wombs. Plasma and amniotic fluid are the two most vital ingredients for their lives. Also, the 'sap' of some plants can keep them alive for months. Most of the plants are parasitic in nature, but red grapes and okra plants can also be added to the formula to keep them alive, if they have no 'regular' formula.

Q -- Female abductees report being inseminated by aliens. Are they trying to hybridize our species?

A -- Yes, they are breeding slave-warriors for the upcoming war with the alien races (the Nordic races? - Branton). The serpentine races are in orbit around Earth, Venus and Mars.

Q -- Abductees have reported that the aliens can pass their bodies and that of the abductee through window glass. Is this a feat of magic achieved by advanced technology or is it a psychic power?

A -- The aliens have mastered atomic matter. They can go through walls like we go through water! It is not magic, just physics. We can learn to do the same thing. It has to do with controlling atoms at will.

Q -- Are you in communication with benevolent aliens or do you have contacts that are? If you are, can you tell us how we can communicate with their teams?

A -- I am not at liberty to discuss communications with any friendly alien life forms. I can tell you there is a friendly factor active in Costa Rica, I am in direct communication with that factor. I am an active member of the Sub-Galactic League of Costa Rica. This organization, using a small satellite dish, a television set and ham radio equipment reached this factor. I might suggest that by using similar equipment and a low band frequency, you may reach the same factor.

Q -- Do you stay in the U.S.A., or do you live abroad? Do you work now? I know you have been on the run for several years.

A -- Yeah, quite a few years. I visit the U.S., but it's really dangerous when I do. I've lived in several countries. I spent a few years in Mexico, working as a mercenary soldier. It's rough work, frequently living in the bush, eating what ever I can find. I spent time in South America, fighting the drug cartel [it's not the citizens, it's the secret government, top officials AND American alphabet boys -- CIA, FBI, etc.]. I settled in Costa Rica, 'bought' a small house in Limon. Actually it is a shanty that some one abandoned. I paid the equivalency of $11 to one of the local constables for the right to call it 'mine'. My name changes when I think some one is asking questions. I've worked in one of the underground bases near the Panama border. It's in the mountains, not very far from a passive but 'active' volcano. It is not as fancy as Dulce, but the people are wonderful.

Q -- What is the best city in Costa Rica for an American to visit and maybe move to live?

A -- None of them are worth anything [by comparison], but I like Limon. There is a real culture shock when you get past the tourist sections. Inside the urban areas, it's not so bad, but away from the beaten path the picture changes. There are no improvements in the shanties, no sewers, plumbing, or paved roads. But if you stay in the cities, and you don't mind the big difference in the cultures, the countries have a lot to offer. Nice weather, great beaches and beautiful trees with fruit growing everywhere.

Q -- Are there any other security level names [other than 'secret' - 'top secret' - 'ultra']?

A -- There are many other security clearances, here are a few, UMBRA, STELLAR, G2-7Z, TRIAD, UMT [Universal Military Training] and UMS [Universal Military Service], ASTRAL and SUB-ASTRAL. UMBRA is higher than ULTRA (Note: It may be conceivable that some of the higher security clearances are used for the joint human-alien interstellar projects. For instance Whitley Streiber described an abduction to another planetary sphere where he encountered ancient ruins, aliens and human personnel dressed in military kackies and carrying camcorders, automatic weapons, etc. Obviously such personnel would have to possess an extremely high security classification, such as

121

"Universal Military Service" for instance? The joint alien-illuminati "Alternative-3" projects have reportedly taken part in joint offensive operations against the peaceful residents of other worlds, this according to a couple who 'defected' from the Alternative-3 movement after an agent from the 'Federation' warned them about such atrocities. - Branton)

Q -- Ever see a badge with 'MAJI'?

A -- No.

Q -- Since you have lived in Spanish speaking countries, it's obvious that you are bilingual. What other languages do you speak?

A -- Other than English, the only other languages I speak are Spanish and Eusshu, the common language [alien] spoken at Dulce. I speak Spanish fluently, and enough Eusshu to keep my self out of trouble. Shortly after I first transferred to Dulce, I took a crash course in Eusshu. Any one that plans to spend more than one week working at that base, they are wise to learn the basics. Other wise, you are required to wait for an escort to get around. All the signs at that base are written in the universally recognized symbolic language. Eusshu is logical and easy to learn.

Q -- What are the eating habits of the aliens? Are they carnivores?

A -- That depends weather they are one of the gray worker caste, one of the reptilian worker caste, or one of the higher developed Draconian Leaders. Also, the created beings, replicants, type two being, or one of the really strange [genetic] mixtures. I'll try to cover a little of each. The formula includes amniotic water, plasma and several other body parts [raw, usually bovine]. This nearly clear mixture with a texture of pureed peaches, and almost in that color. The Greys make the attempt not to 'eat' around the humans, because the odor of it is VERY unpleasant to ANY human. They can spend days or even weeks between feedings. The working caste of the reptilians eat meat, insects and a large variety of plants including vegetables and fruit. They prefer their meat raw and very fresh, but have learned to enjoy some cooked meat like rare beef steak (Note: According to many abductees, the reptiloids are not above eating human flesh. It has been said that they prefer flesh that is young enough to be free of toxins, yet old enough to be imbued with a lifetime of accumulated "emotional energy residue" which is resident within the human body. Some abductees claim that certain reptilian factions have such complex bio-technologies that they are able to remove a human's soul-energy-matrix and place it in a containment 'box', and use the controlled 'body' for whatever purpose they choose. Some abductees also insist that in some cases the reptiloids can create a cloned duplicate of a person in a short amount of time through time warping and replace the soul-energy-matrix of a person back into the new cloned body if their disappearance from society would otherwise create too many problems. This way they can ingest the emotional-residue-imbued original body without the abductee realizing [in most cases] that their soul-memory-matrix has been transferred to a cloned body, because they would have experienced a total 'soul-matrix' energy transfer and a suppression of any memories relating to the transfer process. The cloned bodies do not possess the integrated emotional residue that the vampirialistic reptiloids apparently crave and find intoxicating in a similar manner as a human on earth who is addicted to hard drugs. - Branton). Unlike the Greys, they eat frequently and usually carry or send for food on their breaks. The Ruling Caste is SECRETIVE about their foods. They have created several dietary myths that they carefully embellish when the chance arrives. One of their favorite legends involves one of their ancestors' ability to eat an entire flock of geese in one setting. They RARELY eat in sight of any other species. They carefully choose their food, then carry their meal to their quarters. It was only when dignitaries arrive at the base did they join their meals. They enjoy the same foods we do, and they have been seen secretly munching on a freshly found snail. The "human looking" replicants eat some cooked vegetables. They rely on vitamins and liquid protein for sustenance. If they have to eat on the surface world, they can eat what ever they are served, but as soon as possible they regurgitate. Their digestive systems frequently fail to process the food properly. The engineered beings have a special diet, created for their dietary needs. The mixture includes several organ foods blended with plasmatic fluids, amniotic liquids and parasitiplasm materials. These unique 'animals' also enjoy occasional green plants, usually grasses or lettuce. The creatures that are designed to become warriors, eat protein filled liquids.

Q -- In the Dulce Papers, copper seems to be high on the importance list. In what methods is copper used?

A -- One of the main uses of copper at Dulce is containment of the magnetic flow, magnets are used every where at that base. The infamous vats' interiors are lined with copper, and the exterior walls are clad with stainless steel. The mechanical arm that stirs the liquid is made of a copper alloy. Other uses include dietary needs in a few of the transbiotic beings. There are several specially made cells or rooms built first with lead, then magnetic steel then clad in copper. It is in those cells on the Fourth Level that contain living aural essence. This essence is what you would call [a captured disembodied] 'soul' or..."astral body". (Note: This may tie-in with the reports of certain remote-viewing "astral spies" who claim to have "projected" into underground facilities like Dulce New Mexico or Pine Gap Australia, only to have close encounters with these astral containment fields, or have been captured by the same and released after being 'interrogated' via super-sensitive electronic equipment. In one case an Australian remote-viewer was probing the Pine Gap facility where he also "saw" three other astral spys.

The magnetic or astral body of one of these people had been captured by such a containment field, which really disturbed him. This man, Robert, also saw Greys and Reptiloids operating in the deeper levels of Pine Gap and also Nordic-type humans who were apparently captives and who did NOT seem to be very happy about being there. - Branton)

Q -- Growing multi-species beings, blood formulas and human parts in vats sounds like a bad plot to a science fiction movie. The doctors and scientists of the world claim you can't mix the species (Note: Naturally this may be true, however through genetic bioengineering and gene-splicing this has apparently been accomplished to some extent - Branton). The concepts mentioned in the Dulce Papers sounds far fetched. Could you provide information that the average "surface world" reader could understand about similar things?

A -- The doctors and scientists on the SURFACE world may say that, but underground, away from the prying eyes of ethics boards, they DO GROW TRANS-GENUS BEINGS! There is a lot of written material available at libraries. One of the best sources is an easy to read book published back in 1969, by Prentice-Hall International, with the title of "THE SECOND GENESIS, THE COMING CONTROL OF LIFE" by Albert Rosenfelt. In this book, they discuss "animals that may be especially bred to supply genetically reliable organs for people." -- and "...the use of fetal or embryonic material from which adult sized organs and tissues may be grown..." Also he discusses the fact that embryonic tissue has no immunological activity, therefore it cannot provoke the defense mechanism in the recipient. IT WILL JOIN THE BODY NOT AS A FOREIGN ANTIGEN, BUT AS A NATURAL PROTEIN. He further discusses solitary generation, commonly called virgin birth, but also known as parthenogenesis. With one "virgin birth" in 1.6 million births average ON THE SURFACE of the world, in Dulce that rate is reversed. Occasionally, a "normally born" human infant is born in the hospital wards on the Seventh Level. Parthenogenesis is the method used to grow type two beings. The now common transsexual surgery on the surface world, began at the Dulce Base. Men became women on a whim in the Seventh Level labs, and with the Fourth Level technology, the brain washing [resulted in] the "eager desire to become a woman" and that poor man [whether a willing or unwilling participant] FIRMLY BELIEVES he always wanted to be a woman. No one could convince him to believe the truth. ALL THINGS ARE TWISTED AT DULCE. A quote by Dr. Ralph W. Gerard [in THE SECOND GENESIS] put in his now classic statement: "There can be no twisted thought without a twisted molecule". MOST have originated at Dulce.

Q -- How are the human workers stopped from telling everything about Dulce?

A -- Implants, fear threats to harm the families, EM control, also reprogramming with ELF [Extremely Low Frequency] and drugs are the most common methods to 'encourage' the workers not to divulge the location or daily routine.

Q -- A construction worker at "The Ant Hill" [The Northrup's Tehachapi Base] reports seeing 10-12 foot tall human looking beings in lab coats. Who are these guys, are they from the hollow earth? (Note: The Hollow Earth theory is one that was postulated by various well known individuals, including Marshall B. Gardner, Raymond Bernard, William Halley - discoverer of Halley's comet, Edgar Allen Poe, Edgar Rice Burroughs, John Cleves Symmes, John Uri Lloyd and others. Basically the thesis involves what one might refer to as the Geoconcavitic sphere theory, or that as the earth was forming in its molten state the planetary spin created a hollow or concavity within the center similar to the hollow created by the centrifugal force of a horizontal washing machine following a spin cycle. The theory, which has been postulated in para-geological theories, in adventure novels, and in some cases even in alleged visits to the "inner world", states that the 'shell' of the earth averages between 800-1000 miles thick, with an interior surface consisting of oceans and land illuminated perpetually by a sphere of electromagnetic and/or nuclear energy suspended at the very center of the "empty space".

There are reputedly funnel-like openings near the polar regions, perpetually concealed by mist created by the collision of cold air from the outside and hot air from the inside, which permits ingress and egress to and from this inner 'world'. The theory states that the inner surface has its own gravity, yet slightly less than the outer surface gravity. One side-theory is that between the inner and outer surface where gravity is nullified there exists a layer of weightless or low-weight caverns in an eternal state of chaos where minerals, liquids, gases and chemicals continually slam together from the earth's rotation, causing intense magmatic activity, a virtual inferno, or "bottomless pit". Some have theorized that -- based on the Apocryphal book of Estrus, chapter 13, which contains non-canonized Jewish legends -- that the 10 'lost' tribes of Israel disappeared beyond the river Sambatyon and to a place in the far north where humans never lived before called 'Arzareth'. In the last days, a path would be made through the ice and waters of the north and the lost tribes would return. There are three tribes accounted for as of this writing, or rather two tribes and two half tribes: Judah, Benjamin, half of the Levite tribe, and apparently half of the tribe of Dan if we are to believe the

Ethiopian 'Jews' who claim to be descended from Dan. The '13th' tribe would be accounted for by the fact that the two Josephite tribes of Ephraim and Manasseh are considered distinctive tribes in and of themselves. As for the 'giants', some believe that these have a direct connection to the 10-12 foot tall 'Anakim' people mentioned in the Old Testament who were driven out of Palestine, following which the Torah gives no further details as to their fate, although there have been many reports of such 'giants' being encountered in large cavern systems below Alaska, Oregon, California, Utah, Texas and Mexico, and also reports of ancient gravesites in the western U.S. and elsewhere where the remains of human giants have reportedly been discovered. Most often they -- like the fifth dimensional "Sasquatch people" themselves -- have been described as being benevolent, unless provoked. - Branton)

A. They are probably inner earth drones [workers]. The deeper you get, the stranger the life forms. The tall men are from the subterranean levels, lower yet are the dwarfed deformed forms. I don't trust either of them. There are other forms, that both the tall men and the dwarfed men fear and loathe, they are similar to Bigfoot in appearance, but extremely violent and enjoy eating what ever they find while it is still alive! They are subhuman and demented, with an IQ around 15 (Note: Apparently, according to another source, these lower 'Bigfoot' type creatures -- having more of a resemblance to apes than to the more "human-like" faces and features of the much friendlier Sasquatch people who frequent the surface -- dwell in wild cavern systems some 6 or more miles deep, along with other very large and dangerous insectoid and quadruped or serpentine reptilian life forms reminiscent to something from out of a hadean nightmare. This is according to a report I investigated some years ago of a group of speleonauts who reportedly broke into a vast underground labyrinth west and northwest of Cushman, Arkansas, where they encountered these types of creatures as well as friendly blue-skinned humans who claimed to be descended from a family that had survived an ancient global deluge by taking refuge within a large ship. These ancient people claimed that their ancestors had come to the Americas and discovered the cavern 'world', wherein they commenced to establish their hidden civilization. - Branton).

The reptiloid [hominoid as opposed to quadruped or serpentine] life forms stay in caves or caverns that aren't very deep. They prefer the desert mountains. They use camouflage rather than fighting, but they do carry vril rods for protection [flash guns]. They do have a symbol, not the hokey "snake-with-wings" that I keep seeing in the public (which is used mostly by the GREYS and also as a medical symbol for the Delta Force - Branton). The REPTOIDS use a dragon with its tail in its mouth [a circle] with seven pointed stars in the middle.

Q -- There have been reports of the Delta Force having black vans with no tires that hover over the ground. How much are we [U.S.A.] already inter-working with alien cultures?

A -- I haven't seen the black vans you mentioned. We are totally submerged with alien cultures. Very little of the original human cultures have survived.

Q -- How can WE [the public] go after, or expose an alien culture which is covert and hidden?

A -- Go for the best shot. That means go after the REPTOID. They stay near the surface, they choose to try to hide and avoid contact. They are soldiers, doing a job and usually there are two or three at each job site. They are 'manning' a remote post. They are not to bother the humans unless they are endangering the post. Most of them are not hostile and won't kidnap you, they may blast you with a flash gun that may paralyze you [you won't remember the flash] for an hour or two and cause confusion and mild fear. It could cause you to black out [pass out] for a while. It is their way to escape and buy time to hide any visible equipment. If you know any areas with repeated reptilian sightings, then that is the place for you to look. They are fearsome to meet face to face, and their voices are harsh and whispery with heavy ss's, but most of them understand English [and several other languages]. Wear something with a reptile [not something violent, like St. George killing the Dragon!] in sight. If you see one, keep your hands OPEN, palm forward, arms DOWN. That is the non-aggression approach. DON'T raise your arms, unless told to. DON'T carry anything in your hands or arms. If he doesn't run, walk SLOWLY towards him. Let him speak first. They consider humans repulsive and hostile and threatening [with good reason!]. DON'T try to offer him anything, DON'T touch him or anything of his. If he hisses at you, back up a couple feet, but DON'T LOOK AWAY! It simply means he finds you smelly. DON'T try to overpower him, he is stronger than ten or twelve men! Usually, if he hasn't run so far, he is curious and wants to talk to you. FIGHT YOUR FEAR and your thoughts of panic.

Q -- How do we get closer to some kind of data to prove to others that there really is a danger from non-human beings?

A -- Good question. I'm afraid we will find the proof the hard way, when we are invaded. Try to keep a small camera with you at all times. When you search for reptoids, keep it in your pocket.

Q -- Is there a specific location where the public can set up their cameras and equipment to DOCUMENT an alien-government base, and/or their activities?

A -- The problem is, most of the meetings are held in military bases or underground. The Groom Lake Facility does fly several alien craft that regularly fly over unpopulated land that go back and forth from several bases, Southern California has several notable areas. Twenty Nine Palms -- Lancaster or Chocolate Mountains are well know for such activities.

Q -- Could you provide us with a copy of your badge or card you used at Dulce?

A -- Badges or cards never leave the bases. All exits have bars or walls of metal... to open, to go out requires using the card. When you use it for an exit slot, the card won't come out. Each time you leave the base, you are issued a new card, with all the usual data about you, plus your weight added, corrected daily. There are several mines in the Chocolate Mts. that open into a base highway, but be aware that they are patrolled regularly and there are cameras there.

Q -- There are so many types of really far out 'Aliens' seen in TV, movies, magazines and popular fiction, is there one type of a fictional unknown race, in your opinion, that fits the term 'Alien'?

A -- Yes! There are two, an alien that is totally indescribable, and another would be a pseudo-alien.

129

Q -- What are the dimensions of the Dulce Facility?

A -- There are 1,700 paved miles of roads under Dulce and Northern New Mexico., towards Los Alamos is another 800 miles of tunnels. The base is STILL GROWING [due west].

Q -- What is the top depth?

A -- The First Level starts 200 feet from the surface. Each level has a ceiling of seven feet, except levels six and seven, the ceiling there is 45 and 60 feet. There are approximately 45 feet or more between each level. The average highway ceiling is twenty five feet. The HUB at the base is 3,000 feet wide. Use a 7.5 minute scale map to try to comprehend the size of the place.

Q -- Are there "regular vehicle" exits that can be observed from the ground?

A -- Yes, but they are inside Los Alamos.

Q -- Are there aerial exits that can be observed?

A -- Twenty miles due north of Dulce (across the border into southern Colorado? - Branton) is a large hanger, it is hidden by a facade of cliffs. Look for an isolated short road on the top of a mesa, with no road to or from the top.

Q -- Are the ventilation shafts visible?

A -- The ventilation shafts are hidden by bushes or vents inside caves. There are five on the top of the mesa, be aware there are cameras inside most of the vents.

Q -- Is there external security, and could we recognize them in or around the town itself?

A -- There is minimal security on the surface, most of the men [and women] are Air Force or "highway crew" men. There used to be a Best Western motel that hosts or hires a lot of Base workers from Level One. I don't know if that motel is still operational. Most of the security force live in Santa Fe. Others live at White Pine [Los Alamos].

Q -- Are there security sensors? What type? If so, what is their power source?

A -- Yes there are many types of sensors, radar, infrared, heat sensors, microwave, EMGW, and satellite. Most of the sensors are powered by magnetic power. The only thing you may notice on the surface, would be an occasional satellite dish.

Q -- If you can, give us some information on the upcoming war with the aliens. When does it start? Do you recommend going underground?

A -- The war has already begun. To start, they use "weather control" devices that can cripple a city in hours. Storms, flood and drought -- with those few things they can bring any country to their knees in a hurry. Yes, I do recommend going underground. Choose a location that has a higher elevation than the surrounding terrain. Pick out a cave or even an abandoned mining shaft or two, bury a cache of supplies [including food and water!] near these locations. Place the supplies in heavy plastic boxes that have tight lids [to prevent the destruction by earth burrowing rodents and insects]. Then plan to live like a squatter when it becomes necessary. If you own land, create a system of tunnels and tell no one. Use your tunnels to secrete your supplies, and plan to live in those corridors when you must.

Q -- What about the reptilian ships that are in orbit around the equator (presumably including the original two 'planetoids' that arrived in geosynchronous orbits around earth at 400 and 600 miles up in 1953. This reportedly led to an NSA project which successfully communicated with the Grey aliens and resulted in a contact-landing-treaty scenario involving president Eisenhower and other Executive-Military-Industrial officials at Muroc/Edwards/Holloman Air Force Bases in 1954 - Branton), are they cloaked?

A -- They are not cloaked the way you may think. It's more like nobody is learning to SEE, even though it is in plain sight. Like the mail man becomes invisible because you are so used to seeing him you never noticed he is alive. One of the favorite methods of covert activities is to 'hide' their operation in such an OBVIOUS way [or place] that no one would suspect it is covert (for instance, hiding entrances to underground bases beneath religious shrines, federal buildings, mining works, malls, libraries, lodges, hotels or basically areas that one would consider the least likely places to hide or accommodate an entrance to an underground facility. The underground New World Order 'FEMA' facilities throughout the United States apparently utilize this type of concealment with many of their bases. - Branton)!

Q -- What are the Greys susceptible to?

A -- The Greys are photosensitive, any bright light hurts their eyes. They avoid sunlight, and travel at night. Camera flashes causes them to back up. It could be used as a weapon against them, but they recover quickly. It could buy enough time to escape. Use commands, or nonsensical words in the form of commands and they will back up. Their brain is more logical than ours and they do not create 'fun'. They do not understand poetry either. What really confuses them is saying things in "pig-latin". We learned that in a hurry, and used it against them [the GREYS] in the Dulce Wars.

Q -- Can greys read your intentions if you came up behind one?

A -- Yes. They read your INTENT, because they use your body's frequency. The human race broadcasts a frequency that they recognize as an electromagnetic impulse. Each person has a slightly different frequency - that difference is what we call 'personality'. When a human thinks, they broadcast strong impulses, in the case of 'fear' the frequency is 'loud' and easy to recognize (by the same right, a calm and composed mind-set should be far more difficult to 'recognize' - Branton).

Q -- Can we shield ourselves against their mental control?

A -- We CAN shield ourselves against them, however 95% of the human race never try to control their thoughts, and controlling our own thoughts is the best weapon. The average person rarely thinks in a clear pattern. That allows the brain to think in a chaotic way. Control your thoughts, AND YOU CAN STOP THE ALIENS ATTEMPTING TO ABDUCT AND CONTROL YOU. Controlling my own thoughts have kept me alive for years.

Q -- Could you shed some light on the type of human the aliens are looking for when they abduct?

A -- I can tell you that the most common are petite women in their early twenties or early thirties, dark haired boys between five to nine, small to medium size men in their mid-twenties to mid-forties. But, let me stress that there are ALL TYPES of people being held against their will in the Dulce Base! There are tall heavy men and women, teenagers, elderly folks and very young girls in the cages AND the vats. I only mention the most common age-size are the small young men and petite women. The boys are favored because at that age their bodies are rapidly growing, and their atomic material is adaptable in the transfer chamber. The young small women are frequently very fertile. The men are used for sperm. I have no idea why they prefer small to average size men.

Q -- Did you ever see twins or triplets, etc.?

A -- Since you mentioned it, no. It never crossed my mind to search for them. But then that doesn't mean they aren't there. There is no way I could have seen everybody at that huge complex.

Q -- What is the prevalent human race at the Dulce Base? I am curious about both the human workers, and the inmates.

A -- The human work force is made of people from every nation on the surface world. The one thing they share is that they all speak English. If you are asking if there are white, black, red, yellow and brown skin color, again I'll have to say that there is no 'prevalent' race there. As for inmates, I could see ALL races there. From what I could see, it looked like there were more 'white' people, but again, I saw a constant flow of different people, many I think, were only there for a few hours.

Q -- Please explain the method they use to identify each inmate.

A -- No one has a name. When first brought to this facility, they were issued one large 'number'. Usually that code has a mixture of numbers and letters. They show the place, how, and by who, followed by the time, age, sex and finally the personal number [their S.S. number]. For example it might look like this: NVLV-00A-00700-P00:00:00-00-M-000-00-000

Q -- With that huge facility, trash and garbage must be a real problem, how do they dispose it?

A -- It was never a problem. Some of it is 'reformed' or melted down then remade. Some of the wet garbage is 'eaten' by bacterial forms, and what's left is vaporized in a vat like chamber. The residue of that action [it takes them months to get enough to measure] is used in a complex lye and used to fertilize crops.

Q -- Where is your family? Not just your wife and son, but parents and siblings?

A -- Cathy and Eric are still missing. My parents died in a car crash when I was in my teens. I have one brother, if he is alive I suspect he is inside an underground base some where. I haven't heard from him for several years. Please pray for them, please!

Q -- What is your birth date, and where were you born?

A -- 23 April 1941, Glen Ellyn, IL [actually in a farm at home, in the place now called Glen Ellyn, my birth certificate list is at Wheaton, IL]

Q -- You have been through so much, and yet keep fighting, what is your biggest fear?

A -- That the general public will forget THE TRAPPED INNOCENT PEOPLE in the despicable place, and will ignore THE HUNDREDS OF CHILDREN, WOMEN AND MEN ADDED TO THAT PLACE EVERY MONTH.

Dulce, New Mexico
Both Above and Below Ground

By Sean Casteel

§ Dulce, New Mexico, has been the location of myriad paranormal phenomena, including UFO sightings, ghostly apparitions and cattle mutilations, for more than 30 years. Read what expert researchers Norio Hayakawa, Bill Birnes and J.C. Johnson have to say about the bizarre events witnessed there.

§ Do humans and aliens work side by side in a secret underground base beneath the Archuleta Mesa? What kind of sinister experiments on hapless human beings take place there?

§ Are the many UFO sightings happening in the Dulce area staged by the government using holographic projection technology? Are UFOs a convenient cover story for secret military black projects?

§ Read about J.C. Johnson's theory that the activity in the underground base may be much worse than imagined. Are the beings working with the government there in fact demons whose evil exceeds anything we may think we know about aliens in Dulce?

The twisted trail that is the story of Paul Bennewitz took many bizarre turns on its path to UFO and conspiracy theory legend. And one of the mysterious places it led to is the tiny New Mexico town of Dulce, located not far from the Four Corners region of the American Southwest. We spoke to three researchers about the strange rumors continually floating around Dulce, which together form one of the most interesting enigmas of the present age.

NORIO HAYAKAWA

Perhaps the most vocal and visible expert on the Dulce mysteries is Norio Hayakawa, who has written many articles on the subject and appeared numerous times on radio and television programs dealing with the town.

135

In 1990, Hayakawa formed an organization called the Civilian Intelligence Network, a loosely knit network of civilian researchers and intelligence gatherers whose primary goal was to function as a citizens' oversight group on governmental projects, such as deep black operations.

"Our main concern was in the environmental safety," Hayakawa said, "that needs to be observed with these military black projects."

Hayakawa disbanded his watchdog group some years later in deference to larger groups like the Federation of American Scientists, who it was felt was better- equipped in terms of funds and personnel.

"Their goal is similar to ours," he said, "to monitor government activities and make sure that these projects are conducted in accordance with environmental protection."

Hayakawa was very interested in the government's secret activities at Area 51 in Nevada, and helped to stage a people's rally there in 1998 that eventually resulted in the government's acknowledgement that an operating base existed there at all. Compensation for former workers at Area 51 made sick by the toxic chemical substances stored there followed soon after.

"So this was a tremendous victory and proved that activism such as this, by the civilian oversight committees, is very important and does have a tremendous impact," he said.

MORE IMPORTANT THAN ROSWELL

Hayakawa relocated from Los Angeles to New Mexico in 2008, and has made a thorough study of Dulce from a closer vantage point ever since.

"Dulce, New Mexico," he said, "is a location filled with mysteries that are still ongoing. I believe it is far more interesting than Roswell. Yes, Roswell was significant in that it is the alleged location of the crash of extraterrestrial vehicles in 1947, but, you know, that was it. But Dulce is something different. It is an ongoing thing that is taking place.

"Not only that," Hayakawa continued, "but Dulce has the highest percentage per population of UFO sightings. This is a fact. Almost the entire town of Dulce, which has a population of about 2,600 now, almost the entire population has experienced a sighting of strange objects in the past 30 years. This is the highest percentage of any community in the United States. Most of the residents of Dulce have sighted military helicopters flying over the town and even into the Archuleta Mesa."

On March 29, 2009, Hayakawa sponsored a conference in Dulce about the many rumors and tall tales associated with the town. At 6 A.M. that morning, the guests at the Best Western Jicarilla Inn were awakened by the sound of military helicopters flying very low over the hotel. If it was intended to send some kind of signal, its message got through loud and clear.

Without a doubt the most persistent researcher of the Dulce phenomenon has been Norio Hayakawa who insists the answer to what is going on lies in the nature of what might be buried beneath the town.

THE DULCE CONFERENCE

Hayakawa's conference drew a great many locals who came to speak about their own experiences with the mysteries of Dulce. One was former rancher Edmond Gomez.

"Edmond Gomez was the spokesman for the entire Gomez family," Hayakawa said, "who had been operating a huge ranch in Dulce. In fact, the family and their descendants had been living in Dulce since the 1800s, even before the Jicarilla Apache Nation came here to the reservation. Edmond Gomez grew up during the height of the cattle mutilations in the mid-70s. The family suffered tremendously. They lost 17 cows during the period of 1975 to 1985, the equivalent of $115,000 in today's money."

The lost revenue from the mutilated cows eventually drove the Gomez ranch out of business. They now operate a small grocery store in Dulce. Edmond Gomez continued his research into the cattle mutilations, however, and has come to the conclusion that the government and not some cow-butchering aliens are responsible.

"He showed some fascinating photos of gas masks," Hayakawa said, "some of which were found not too far from the mutilation sites. He is convinced that the government had conducted clandestine bio-warfare experiments and programs in Dulce. Even today, he believes there is a governmental facility, maybe not as expansive as imagined in the wild stories about underground bases, but possibly a minor scale governmental facility in the Archuleta Mountain."

Hayakawa said that he concurs with much of what Gomez has to say, including the idea that a program involving bovine diseases and anthrax may have been conducted in Dulce, conveniently close to the Jicarilla Apache reservation. Hayakawa also feels that the many UFO sightings associated with the cattle mutilation phenomenon may have been staged by the government using holographic projection devices, something similar to Project Blue Beam, an alleged NASA operation intended to create a false belief in alien visitation. If a given area gets a reputation as a UFO spot hot, the thinking goes, then it provides a helpful distraction from what's really going on there. The government does indeed work in mysterious ways.

HOYT VELARDE CHANGES HIS TUNE

Another speaker at Hayakawa's conference was former law enforcement officer Hoyt Velarde. The two gentlemen have an interesting history together.

"It was he who arrested us," Hayakawa explained, "back in 1990 when I took a Japanese film crew to Dulce to interview some of the residents on the street about the existence of an underground joint U.S./alien biological lab rumored to exist deep under the Archuleta Mesa.

"Velarde arrested us for no reason. We were detained at his office for about an hour and questioned. We had asked him if we were doing anything illegal by interviewing the people, a question to which he never responded. I clearly remember that, just before he released us, he told us in a rather warning tone, 'Don't you ever ask any more questions regarding such a base. I have nothing to do with it and I do not want to talk about it.' An enigmatic answer indeed."

When the two met again several years later, Velarde told Hayakawa the arrest had been necessary for "safety reasons." Velarde agreed to speak at the March 2009 conference and told the attendees that he is himself investigating the rumors having to do with an alien presence in Dulce.

"He indicated that the whole area of Dulce," Hayakawa said, "is filled with paranormal activity. There are frequent sightings of Bigfoot near the Navajo River area, and apparitions of various types are very common. People have often heard strange sounds and chanting, such as Indian war chants, when there is nobody there in the woods."

The area's reputation as the location of that type of unusual phenomena is also borne out by the rich cultural and spiritual beliefs of the Jicarilla Apache Nation, according to Hayakawa, and goes hand in hand with the possible governmental operations being conducted there.

GREG BISHOP AND THE BENNEWITZ AFFAIR

Another speaker at Hayakawa's conference was researcher and author Greg Bishop. Bishop wrote a book on the origin of the rumors around Dulce called "Project Beta" in which he investigated the claims of Paul Bennewitz, a scientist who lived close to Kirtland Air Force Base in Albuquerque.

In 1979, Bennewitz began to observe the flights of mysterious objects from his home, which was also adjacent to the Monzano Storage Area, the country's largest underground nuclear storage facility, as well as the Coyote Canyon Test Range.

"Albuquerque is very significant," Hayakawa said, "because it is where German scientists were first transferred in 1945, immediately after World War II, through the Operation Paperclip Program in which the U.S. brought in to the country not only scientists from Germany but also many skilled intelligence officers."

In any case, when Bennewitz began to film and attempt to report on the strange aerial activity he was witnessing, he immediately drew the attention of the government. One theory is that the bewildered scientist was seeing test flights of what are called "UAVs," or Unmanned Aerial Vehicles, pilot-less aircraft that are remotely controlled either on the ground or programmed by onboard computer systems. Whatever the secret flights involved, the government did not want Bennewitz to know the truth.

"According to Greg Bishop," Hayakawa said, "the government brainwashed Paul Bennewitz into believing that he was witnessing a flight of flying discs over Kirtland Air Force Base. The government allegedly sent Bennewitz, through the use of computers, a message stating that there is a secret base 150 miles north of Albuquerque in the mountains. They gave Bennewitz the exact coordinates of this alien base. And that was of course Dulce."

Hayakawa believes that Bennewitz may only have pretended to be disinformed while conducting his own independent investigation of what was happening at Dulce. Bishop, meanwhile, has come to doubt his initial skepticism about an alien presence in the area and readily admits there are still many unanswered questions about Dulce, whether there are aliens there or not.

NEW BUILDINGS AND OLD PROBLEMS

Hayakawa has visited Dulce many times over the years, and has recently noticed some important changes there.

"In spite of being a town of only 2,600 in population," Hayakawa said, "there are many, many new, modern-looking structures there now. A new elementary school, a new high school building, a new medical emergency building."

Although he was visiting the area on a normal weekday, there were no students to be seen at either of the new schools.

"There have been rumors that some of these buildings could be a façade under which there could be passageways leading to some underground facilities either under Dulce or under the Archuleta Mesa or Archuleta Mountain," he said.

Another disturbing fact is that Dulce used to have a population of about 4,000 in the mid-1970s.

"But now it's dwindled down to 2,600, and the reason for this is that in the past 25 years many young people were attracted to larger cities like Albuquerque and moved out of Dulce. That's true. But on the other hand, there have been many sicknesses and a high rate of cancer in the area. There is also a problem of fertility among the young women. I suspect that during the 70s and 80s, the government may have dumped toxic chemicals and bio-hazardous material in Dulce and this may have contributed to the unusually high cancer rate.

"Not to mention the fact that in 1967 the government exploded an atomic bomb underground about 22 miles south of Dulce. The government called it Project Gasbuggy, and it was part of the post-World War II peaceful use of atomic energy program, called the Ploughshare Program. They were attempting to ease the flow of natural gas in the area. But the government knew well in advance that such an underground explosion could cause dangerous radiation leaks."

ANOTHER ALIEN INCIDENT

Returning to the speakers at Hayakawa's conference, a former Dulce police officer named Gabe Julian stated that he had had many encounters with unknown UFO-type objects. One story in particular is very noteworthy.

"He testified that in the mid-1970s he was dispatched from his patrol car to a ranch near Dulce. A woman had been frantically calling the police saying that she was being harassed by a small being standing outside the house on her ranch. The being was carrying some kind of square black box in hands."

Julian immediately responded to the nighttime distress call.

"When he reached the ranch," Hayakawa continued, "he was astounded first of all to witness three shiny, metallic, oval-shaped objects floating at treetop level. He was so shaken up that he felt powerless to do anything about it or to calm down the lady who was already so frightened. In spite of being a trained police officer, he felt totally immobilized because of the shock of this unbelievable scene. His testimony was very, very important in this conference."

And what does Hayakawa himself think of these stories of UFOs and underground alien bases?

"I am a person who can only think in terms of the empirical method," he answered. "I am a physical nuts-and-bolts type person, and I think many times in linear fashion. So when somebody tells me that there is a joint U.S./alien underground biological laboratory and base, I just can't say, because there is no physical evidence so far that such a base exists in Dulce.

"But it's very interesting, because the Jicarilla Apache people many times are superstitious. Many of them know that something is there but they are afraid to go into those areas because of their cultural and spiritual beliefs. They believe that their ancestors may have come from underground. In fact, this is in common with many of the Native-Americans in the U.S., like the Hopis and so on, who believe that their ancestry is from underground. And there is some kind of a fear about that. They don't want to get involved."

Another possibility that Hayakawa considers is that perhaps some kind of time/space portal is located in the Dulce area.

"I'm very open to that possibility," he said. "We don't know what reality is because we judge it only by what we can see. Perhaps there are alternate realities that coexist with our perception of physical reality. This is the conclusion of not only myself but also a couple of well known researchers, Dr. Jacques Vallee and John Keel, who also believe that there is more to the physical reality of this world than we can see. And this is the whole thing about Dulce: it's a mixture of possible nonphysical reality intertwined with physical reality. And the government may have conveniently manipulated and targeted this area to conduct certain types of physical clandestine operations.

"It's a subject that should come out in the open more," he said. "Because people know about Area 51, yes, the American public. But the American public does not know about Dulce."

BILL BIRNES ON THE DULCE MYSTERY

Bill Birnes is the publisher of "UFO Magazine" and the head of the research team that is featured regularly on the popular History Channel program "UFO Hunters." He also coauthored with Philip Corso the landmark book "The Day After Roswell" in which it is argued that the Roswell crash was that of an alien spacecraft from which we were able to back-engineer many technological breakthroughs.

On a 2009 episode of "UFO Hunters," Birnes and his crew visited Dulce and looked into some of the mysteries and rumors emanating from the small, tightly-knit community.

"The rumors about Dulce," Birnes said, "stem from the fact that it's simply a place, an underground facility, where all kinds of experiments are taking place with certain kinds of very virulent diseases and certain kinds of bacteria. That's one explanation. And that's why the base is so secretive. And that's also why it's at an Indian reservation, because the government controls some of the land. It's Bureau of Land Management land and they may lease part of it from the Indians. So it's nothing really extraterrestrial. But what it is is very frightening because of the kinds of diseases they're experimenting with, for weapons, weaponizing certain kinds of bacteria. And the way to test them is on cows, on certain cows and certain herds. That's one rumor, one theory.

"Another theory," he continued, "is that mad cow disease has really penetrated the American beef stock, far more and far deeper than anybody understands. And the way to test for mad cow disease is in the soft tissue. So the government can't possibly say, 'Oh, this is what we're doing.' They can't possibly say that. So what they're saying basically is, 'Oh, let people think it's UFOs. We're just going after the beef stock to test the soft tissue and we're testing it on certain bovine genetic lines to see if it's transmitted through the bloodstream.' That's another theory."

There is still another possibility that Birnes has discovered.

"Yet another theory," he said, "is that, because of all the nuclear testing that was done in Nevada and places like that, during the 1950s, we really don't know how much the ground was penetrated by nuclear fallout. The only way to test that is not on humans, but to test it on beef stock. So that's why they're doing it. They're doing the lips and the anus and all kinds of soft tissue—the tongue—because that's where radioactive material would coalesce and they can check it that way. It's an ongoing program, ongoing basically since the late 1950s. And so these are like conventional theories."

Surely one of the stranger theories out there is this one from Birnes:

"Another theory, he said, "is that they are really hybridizing certain kinds of species trying to find the best created warrior or intelligence agent. Since they can't go ahead and implant these in test tubes, what they're doing is using the wombs of cattle to gestate some of these interbred species and that's what's going on as well."

THE ALIEN STUFF

"Then there's the alien stuff," Birnes said. "The alien stuff is that it indeed is a base, and this comes from John Rhodes and John Lear, and this comes from a person known as Thomas Costello, who was a self-described security guard at the base and who disappeared. He'd run away from the base, told his story to a number of people, made some drawings, took some photographs of the base, and described the base as a multileveled, multi-tiered base built inside the Archuleta Mesa which is run by the U.S. military, the U.S. government, as well as extraterrestrials. And on certain levels all the way at the bottom of the facility it's controlled by aliens who are conducting experiments on human beings."

And what does Birnes think about all that himself?

"There's no way of knowing," he replied. "When you start talking about extraterrestrials at the base, you're really talking about what kinds of species. Are you talking about grays, are you talking about reptiles, are you talking about other kinds of species? Humanoids? Nordics? And the fact is, according to what we've heard, there are all kinds of species that are involved.

"Quite frankly," he continued, "I can understand the alien hypothesis. I really do believe that there are areas where aliens and humans are working together, such as Area 51 and S-4. But whether Dulce is indeed that kind of a base or not, everything we've seen—when you talk to Norio Hayakawa, when you talk to Gabe Valdez, a New Mexico state trooper, they really discount the alien connection and talk more about the New World Order. Norio Hayakawa has now gone into the whole time portal/gateway theory. But I mean, the base is top secret, and there are serious things happening at the base. But whether it's because of aliens or because the aliens are a very convenient cover for even more dastardly goings on there—that I can't tell you."

THE FIREFIGHT AT DULCE

While Birnes obviously has his doubts about an alien presence in Dulce, he did relate an interesting story about what has come to be called the Firefight at Dulce.

"The story goes that all the way back in the 1980s," he said, "the extraterrestrials were giving a lecture to some scientists. In that demonstration, a lot of the scientists were getting sick because of what the aliens were doing. So some of our military guards, who were prohibited from entering that area and prohibited from carrying any kinds of weapons into that area, suddenly burst in to protect the scientists.

"And the aliens reacted," Birnes went on, "by basically turning their weapons on the security guards, killing them. Some aliens were killed and some scientists were killed. And supposedly we all worked very hard to try to patch it together so there wouldn't be any more incidents like that."

Birnes also doubts that nuclear material is secretly stored there.

"If there were," he said, "and we were crawling around a nuclear testing or storage site, on top of the mesa, I think we would have been stopped. There is an arm of the Nuclear Regulatory Commission that is absolutely frightening in its ability to protect America's nuclear assets."

J.C. JOHNSON GOES UP THE RIVER

J.C. Johnson is a paranormal researcher who is also an adventurer. Just prior to this interview being conducted, he had recently spent an eventful weekend traveling an isolated section of the San Juan River in the Four Corners area where Colorado, New Mexico, Arizona and Utah all converge. While on his journey through a wilderness devoid of other human beings, he and a partner experienced three hours of missing time and saw the footprint of some invisible entity appear and disappear in front of their incredulous eyes. Such strange moments seem to be the norm for Johnson these days.

A colleague of Norio Hayakawa, Johnson has also done his share of research into the Dulce mystery.

"I live in the Four Corners area," Johnson said, "and Dulce is like an hour and twenty minutes from me. I've got friends up there."

According to Johnson, he also has a source of inside information that he prefers to keep anonymous.

"I won't call him Mr. X or give him a fancy name," Johnson said. "This is probably no one that you've read about. This is someone else who came out of this supposed underground facility as a government employee and made a break for it and got out. My 'Deep Throat' is in South America and he's not coming back."

The informant confirmed for Johnson that a combined effort between U.S. government personnel and an alien race or races did in fact operate in Dulce.

A RACE ORIGINATING ON EARTH

But from that point, Johnson chooses to differ with the conventional wisdom.

"I think these things can air travel, space travel," he said. "They've got all kinds of modes of transportation. But I think their origin is from this Earth. When Satan fell from heaven, he took a third of heaven with him. And they're down here with him now. We've talked with Christian abductees and they've said that these things came right out and said, you know, 'We're fallen angels. That's what we are.' That's kind of where I'm at with this, up to a point.

"There's also a lot of government disinformation out there. I know there were some holographic things going on. Norio touched on that. And if, as Norio says, this is an underground nuclear waste storage facility, then who wants to go up there and poke around? Nobody. I don't want to go up there and get radiated. But there is so much speculation.

"If one percent," Johnson said, "of what my Deep Throat says is true, it makes me very, very ill. It makes me sick to my stomach. There are things I don't even want to ponder or think about. But there is an information exchange going on. If our government is actually involved in this, and the guy I'm talking to isn't out of his mind, there's an information exchange going on."

FURTHER STORIES OF DEMONIC ACTIVITY

Another story that has filtered down to Johnson concerns a woman who claims she was raped in the underground base.

"This gal said this thing walked right through the wall," he recounted. "It didn't come through a door. It walked right through the wall and raped her. It's a clean, sterile-type facility, much like a hospital. And the people that are there have been snapped up and kidnapped and everything else, if it's true."

The race of aliens in Dulce are called the Draculians, which Johnson says is another name for Satan or the devil. What are the demons trying to achieve down there?

"You have to realize," he answered, "that they came here in spirit form, and they're probably going through all kinds of bodies. They want to design something that they can be comfortable in and do whatever it is they're going to do. They can pop right in. Don't even worry about a brain. It doesn't need a brain. It can just pop right in and this thing will be 'occupied.' 'I'll bring a half dozen of my buddies and we'll share this human hybrid. It has no soul in the first place, so we become all that this working piece of flesh is.' So that would allow for possession.

"Imagine," he added, "if you could create something without a soul and just occupy it. I'm sure that's very convenient for them. To get around and do what they have to do. Obviously they would want to be in the flesh form to do whatever it is they're going to do. This would be a wonderful opportunity."

In the meantime, it is only the power of God that is holding back the fulfillment of all that evil. If God were to withdraw his presence from the Earth, the results would not be pleasant.

"And all of these things I've investigated and seen," Johnson said, "what if they all have a job and they're turned loose? That's very terrifying. We are unfortunately involved in the paranormal. It's a house of mirrors, where nothing is as it seems."

THE DARKNESS CONTINUES

Meanwhile, local superstition adds its own coloration to the myths surrounding Dulce.

"If you want to hide out," Johnson said, "go to a reservation. Go to a superstitious people that, when they see something they can't explain, they're going to put it in a genre or a box or whatever—'This is something I'm not supposed to look at. I'm going to leave this alone. I'm not going to pursue it. I never saw this, this never happened.' Because everything on the reservation, if you see it, it's got something tagged with it. 'If I see a Bigfoot, I'll be dead in a year. I'll turn instantly old and my hair will instantly turn white and my bones will turn into dust.' There's a consequence for looking and seeing or pursuing."

Which is another way of saying that the local Native-American population is apparently not as driven to find answers to the same mysteries that seem to trouble outsiders so much. Their wisdom in that sense is certainly their own. Perhaps they take the manifestations of the paranormal to be par for the course, a continuation of traditions handed down for millennia and best kept quiet about.

Johnson echoed Hayakawa's sadness about the decreasing population in Dulce.

"There used to be four or five thousand people there," Johnson said. "Now there's two thousand. A lot of them moved away. Most of them died. A lot of prominent people who were well known in the community simply disappeared with no explanation. I want to bring that up. I want to bring up that we've probably got four times the cancer rate up there per capita than we have anywhere else, as an average, as a norm.

"The overall statistics for Dulce suck," Johnson said. "That is not a good thing. This is a city quietly under attack."

For more information, visit these websites!

The website for Norio Hayakawa is:
www.myspace.com/noriohayakawa

The website for Bill Birnes and "UFO Magazine" is www.ufomag.com

The website for J.C. Johnson is:
www.untameddimensions.com/c.html

The website for Sean Casteel is:
www.seancasteel.com

Exclusive Interview With Paul Bennewitz

Conducted By Jim Mccampbell

SUMMARY OF NOTES TAKEN BY JIM McCAMPBELL CONCERNING TWO TELEPHONE INTERVIEWS WITH DR. PAUL F. BENNEWITZ. (Signed by Walt Andrus, Past Director - MUFON. Dated September 19, 1984)

For those of you who are not familiar with the Bennewitz case, this will be new material but for those of you who are, perhaps you have never read this particular interview.

––––––––

This is Jim McCampbell making a recording of a remarkable episode on July 13, 1984. It has to do with a UFO base, cattle mutilations, advanced weaponry, contact with aliens, etc.

The episode began about a week ago when I received a little semiannual periodical titled Stigmata. It is Number 21, the First Half of 1984. This little bulletin is prepared by Thomas Adams of Paris, Texas.

He has a rather lengthy article. One finds points of interest on page 9 and I suppose the only way to pursue this is to read what he has here as it is fundamental to the entire story.

Quoting "In May of 1980 a most interesting event occurred in northern New Mexico. An event similar in many respects to the Doraty case. A mother and her young son were driving on a rural highway near Cimarron, New Mexico. They observed two or more craft and as Judy Doraty did, they observed a calf being abducted. Both observers were themselves abducted and taken on separate craft to what was apparently an underground installation, as well as the dead animal she had observed being mutilate in the field. It has been alleged that she also observed a vat containing unidentified cattle body parts floating in a liquid, and another vat containing the body of a male human.

The woman was subjected to an examination and it has been further alleged that small metallic objects were implanted into her body as well as into her son's body. More than one source has informed us that CAT scans have confirmed the presence of these implants.

Paul Bennewitz, President of his own scientific company in Albuquerque and an investigator with the Aerial Phenomenon Research Organization, has been the principal investigator of the case. Interviewed in his office in April 1983, Bennewitz reports that through regressive hypnosis of the mother and child and his own follow-up investigation (including communications received via his computer terminal which ostensibly is from a UFO related source), he was able to determine the location of the underground facility; a kilometer underground beneath the Jicarilla Apache Indian Reservation near Dulce, New Mexico. (Since 1978, one of the areas of the US hardest hit by mutilations or whatever.) Bennewitz's information is that this installation is operated jointly as part of an ongoing program of cooperation between the US government and extraterrestrial UFOnauts. The story continues that after initial contacts years ago, the aliens agreed to give "us" certain technological advances while we provided them with the location for the New Mexico base and at least three others. Plus, the aliens were to be allowed to carry out certain operations, abductions and mutilations without our intervention. The mother and son, by the way, were returned back to their car that night. Since the incident, they have suffered repeated trauma and difficulties as they attempt to recover from the episode. We pass this along because the account is, of course, most crucial if true; but we are not in a position to confirm the alleged findings. Hopefully, more information regarding this incident will be aired in the near future. We can only consider such reports while continuing to seek the evidence to refute or confirm." That's the end of this remarkable quotation from Stigmata.

As I have been studying the idea of bases for aliens for some time, this has caught my attention and I also suspected cooperation between the US Government and the aliens. It also gives the name and locations of a man who has his own scientific operation, Dr. Paul Bennewitz. I tried to get in touch with him. Through the telephone information service I was able to do so. I got in touch with Dr. Bennewitz by telephone and indicated that I had seen this reference to him and his work and I wanted to find out whether he was being misrepresented or whatever. I told him that I would Xerox a copy of it and forward it to him for comments, which I did. This morning, July 13, 1984, he telephoned me and said that he, having looked over the article, found that it was substantially correct. I forgot to mention that in my letter to him I said that none of the details that wre in this particular article gave me any strain. Then Dr. Bennewitz, who I will refer to as Paul... He took time to close the door to his office and elaborated upon the whole story and the conversation lasted somewhere near an hour. It is rather mind boggling and here is the substance of that telephone conversation.

The article is basically accurate and he does have the coordinates of the base. He is a physicist and he started four years ago to determine in his own mind whether UFOs exist or do not and he has gotten much more deeply involved than he ever intended. It has caused him a great deal of trouble from the government intelligence groups. He has pictures from the location. He went with a Highway Patrol Officer and they saw a UFO take off from a mesa at the location. He obtained photographs and what he calls launch ships were 330 ft. long and 130 ft. across. The cattle rancher named Gomez and he went back to this location which is a mesa and saw a surveillance vehicle which was about 5 ft by 10 ft, like a satellite, he said. Hehad been using a Polaroid camera and then got a Hasselblad to produce much better pictures. He set up a monitoring station and observed that UFOs are all over the area. He was also able to pick up signals and obtain video pictures that are transmissions from the aliens screens. He has been dealing heavily with a Major Edwards, Security Commander of Manzano Security. He and his wife saw four objects outside of a warhead storage area at a range of about 2500 feet and obtained movies of them. He now has about 6000 feet of movie footage, of which 5000 ft is in Super Eight. The objects have the ability to "cloak." That is his word, spells CLOAK like cloak and danger, like cover up and he says that they can cause themselves to go invisible by a field that causes the light waves to bend around the object and that one sees the sky behind them.

He confirmed the fact that the woman was picked up when she accidentally observed the calf being abducted. He has paid for a pathology work and a medical doctor work. The pathologist is a former head of the microbiology department of New Mexico University. They have done CAT scans to show that the woman did in fact have an implant in her body.

She has a vaginal disease like streptococci-bacillus and tried many antibiotics to destroy the bacteria. That it has survived off the antibodies themselves. The aliens keep hassling her.

Paul kept the woman and her mother at his house and the UFOs were flying overhead constantly. There is no ESP involved, but it is just plain physics.

They send a beam down. They have a beam through which they can sense her thoughts. They can communicate through this beam. She picked up their transmissions. He devised a means of communication based upon hex ASCII code; one is equal to "no" and two being "yes." Through this code he has been able to talk to the aliens. He then computerized the system that would reject extraneous inputs. He said that they can be very threatening and malevolent. One of them he talked to said that he would drop off communication if he became too familiar. He was told about the base.

He then told the OSI of the Air Force and gave several presentations to high level Air Force people in briefings on the subject, Wing Level Command, and many others, including this fellow Edwards.

After he gave his presentation he was taken twice by helicopter to the site; once with an OSI agent and the next time with a Col. Carpenter. He made photographs.

Part TWO

He telephones shortly after noon today, July 17, 1984, and excused himself then to close the office door. I suggested I would use that time to pick up some note paper, which I did. He indicated that in a separate incident; it must have been a court order or something like that, to Kodak Corp. to intercept some of his film; to either take it or copy it. He has a secret report where apparently his pictures that were missing are included. There are some reference numbers involved there and also including his case number. He is going to be sending me that information. He asked if MUFON would search it out and I said I couldn't say, although I might have sufficient interest to pursue it myself, and asked why he would not do it and he said that "perhaps somebody else could be more successful." This material came to him anonymously and I'm being very specific because it has some bearing on a piece of paper that we know about in northern California. "It is a piece of paper," quote. It describes this film and the tests that were performed on them, being very sophisticated. He indicated something else about a case number and referring to intelligence groups access, to a very highly classified--up in the 20 hundreds, which is a reference figure that I am not familiar with. The Air Force has claimed that this document is a forgery. The former Major Edwards is now a Lt. Colonel.

Paul offered, because he just voluntarily offered this information that Edwards is at Hann AFB in Germany and his home telephone number is _____. (On 1-8-86 he was Vice Commander AF Security in Albuquerque.) He is in charge of security there and has around 500 people. He said that Edwards might be somewhat reticent to speak freely because he knows that the National Security Agency monitors all the international calls.

I inquired about the other bases that were referred to in the Stigmata report or article. He said all that he knew that one was to the south, one to the west and one to the east and he doesn't want to know anything more about it.

I discussed the prospect of using the paper in the MUFON 1984 Proceedings to try to find the center of gravity for the mutilation cases from those maps that run from about 1972 to 1982 or 1983. The word gravity triggered in his mind another connection having to do with the Department of Interior that has a gravity department and they do in fact survey the US and publish maps indicating the gravity contours. There is a very weak gravity at the site near Dulce. He said that the craft are very sensitive to the gravity levels and that suggested that perhaps the other sites might also be located relative to weak gravity.

He indicated that the objects fly in a wobbly way. His pictures have shown that. He says "like the rocking of a boat." He has measured many right angle turns and also full 180 degree turns in a 20th of a second with the object still inside of the bow-wave. He has also observed and photographed the object or lights moving in a triangular pattern and square patterns. He says high powered radar can interfere with them.

I reported on the meeting that we had on Sunday afternoon and raised some of the questions that came out of that meeting. One of them was why not remove the implant? He said that this had been discussed and the lady witness finds that acceptable if she can be assured that there can be no nerve damage. He then went into great detail, which exceeds my knowledge of anatomy, in describing the location of the implants. One appears to be adjacent to and external to the cortex, which I think he indicated was at the base of the brain. The image in the CAT scan is of a very small helix, like it was joining two major nerves near the spinal column. Then on the lateral right side from the back, there is an implant of perhaps like the one above. Another is on the left side. Two others are on the forward part of the skull, which appear to be small 2 millimeter electrodes against the radial nerve. There is a shape to these things which he indicated is like a baby bottle nipple upside down, not the cap part, but just the nipple itself. (A note from Bennewitz: This shape is not the implants which are just round disks. ([On the top part of the skull]) The nipple things are worn externally as pick offs by the alien.)

(I raised the question of the USSR satellites seeing the base) He acknowledged that, and also that ours can certainly see it. He had a discussion with an OSI Photo Analyst who indicated that he had seen tracks up a hill and a launch location that was definitely not a rock but some kind of artificial construction. On the hazard of entering the area, I asked about that. He said that there is a risk if we went in on foot, but if a person tried to do that likely that the people would "zap" them. The odds are one might be accosted. But he thinks a helicopter would be safe. But what he wants to do is to do additional surveillance, then go in with a group. The larger number of people the better. A highway patrolman, a friend of his, is ready to go in at any time. He says one can't act on impulse. You have to plan out a program. He said four times he had near encounters and one was with this Major Edwards. He asked them mentally to be picked up. They were apparently scanning him. He doesn't "receive" anything mentally. He asked them to blink their force field twice if they were willing to do it and all four UFOs under surveillance did blink twice. He asked to be picked up on Sunday if he received one blink from all four UFOs, which were reported about 300 ft. from each other. He took this to mean "no." He asked if they were not authorized and he got a similar response. This established a code system by which some further communication was accomplished.

At some later time, an agreement had been reached for a meeting. He was on his roof and observed a UFO on the ground near an outer fence of the base. (This appears to be in reference to a government reservation.) An agreement seemed to have been reached to meet at the Northeast corner of the inner compound. Major Edwards picked him up and they went to this meeting place. He said "don't use the radio." They encountered two guards in India Section who had been ordered to fire upon anything that moves. They stopped their jeep and walked into the desert. There had been a miscalculation and they were in the wrong place. On three other occasions on some property he owns on 95 acres, UFOs came within 400 yards of him during daylight. Apparently, both he and the aliens "chickened out" on a definite meeting. We had a recorder at one time and waited until after dark (8:00 p.m.) and then pulled back for he said his voice on the recorder showed confusion. He said you monitor yourself constantly for confusion and psychological variations.

I asked who was flying the UFOs? He said aliens. He says they call the implants "alterations."

He thinks something should be done about all this and quick. UFO activity is still going on all around Albuquerque. It is hard to separate their activity from ground lights because they move slowly at less than 200 ft. Elevation, particularly over West Mesa where a lot of lovers go.

He has been observing that area with binoculars and then he talked about rotating the binoculars. (I inquired about this in some length.) If you rotate the ends of the binoculars, you will get vertical stripes that represent 60 cycle input to the light. For airplanes, you get 400 cycles -- you get the same type of bright stripes with different separation. On DC one sees only a spread out change their positions so apparently what he calls the MPS (manipulations per sequence/second) changes its frequency on a periodic basis, I guess. The MPS is visible on film in color at night. I suggested I would be helpful if he had a photographic record oft this spec and he said that this could never be possible. (Note from Bennewitz: What I meant was the binocular phenomena had to be observed. Photographing the phenomena would be difficult through binoculars.)

I inquired about his business and his solid state physics. I told him that was my bag too and I studied physics at night school in years after college and got just up to doctoral level, but never got a Ph.D. because I was skipping around the country trying to maximize my income and raise three children. He said that was his experience also. Specifically being temperature and humidity devises. Their equipment has been on the shuttle and most of their business is with the top 500 corporations.

His company is by Sandia on 1/2 acre and now building an additional 3500 sq. ft. building. There is another organization called Bennewitz Laboratory which is the research arm of Thunder Science Corporation owned 0% by the latter and operated by his three sons. They have invented a hearing device that has no moving parts that makes totally deaf people able to hear and in addition, expanding the frequency range plus 1000 Hz on the high side and down to less than 10 Hz on the low frequency end.

He said that he got involved in all of this merely as a hobby and it became an obsession. He simply wanted to know what was going on and to develop instrumentation to measure data, etc. Since the signals from the UFOs are very low frequency, down around 200 Hz and with an analyzer you just think you are looking at some noise. But I believe he said it was a memory scope that was able to filter out the signal involved there whereas ordinary filters do not. They trigger signals in an on and off fashion, instead of 0 and 1 volt representing that type of communication or signal a distinction is made between a narrow pulse and wide pulse. Each communication is preceded by four or five pulses.

He had previously been in touch with the OSI which has been verified in Clear Intent. But now he says that when he calls them, they won't speak to him so he is in a "shut out" situation. I pointed out that there were two OSI (Office of Special Investigation) and the other is CIA. He assures me that it was not the CIA group. He said the actual title of the group that he was dealing with was the "Office of Secret Investigation or Intelligence." He says they investigate the humans, that is the government. I mentioned to him that in Clear Intent that it said he was under surveillance. That happens to be in error. That information comes from somewhere else. But he quickly said "I know that I am under surveillance."

They set up a site across the street from his house with computers and recorders. A girl rented the house. He had a detective look into this and found that she was operating under an assumed name and she had no social security number. He has photographs of people coming and going with NORAD license plates, Air Force, A.F. Weapons Lab. He thinks NSA is orchestrating this.

For an entirely separate subject, he was told that it was a Washington source. The whole operation, the UFO base detail, is classified higher than the President. The President doesn't know about all of this.

He is also concerned that there are two levels of security involved. (1) Project Aquarius, which is TOP SECRET and another (2) higher than that; where people in charge of the higher level information having these new vehicles could simply take over the government. He called the Air Force intelligence headquarters in Washington. The Commanding Officer was not present but he talked to a Captain who was the adjutant or executive and started talking. He said "I know all of these facts, and this and that, and what do you think about that?" The Captain said, "Just write us a report and tell us what we should do about 'it". So he prepared a 20 page report and Edwards saw it. He forwarded it by Federal Express and also a copy to the White House in a double envelope, indicating that sensitive material was in the inner envelope. Edwards got a call from Colonel Don _____ who was the White House Liaison to inquire who this Bennewitz fellow was. Edwards gave a positive report. The White House was extremely interested and issued orders "to get on with it; to do something, assuring Edwards that Bennewitz would receive a letter within two weeks." Such a letter was never received. Finally, Col. _____ from the Air Force Secretary sent him a letter eventually just pursuing the "Old Party Line" that said he should not be troubling the headquarters of the Air Force and the Executive offices of the White House with all of his stuff. Bennewitz showed this letter to Edwards who blew up and called Col. Don _____. They got an answer from the Air Force that they were not interested and knew nothing about it.

On another point: referencing the Stigmata article where the farmer thought that the two humanoids may have been naked. In the case with which he is dealing -- the woman and the son, the boy upon being questioned laughed, and he said "they had no fronts or behinds." I asked, "No sexual organs," and he said "Yes, no organs at all." He has received information concerning a high metabolism rate of the creatures, even birdlike. One of the witnesses, I think the woman who was being taken by the hand, said the hand of the creature was "red hot." He guesses that it must have been 115 degrees F. The creatures cannot stand uncontrolled environment. They wear suits for protection against excessive heat. They are fed by a formula and if they are short of that intake they will turn gray. They are a light -- yellow green when healthy. The heart is on the right side and they have one lung. Elimination is through the skin. The creatures are very strong.

(He seems to have very little knowledge of the literature and the organizations working on UFOs. I promised to scare up a copy of my book to send to him and also a personal resume to give him an idea of my background and copies of one or more of my papers.)

I asked about his reaction to the summary of the UFOs fields that I deduced that I relayed to him in the first call. (He thinks that I may be right.) He says that the UFOs can be detected by radar detectors and they also trigger highway patrol radar or police radar guns.

His friend Valdez, at his suggestion, was looking for a water intake to the site and within about 1 1/2 miles he came upon a flying saucer at a distance of about 300 ft. The Indians own the area -- are quite scared and very superstitious and 90% of them have moved into town.

The Chief of Police told him about an experience he had. A tribal chief had gone deer hunting on a mesa south of Dulce. Two days went by. When he didn't return, a search party was sent out. In the daylight on the mesa, a ship "hopped up" from down below and came up above the mesa. Two guys (human) kicked the tribal chief to the ground. Then they got into the ship and disappeared. He had been hunting and had "fell." He had a broken leg and he was picked up by these human people in the craft. The ship was black. Some of these humans wear black uniforms.

He discussed something about some devices called sphericals that have a sound when they move abruptly; and they are apparently remotely controlled little vehicles. Spheres are from 1 1/2" to 12' in diameter. We discussed weapons used by aliens and whether or not they are used to paralyze people. Yes, they consist of a cube about 2" on a side -- called a lens hung around the neck that emits a beam. Another on the ship produces a blue light that he has seen. It comes from a device about 4' high and 14" long with grid black lines on it. The color produced is very light blue which is like ionized oxygen.

He has not sought publicity on any of this. He is interested only in getting the facts. He did not object to the idea that I would send a copy of our telephone conversation to Tom Adams when I told him about my plan. He had received a call from a William Allen from Seattle, concerning an English publication of the Kirtland AFB case. I told him that if it was the same Bill Allen that I knew, it was a good contact, since I had become very well acquainted with Bill Allen at the 1983 MUFON Symposium in Pasadena. (NOTE: William K. Allen lived in Kelowna, BC, Canada. Bill Allen from Seattle recently died. He is not the same person as Bill Allen from Kelowna. I knew both of them. Bill Allen from Seattle wrote several books, one of them was "Spacecraft from Beyond theThird dimension." He was a Boeing engineer. Bill Allen in Kelowna was an APRO investigator.) The English publication seemed to be the Flying Saucer Review which I assured him was the leading publiication of its kind in the world. (Now defunct)

(So there is some more information that we can put into the equation of Paul Bennewitz and it is indeed a puzzling situation. I continue to get a reassurance that the guy is continually on the level and what he has to say should be taken seriously and not look into it in great details without being overly skeptical at the outset.) Jim McCampbell comments.

(A note on the bottom from Paul Bennewitz: "You are skeptical? If it were not happening in "first person" I wouldn't believe it either.) This paper was signed by Walt Andrus - September 19, 1984.

Someone in the government took what Bennewitz said very seriously even though they said they weren't interested. They ended up by putting him in a mental facility saying he had a nervous breakdown. A usual tactic to shut a person up that they don't want "spilling the beans!" How disgusting.

Part Three

He says that you can see saucers on the ground. He says there is a kind of a cone -- a large cone and the larger vehicles come and land on top of the cone with the top of the cone fitting into a hole in the bottom. There is an elevator inside of the cone and that goes down into the mountain or ground about one kilometer. You can see the aliens running around the base getting into the vehicles. They use small vehicles to get around that have no wheels. They are rectangular in shape and they levitate. They do not show up in color because they are highly reflective, but in black and white they are visible. He says that there are beam weapons that are floating in strategic locations and there is a road into the base. He obtained infrared photos of the area from an altitude of 14,000 ft. There is a level highway going into the area that is 36 ft. Wide. It is a government road. One can see telemetry trailers and buildings that are five sided with a dome. It is standard military procedure. There are many guard points and "stakes" and there are launch domes that one can see. Next to the launch dome he saw a black limousine and another at some distance off. The careful measurements showed that the limousine was the same length as his Lincoln Town car. It is a CIA vehicle. Also there was a blue van. He has been cautioned about these limousines as they will run you off the road if you try to get into the area and in fact somebody has been killed in that manner. To the North is a launch site. There are two wrecked ships there: they are 36 feet with wings, and one can see oxygen and hydrogen tanks. There are four cylindrical objects Socorro type -- two carrying something while flying. The whole operation is based upon a government agreement and a technology trade. We get out of it atomic ships that are operated by plutonium. The Cash-Landrum case was one of them. The doors jammed open and neutron radiation came out.

One is based at Holloman Air Force base and possible Ft. Hood, Texas. Refueling of the plutonium is accomplished at Los Alamos.

He had traced pictures of this base back to 1948 and it has been there starting in 1948. Pictures in 1952, you can see many saucers and the base and trucks in winter time. The road was "passed off" to the local inhabitants as a lumber contract. He has photographs (I believed) of the firing of a beam weapon that ejects in two directions. (That would be necessary on a flying saucer. The reaction forces would impede the vehicle.) He has computed the speeds of flying saucers at 15,000 mph an indicates that the pilots of ours are from NSA, the National Security Agency. The aliens have had the atomic propulsion system for 48 years and the saucers themselves operate on an electric charge basis having to do with a crystal semiconductor and maybe a super lattice. I think he said "as you increase the voltage, the current goes down." At present there are six to eight vehicles, maybe up to ten over the area and sometimes up to 100. They can be seen in the clouds. They go into the cumulus clouds and produce nitrogen nitrade. I speculate it is this you will see when you see black spots in the cloud. They eat holes in the cloud. If you can see black spots in a cloud, then you can tell that a vehicle is in there.

He says they come from six different cultures and in his communications that some come from a binary system, possible Zeta Reticuli and from distances up to and larger than 32 light years away. They appear to have one to three ships in earth orbit at 50,000 KM altitude. Based upon data he had to form the words to try to communicate and he produced a vocabulary of 627 words in a matrix form and uses a computer. The Flying Saucers we see are limited to operation in the atmosphere.

Now with regard to the cattle problem, the aliens are using the DNA from the cattle and are making humanoids. He got pictures of their video screen. Some of these creatures are animal like, some are near human and some are human and short with large heads. They grow the embryos. After the embryos become active by a year of training, presumably that is required for them to become operational. When they die, they go back into a tank. Their parts are recovered.

In 1979 something happened and the base was closed. There was an argument over weapons and our people wre chased out, more than 100 people involved. (Some place later he indicates further details on this point.)

The base is 4000 ft. long and our helicopters are going in there all the time. When it became known that he was familiar with all this, the mutilations stopped. They are taking humanoid embryos out of this base to Albuquerque.

He said there are still quite a few of the helicopters in operation. All are unmarked. They fly at night. He went up there himself in a helicopter and the OSI briefed the copter pilot and he thought perhaps the copter pilot himself was an undercover man. They saw helicopter pads up there - Viet Nam type, with bearing markers and the trees pushed off away from the location. It is such a wild area he said. He agreed to send me the coordinates of this base.

Regarding abductions of people, they pick out medium to low IQ personnel. They are able to scope out each one. They pick up these people and then put implants into them and take tissue samples; including ovum from the women, sperm from the men and DNA.

They can program these people as slaves to do whatever they wish and they will have no memory of it. The hard core type refuse to be x-rayed or hypnotically regressed. You can recognize them because of their eyes. He says "peculiar look in the eyes and expression -- with a funny smile." Hynek knows about all of this and has been in contact with Coral Lorenzen. (Editor's Note: Remember this was before Hynek died, also Coral died.) He regards Hynek as a government cover. At his house, he showed Hynek films and out in the back yard a flying saucer. He asked Hynek about his view with regard to abductions as to how many people might have been abducted. Hynek, unhesitatingly said about one out of forty.

He said that many people come to his door to see him, just "out of the blue" and he sees scars on the back of their necks. That previous old scars are easy to detect and that new ones are hard to detect. He feels that this is a sickening situation.

The aliens have gone wild and use hypodermics. He has been paralyzed four times and has been hit 250 times by hypodermics. He says they know you could and they do whatever they want to do and the above points have been verified medically.

A man came to see him with a top secret document that was dated in the 50's, indicating if anybody found out about all of this they would kill them. He was asked "doesn't that bother you? He said "no it didn't."

He said he had sent in some film to Kodak and there were seven rolls. They were Ectokrome G which could not be processed locally, so they had to go to Kodak. He does all of the film work commercially so that nobody could claim that he had monkeyed" with the film. His films come back, but one of them which was plain Ectokrome was missing for about 2 months -- when received nine feet was missing and this was close-ups of UFOs that he had taken. Missing pictures known to him showed up in a top secret document that he studied and the code name is Aquarius and it is a project of NASA. They are the ones that kept the film and copied it with deletions on Ectokrome and sent it back he suspects.

There have been indirect threats by the air force intelligence against him.

The location of the base is 2 1/2 miles northwest of Dulce and almost overlooks the town. It is up on a mesa. We discussed the similarity between everything we have been talking about here and the movie Close Encounters of the Third Kind. He said he speculated the movie seemed to be a plan of disclosure. The coordinates of the location are not far off and the mountain where the actual base is looks much like the mountain the movie.

Here is what we got in the trade off. We got the atomic technology, the atomic flying ships. Several of them. The first one was wrecked on the ground and it can be seen and photographed from the air. A second one was wrecked. A third one was wrecked. Apparently this last one was repaired and was the one that was in Houston -- near Houston in the Cash-Landrum case. The second item that we get out of it, are the beam weapons. The beam technology and third (he speculates) is the thought beam. That is the means by which communication is accomplished. It is electrostatic in character with a magnetic artifact component and it is the only way of communicating with people. They have to have the implants in order to use it. In the crash that occurred at the base when there was a disturbance of some sort, the aliens killed 66 of our people and 44 got away. This was information from an alien computer input -- true? He does not know. Supposedly it was over an argument and they turned on us.

I discussed with him whether he wished me to relay any of this information to other people. He said he had no objection. He would like to review any writing that I might do, to make sure that it is right in advance, and also to make sure that the source of the information was given. I mentioned in particular, John Schuessler, who would be extremely interested in part of this data. (NOTE: John is now head of MUFON.)

I gave him a summary of my analysis of the electromagnetic environment around UFOs related to propulsion. He was going to study that, but he did not comment offhand. He was familiar with what the aliens called MPS which means manipulations per sequence. In an electromagnetic field that can be manipulated into many configurations and the craft can stall. In order to prevent that, this field is adjusted

163

once every forty milliseconds. He has studied the trails from UFOs and they seem to break down into a pulse rate of 62 per second. Based upon the color movie pictures, there seems to be a blast of light and a spectral components and composition in there, with a Bow-Wave in front of the UFO with nitrogen showing green and oxygen showing blue but with the saucer being invisible. They can run into a car or airplane and this Bow-Wave will destroy them. Rockets can hit this Bow-Wave and be destroyed. They can't penetrate it. At White Sands he was shown pictures of an F-15 shooting rockets with a missile at a target and the saucers came in behind the missile, 30 ft. behind, and then flew through the explosion!! He didn't know what the purpose of the demonstration was, but suspected it might be just to show how invulnerable they are. But sometimes the saucers get into trouble and they are all consumed in some kind of way.

When he went up to Dulce in a helicopter, they landed and left some equipment there, but then when they came back the pilot was extremely nervous. Paul wanted to land on the base, but the pilot wouldn't do that. They came back to Dulce and landed at a small strip there, where they found two large Huey helicopters. The highway patrolman in charge there named Valdez went aboard one of the choppers and they found them to be full of commandos. They estimated a total of 75 commandos, fully armed with M16 rifles and rocket launchers. They did not have any indication of rank. They only had shoulder patches on. The helicopters were part of a project called Blue Light and they were from Ft. Carson, Colorado according to an OSI input. When they left they were escorted by these two large Huey helicopters. As they were flying along -- in the background, they saw rise up -- one of the advanced space technology vehicles that looked like a manta ray with a negative dihedral and projections coming down. It flew vertically past the two accompanying helicopters. Paul feels that it is imperative that this information be released because he feels that it is unconstitutional for the government to be involved in such an arrangement that invades the privacy of the individuals by the implantation's. He said that "once they have been tampered with by the aliens, they are never the same." (I suppose one can easily believe that. Jim McCampbell comment.)

So it appears that for the privilege of collecting the biological materials in the mutilation of and the abductions and the operations on board the craft, the government has allowed this to go on and even to assist for the privilege of getting the nuclear flight technology, the beam weaponry and the thought beam technology, plus also the embryos which are flown out of the base. (A rather fantastic story -- Jim McCampbell comment.)

Paul strikes me as being an extremely conservative, extremely knowledgeable and reliable scientist, who was intimately familiar with sophisticated laboratory equipment. He is thoroughly scientific and reliable. (Jim McCampbell evaluation.)

The base was started in 1948 showed major construction of the base from the photographs that were studied.

Jim McCampbell

Shuttle cars carry supplies and military as well as alien forces about in tunnels that stretch across the United States. Some researchers theorize these tunnels may go back thousands of years.

ROOM LIGHT : PINK-PURPLE
BRIGHT IN SOME AREAS

HUNDREDS OF THESE IN
VARIOUS STAGES OF GROWTH.

WISPY HAIR, "ALMOST NOSE"
MOUTH LOOKS "SEALED"

WOMB LOOKS GREY
VEINS (?) LOOK DARK GREY
CREATURE WHITE- PALE
EYES - DARK LIDS (?)
CAN'T FIND GENDER
2 TOES : 3 FINGERS

LIQUID - AMBER COLOR
NOT COMPLETELY CLEAR

LOOKS LIKE GLASS TUBE,
BUT ABOUT 5 FT TALL

The Dulce Papers were the first seemingly
"official" report on the status of the invasion of aliens at Dulce.

Paul Bennewitz - Lights, Signals and Lies

by Leslie Gunter

For years I wasn't sure what to make of the bizarre things I had heard about Paul Bennewitz. Was he completely mad or were the people saying that trying to cover something up? After researching for a while I am quite sure Bennewitz was not completely mad, somewhat, but not completely. He did finally have a complete breakdown but not until after being tormented by certain sinister individuals for years. If Bennewitz had not been such a bright individual he probably would have been better off because it was bringing attention to one of his inventions and what it was picking up and recording that caused most of the trouble.

Paul Bennewitz had a Masters degree in electronics and was the owner of Thunder Scientific Corp which did work for Sandia Labs, Phillips Labs, Kirtland AFB and many other such organizations. There are many players in this tragic black comedy, Bennewitz himself, Richard Doty the master of disinformation, Bill Moore (the UFO researcher and disinformer), John Lear pops up from time to time and there is also a poor woman who obviously had some horrible experience named Myrna Hansen.

May 5, 1980, Myrna Hansen had what is now known as an abduction experience. She was driving along one night to her home in Eagles Nest, New Mexico when she saw a bright light which was sucking a cow up into what could only be called a UFO, at least two other people witnessed this event. Myrna had expected to arrive home about 9:00 that evening but instead did not get there until 1 a.m.. When she got home she called the police department for help. The officer referred her to Officer Gabe Valdez who in the past had many of his cows mutilated and he referred her to Paul Bennewitz who Gabe knew was interested in cattle mutilation and UFO's. Two days later Myrna came to stay at the Bennewitz residence. Bennewitz became convinced that she had been implanted with some sort of device that was controlling her and keeping her from remembering everything that had happened so he preferred regression sessions, done by Leo Sprinkle a psychologist and Professor at University of Wyoming, be done in his car with many layers of foil over the windows to keep the EM signals from getting in or out. This sounds rather funny now, but as far as I know Bennewitz was the first person to come up with the theory that abductees were being implanted. It was during these sessions that Myrna told about being taken to a underground base that Paul somehow figured out was near Dulce.

In the Bennewitz home sat a receiver he had built that was picking up low frequency EM signals which he said were coming from Kirtland AFB around the Manzano weapons storage area. The neighborhood he lived in is as close as you can get to the Manzano area, the two are separated only by barb wire and electric fences. His house was only about 1 mile away from Manzano mountain. He had also been taking photos and 8mm film of lights he saw hovering and moving rapidly around the Manzano area. Everyone in Albuquerque has known for ages that Manzano Mountain is mostly hollowed out with tunnels throughout. I have known this since I was a child because my Grandfather worked at Sandia Lab and had told us and just about everyone who knew this told everyone they knew so I am sure Paul Bennewitz knew this too. Paul was sure that the signals and pictures he was recording were signs of a eminent alien invasion so he contacted Kirtland AFB along with NM Senators and Congressmen to warn them. Kirtland was very interested in what Paul was recording, since they had many secret projects going on that needed to be protected from eavesdroppers and this is where Richard Doty enters the picture in late 1980.

Richard Doty is on the record saying he worked for the OSI as a disinformation officer. I checked with Linda Howe who tells me that she did meet him at Kirtland where he gave her some information that was true, but at the same time that seems to only be to get her to believe his other information that was not true. He recalls that she did not fall for this and the "operation" with her was a failure. Paul Bennewitz on the other hand was eager to believe whatever Doty told him. It seems that Bill Moore who at the time was working himself as a disinformation agent tried to tell Bennewitz not to believe everything Doty or even Moore himself told him, but to no avail.

Still, Paul Bennewitz was not a complete nut. The signals he was receiving were real signals that Doty says the NSA who had their own offices at the base were doing the sending and receiving. Doty was eventually replaced by NSA agents who wanted to make sure Bennewitz discredited himself by spreading wild stories about UFO's. They also wanted to keep a eye on him to make sure that he wasn't sharing his method of intercepting these signals with Soviet spies posing as UFO enthusiasts. Bennewitz was even sent some sort of software that was suppose to decode the messages which basically gave him a bunch of nonsense about a alien invasion.

Eventually Paul Bennewitz became convinced that the true threat was the underground alien base somewhere near Dulce. According to Richard Doty the military wanted Paul to think the aliens were responsible for cattle mutilations because really they were being done by the military and that the NSA wanted him to concentrate his energy on Dulce rather than Kirtland where there was real stuff going on, so they set up a elaborate hoax to go along with his disillusions. According to Doty they helicoptered in bunches of debris from Kirtland that would look like stuff that belonged to spaceships and even pounded large tubes into the ground of Archuleta Mesa to make it look like air shafts for the underground base. When this was all done Doty flew Bennewitz over the site to show him what the Air Force was concerned about. Bennewitz apparently believed every word. Bennewitz was so interested in the area that he purchased his own plane and began flying reconnaissance missions over the site himself. During one of these flights he came across the wreckage of what may have been a early prototype stealth bomber. He snapped many photos of it, but made the mistake of showing them to Richard Doty. Bennewitz was then told that this was a experimental nuclear aircraft that the aliens had shot down to teach the US a lesson about flying over their base and that Bennewitz and others should stay away do to the radiation. With everyone keeping away, this gave the air force time to clean up the wreckage and the NSA time to steal Bennewitz's photos of it. All that remains is the drawing he made of the crash, but other researchers such as Bill Moore saw the original photos.

In 1988, after 8 years of constant stress and lack of sleep Paul Bennewitz finally had to be taken to a mental hospital. His paranoia had reached a all time high and he had pretty much barricaded himself in his home, he was hardly eating or sleeping and was sure aliens were coming into his home late at night and injecting him with strange chemicals. Richard Doty who says no matter what he had done to Paul he considered him a friend and felt very badly about this turn of events and even rushed to visit him at the hospital. He was released after a month and his family who was very concerned about his health effectively kept him away from the subject of UFO's and ET's until his death in 2003 at the age of 75.

After listening to the February 27, 2005 Art Bell's Coast to Coast interview with Richard Doty and Greg Bishop, author of the book "Project Beta" about Paul Bennewitz and the interview with Greg on Dreamland a couple weeks ago, as well as reading Greg's book, I still had many questions. These questions led to the nagging conclusion that not all about Paul Bennewitz, what he saw and the signals he was receiving had been revealed by Doty. It is highly possible that Doty did not truly know as much about what was going on as he thought or it could be that after years of being a disinformation agent he just cannot tell the truth. I discussed my feelings on this with Linda Moulton Howe who affirmed that I was on the right track, but didn't seem to have all the answers to my questions either.

First off I don't believe Paul Bennewitz was just some crazy nut like he was made out to be. He build this amazing receiver that was picking up low frequency EM signals that appeared to be coming from the Manzano area. This is not disputed by Doty or anyone else, nor is the fact that it was the NSA who were sending and receiving these. What information they were sending and receiving and to whom is the question. They had thought it would be impossible to intercept their signals and Bennewitz proved them wrong. In fact, the NSA and others broke into Paul's house when he was not there and took pictures and back engineered his receiver to build for there own purposes.

Paul Bennewitz was the first to come up with the concept of abductees being implanted with some sort of small device. I think most people in the UFO community now believe this as fact though they believe it to be some sort of tracking device rather than mind control as he believed.

As for Bennewitz's reports of seeing lights hovering and zooming about Kirtland AFB the only explanation we are given in "Project Beta" or by Richard Doty is that it was a laser used to calibrate the large telescope at Kirtland. I have personally seen this green laser on many occasions and while it could be mistaken for what people sometimes report as green fireballs I cannot imagine someone mistaking it for hovering multi colored lights. Some people have suggested that these were only helicopters, but Bennewitz lived only 1 mile from the base, I can hear helicopters taking off and landing there from my house and I am sure he could have heard a helicopter at his house which is much closer.

Besides that, there are a couple well documented UFO events that took place near Manzano during August and September of 1980. Some of these cases are documented in freedom of information act documents and have become known as the Kirtland papers. In one case all air traffic control in Albuquerque completely went off line. Air traffic control at Albuquerque International Airport contacted Kirtland, they traced the problem to somewhere in Coyote Canyon which is the area below and south/east of Manzano Mt., Security personnel were dispatched to this area where they saw a bright object hovering just above the ground. When they tried to approach the object it shot straight up into the sky and disappeared. After that air traffic control came back online. So it seems to me to say that all Paul Bennewitz sightings were of a laser is probably not true. The report obtained by the freedom of information act seems to have been filed by Richard Doty himself so for him to say there was no UFO activity at Kirtland at the time is a complete lie.

Another event that happened during this time also baffles me. Richard Doty was driving Bill Moore around Manzano they stopped to look at a complex of buildings. Doty told Moore to go ahead a take a picture if he wanted and kind of laughed like it was a joke of some sort. Moore did take the picture but when he got it developed none of the building were visible, it just looked like a large white snow drift (there is a copy of this photo in Greg Bishops book "Project Beta"). I think Doty explained to Moore that this was some kind of advanced camouflage used to foil Soviet satellites, but didn't explain how it works. As many of you might know I love using google to have a look around military bases and Lockheed Martin facilities. In many of these areas (including Coyote Canyon)

UNDERGROUND ALIEN BIO LAB AT DULCE

Area 51

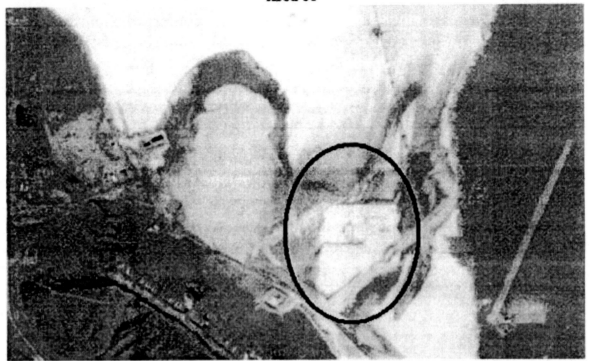

Holloman AFB

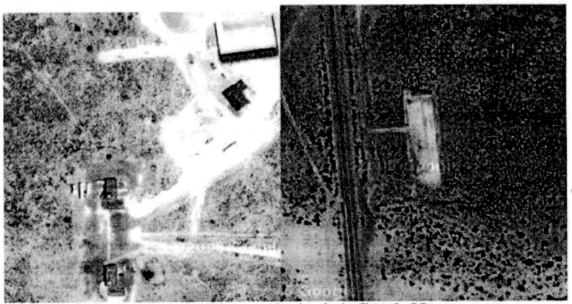

Satelite Map Pictures obtained via Google Maps

I have found large areas of white where all around it is a darker tan colored sand. Sometimes I can make out the outline of what appears to be a building in these areas, but not always. Sometimes I have also found areas that look like huge lakes of fire (yes, like hell itself people).

Both at Area 51 near what looked to be a construction project of some sort and land owned by the Government near the Lockheed facility in Lancaster CA this anomaly appeared right next to a large runway where the hangers should have been located. It is obviously something done to block out areas they don't want us to see. So I pretty much believe Moore's story of buildings that could not be filmed. I have looked around the Dulce area for a base there, knowing what I have found out about camo since then even if it is there I am not sure anyone could find it. At one point I found what I thought could be a underground base, at this point I believe it is a underground type structure however I think it is a old uranium mine given the area it is located.

Paul Bennewitz.

There are so many bizarre events that happened during this time, but one that stands out for me is the mysterious orbs witnessed in Bennewitz house. Moore as well as Doty and others saw these. They are described as glowing yellow/orange balls about the size of a softball they were transparent and seemed to be self illuminating and 3 dimensional. Moore completely freaked out the first time he saw one and immediately asked Bennewitz what it was. Bennewitz replied a bit surprised "oh, you see them too?' He had no idea what they were. They don't seem to have been projections into the room from somewhere else because they often appeared in places with no window for them to be projected through. Doty speculated that they were some sort of NSA spying devices, but didn't have any real knowledge of them.

Many people think Dulce Base is a complete hoax put out by disinformation agents to keep Paul Bennewitz busy somewhere other than Manzano. Richard Doty says it was to make Paul think the aliens were doing cattle mutilation and not the government. It was a very large hoax to pull off just to make him think that aliens were doing cattle mutilations which was something he already believed anyway. Also, he already totally believed there was a base somewhere near

Dulce because that is where Myrna Hansen told him she was taken when she was abducted. Then there was the wreckage Benewitz found on Archuleta Mesa of what could have been a early prototype stealth bomber, whatever it was it was not part of the hoax and the powers that be did their best to keep him away from it. Not to mention the huge amount of cattle mutilations near Dulce in the 1970's and 80's. Why would military personnel from Kirtland fly all the way out there to do cattle mutilations? There are many rural areas with ranches a lot closer to Albuquerque and as far as I know none of these areas ever reported such things happening.

So is there any truth to the Dulce Base rumor? I don't know, but when I spoke with Linda Moulton Howe she seemed to think there was. I am not sure if she interviewed Myrna Hansen, but I know she was lucky enough to interview Bennewitz sometime before his death.

For months before being committed to the mental hospital Bennewitz had reported that aliens were coming into his room at night and shooting him up with chemicals. Moore, Doty and everyone who saw him during this time recalls there being pin pricks all up and down his arms. Were these self inflicted? Doty recalls noticing a ladder on the side on Bennewitz house leading to his bedroom window on one of his many visits, so maybe someone was shooting him up with something, but it is doubtful that we will ever know for sure.

At first glance having the disinformation agent who worked with Bennewitz come forward one would think this would clear up everything, but in a sense it has only muddled things up even more. There is no way to know whether Doty can be trusted or if he even knows the whole scheme of things. He says very confusing things like there was no UFO activity at Manzano during that time, but he files reports that contradict that. Then he says at that time the military were doing the cattle mutilations, but that they are not the ones doing it now. He tells stories of seeing government documents about the Roswell crash and having viewed film of the live alien they captured which was kept at Kirtland and Los Alamos at different times. Also, he insists that aliens really do love strawberry ice cream because they have no teeth.

So at the end of all this supposed "disclosure", I am still left with more questions than answers. Really the thing that has been disclosed here is the biggest disinformation operation in recent history that I am aware of. The years it went on and the elaborate hoaxes that went along with it are amazing. You would think at the very least someone in the mass media would want to question Doty and the Air Force about what gave them the right to drive some poor scientist in NM mad, but they don't and they probably never will because they don't want to question anything the government does under the cloak of National Security. So unless some other individual "in the know" comes forward with a book or shows up on Coast to Coast this is probably the end of the story.

This material originally appeared on the www.BinnallofAmerica.com web site.

LESLIE GUNTER: I have been interested in ufos and the paranormal since childhood. I write the weekly column Grey Matters for Binnall of America and the monthly column Beyond the Dial for UFO Magazine. Interested parties may find my blog at http://thedebrisfield.blogspot.com/

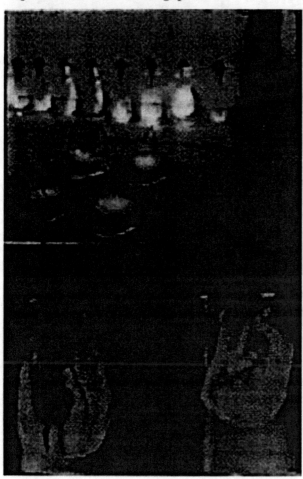

Several stills of the human-alien hybrids -- supposedly taken by a hidden camera -- were released by Commander X during a talk about Dulce as part of his his Underground Lectures DVD. Some researchers feel they are not conclusive evidence and may be from some other incident involving ETs. . . or it could be part of a "false flag" hoax.

Are these stills of special hybrid chambers the real McCoy or are from a science fiction film, or perhaps even a "False Flag" set up by the Secret Government or NWO?

Engineer Paul Bennewitz took this photo of several swiftly moving objects as they entered the side of a mountain overlooking the town of Dulce, NM. Were these objects going to their underground base?

The incident around Dulce all began when Paul Bennewitz started receiving radio messages from a mysterious group of what he assumed to be aliens who had taken up stakes in the area surround the Indian Reservation.

The Dulce Report:
Investigating Alleged
Human Rights Abuses
at a
Joint US Government-
Extraterrestrial Base
at Dulce, New Mexico

An Independent Report by
© Dr Michael E. Salla

September 25, 2003

DrSalla@exopolitics.org

www.exopolitics.org

Abstract

Dr Paul Bennewitz is an electronics specialist who in the late 1979 began to film, photograph, and electronically intercept what appeared to be extensive UFO/ET activity and communications that he traced to the vicinity of the Archuletta Mesa on Jicarilla Apache Reservation land near the town of Dulce. Based on the collected evidence Bennewitz concluded that an underground extraterrestrial (ET) base existed near Dulce that played a role in both cattle mutilations and abduction of civilians. In 1980, the Air Force Office of Special Intelligence (AFOSI) began investigating Bennewitz's evidence, and this eventually led to its disinformation campaign to discredit Bennewitz. Bennewitz's subsequent electronic evidence and field research alleging extensive human rights abuses were occurring at the Dulce underground base became associated with the AFOSI disinformation campaign. Most UFO researchers concluded that Bennewitz had been too influenced by disinformation to be taken seriously

In this report, I investigate Bennewitz's claims regarding massive human rights abuses by ETs at an underground base at Dulce, and his belief that this was a joint US government/ET base that was the site of a significant violent confrontation between military forces and resident ETs in 1979. I begin my analysis of whistleblower testimonies by reviewing whistleblower protection laws, and how National Security statutes eliminate this protection for whistleblowers that disclose classified information such as secret underground military installations. I then review various whistleblower testimonies that involved the disclosure of information about the existence of an underground base at Dulce used by ETs. I subsequently explore whether the evidence for the alleged human rights abuses and a military conflict having occurred at Dulce are persuasive. I then examine criticisms raised against the Dulce underground base hypothesis. Using further whistleblower testimony, I further examine how a secret base at Dulce and other government facilities are funded without US Congressional and Executive Office oversight. Finally, I make recommendations on how to address the alleged human rights abuses identified in this report, and the political implications of the purported joint government-ET underground base at Dulce.

About the Author

Dr. Michael E. Salla has held academic appointments in the School of International Service, American University, Washington DC (1996-2001), and the Department of Political Science, Australian National University, Canberra, Australia (1994-96). He taught as an adjunct faculty member at George Washington University, Washington DC., in 2002. He is currently researching methods of Transformational Peace as a 'Researcher in Residence' at the Center for Global Peace (2001-2003) and directing the Center's Peace Ambassador Program. He has a PhD in Government from the University of Queensland, Australia, and an MA in Philosophy from the University of Melbourne, Australia. He is the author of The Hero's Journey Toward a Second American Century (Greenwood Press, 2002); co-editor of Why the Cold War Ended (Greenwood Press, 1995) and Essays on Peace (Central Queensland University Press, 1995); and authored more than seventy articles, chapters, and book reviews on peace, ethnic conflict and conflict resolution. He has conducted research and fieldwork in the ethnic conflicts in East Timor, Kosovo, Macedonia, and Sri Lanka. He has organized a number of international workshops involving mid to high level participants from these conflicts. He has a website at www.american.edu/salla/. In January 2003, he began publishing a series of scholarly papers dealing with the political implications of a possible extraterrestrial presence on the planet (website URL: www.exopolitics.org). These papers are being published as Exopolitics: Political Implications of the Extraterrestrial Presence (forthcoming Dandelion Books, 2004).

Introduction

[1]Dr Paul Bennewitz is an electronics specialist who in the late 1979 began to film, photograph, and electronically intercept what appeared to be extensive UFO/ET activity and communications over the Manzano mountain range near Albuquerque, New Mexico. He traced this UFO/ET activity to the vicinity of the Archuletta Mesa on Jicarilla Apache Reservation land near the town of Dulce. Bennewitz had earlier researched cattle mutilations in the region and civilians who claimed to have been abducted by extraterrestrials. Based on his film, photographic and electronic evidence, and his field research Bennewitz concluded that an underground extraterrestrial (ET) base existed near Dulce that played a role in both cattle mutilations and abduction of civilians. In 1980, Bennewitz submitted his evidence to the nearby Kirtland Air Force base to alert officials to the possibility that ET races were a threat to the nearby Manzano Nuclear Weapons Storage Area. The Air Force Office of Special Intelligence (AFOSI) quickly became involved in investigating Bennewitz's evidence, and this eventually led to what credible sources conclude was a disinformation campaign to discredit Bennewitz. Bennewitz's subsequent electronic evidence and field research alleging extensive human rights abuses were occurring at the Dulce underground base became associated with the AFOSI disinformation campaign. Most UFO researchers concluded, after Bennewitz had suffered a nervous breakdown in 1987 and the AFOSI disinformation campaign became public knowledge, that Bennewitz had been too influenced by disinformation to be taken seriously.

The strongest support for Bennewitz's claims are a number of individuals claiming to be 'whistleblowers' who in their capacity as former employees of corporations performing a variety military contracts worked at or learned of the Dulce base, and subsequently revealed aspects of what had occurred there. A recurring feature of these whistleblower statements is testimony of a violent conflict in 1979 between US military personnel and ETs at the base that led to a significant number of military fatalities. This seemed to confirm Bennewitz's claim of such a military conflict, and raises the possibility that the conflict's cause was related to his allegations of human rights abuses. Furthermore, Bennewitz's evidence provided an example of how money illegally siphoned from the US economy into 'black budget' programs related to an ET presence, estimated to be as high as 1.1 trillion dollars annually, was being used. [2]

Was Bennewitz just an overzealous UFO researcher that accidentally tapped into highly classified Air Force research and development projects, or was he an electronics genius who single handedly uncovered the existence of a joint US government-ET underground base where ET's conducted gross human rights violations on abducted civilians? Seeking clear answers to these questions have spurred a number of books, articles, and internet websites. [3] The quality of answers has varied greatly since all who have written on Dulce have mixed primary source materials with secondary sources that cross-reference one another without confirming the validity and origins of sources. This has led to much confusion and uncertainty for those seeking clear answers to what was occurring under the ground at Dulce since most of the available Dulce material takes the form of hearsay and speculation. A more scholarly effort of analyzing the primary source material available on Dulce is needed to help answer key questions about the alleged base at Dulce, and the human rights violations that were reported to be occurring there by ETs with US government complicity. This report is an effort to fulfill the need for a scholarly analysis of the primary source material on what has occurred, and may be still occurring, at Dulce and elsewhere in the US and around the planet.

In this report, I begin by investigating Bennewitz's claims regarding massive human rights abuses by ETs at an underground base at Dulce, and his belief that this was a joint US government/ET base that was the site of a significant violent confrontation between military forces and resident ETs in 1979. I begin my analysis of whistleblower testimonies that support Bennewitz's claims by reviewing federal and state whistleblower protection laws, and how National Security statutes eliminate this protection for whistleblowers that disclose classified information such as secret underground military installations. I then review various whistleblower testimonies that involved the disclosure of information about the existence of an underground base at Dulce used by ETs. I subsequently explore whether the evidence for the alleged human rights abuses and a military conflict having occurred at

Dulce are persuasive. I then examine criticisms raised against the Dulce underground base hypothesis. Using further whistleblower testimony, I further examine how a secret base at Dulce and other government facilities are funded without US Congressional and Executive Office oversight. Finally, I make recommendations on how to address the alleged human rights abuses identified in this report, and the political implications of the purported joint government-ET underground base at Dulce.

Paul Bennewitz and Evidence of a Joint Government-Extraterrestrial Base at Dulce

In the mid 1970's, a wave of cattle mutilations began occurring in New Mexico and Dr Paul Bennewitz, a local Albuquerque businessman and electronics specialist, became keenly interested in the phenomenon. [4] In 1979, he did some field trips with Gabe Valdez, a well known New Mexico State Trooper to investigate some of these mutilations, and they concluded that the mutilations were not caused by anything 'natural'. Bennewitz soon began noticing an unusual amount of UFO activity in the Northern New Mexico area. Using his film and photographic equipment, he began accumulating evidence of what appeared to be UFO's. [5] He then began intercepting radio and video transmissions that he believed were used by the UFOs and involved different ET races. He traced these transmissions to a base located under the Archuletta Mesa, near Dulce. Bennewitz believed he had identified the radio and video frequencies used for communications between the ET piloted ships and ground controllers at the underground Dulce base. Bennewitz then created a communication system that he believed enabled him to electronically communicate with what he now was convinced were ET piloted ships flying to and from the base. Furthermore, Bennewitz began to track the electronic frequencies ETs used to control individuals who had been abducted and implanted with miniature electronic devices. Bennewitz tracked down some of these individuals and conducted interviews on what they could remember of their ET encounters. Bennewitz eventually issued a report, Project Beta, in which he summarized the evidence of his filming, photographing, electronic interception, communications and fieldwork:

1. Two years continuous recorded electronic surveillance and tracking with d.F. 24 hr/day data of alien ships plus 6,000 feet motion picture of same.

2. Detection and disassembly of alien communication and video channels - both.

3. Constant reception of video from alien ship and underground base view-screen; typical alien, humanoid and at times apparent homo sapien.

4. A case history of an encounter victim in New Mexico which lead to the communications link and discovery that apparently all encounter victims have deliberate alien implants along with obvious accompanying scars. The victims cat scan. Five other cases were verified.

5. Established constant direct communication with the alien using a computer and a form of hex decimal code communication was instigated apparently.

6. Through the alien communication loop, the true underground base location. [6]

All of the evidence he gathered pointed to the existence of an underground base at Dulce used by different ET races. The communications, video images, and the abductee testimonies he found, provided further information that Bennewitz used in understanding what was occurring at the base and its national security implications.

One of the abductees Bennewitz found was Myrna Hansen whom he had arranged to be placed under hypnotic regression by Dr Leo Sprinkle from the University of Wyoming. [7] Under hypnosis she claimed to have been abducted in 1980 along with her son and taken inside the Dulce base. She proceeded to describe humans placed in cold storage, and large vats filled with the remains of cattle and human body parts. [8] These were the most controversial aspects of Bennewitz's activities but combined with his electronic interceptions, video recordings and communications he became convinced that they fit an overall pattern of ET deception, responsibility for cattle mutilations and massive human rights violations of abducted civilians. [9]

Bennewitz's electronic interceptions and interviews led to him quickly learning much about the activities at the Dulce underground base, the extensive ET presence there and the sizable number of civilians abducted and forcibly taken to the base. His electronic intercepts and communications provided him some basic information that a military conflict had occurred at the Dulce base between ET races and US military personnel. [10] Bennewitz subsequently reported his findings to the Air Force Office of Special Intelligence (AFOSI) at the nearby Kirtland Air force in October 1980 believing the ETs presented a threat to the nearby Manzano Nuclear Weapons Storage Area. In an official report signed by Major Thomas Cseh on October 28, 1980 and later released under the Freedom of Information Act, Major Cseh wrote:

On 26 Oct 80, SA [Special Agent] Doty, with the assistance of JERRY MILLER, GS-15, Chief, Scientific Advisor for Air Force Test and Evaluation Center, KAFB, interviewed Dr. Bennewitz at his home in the Four Hills section of Albuquerque, which is adjacent to the northern boundary of Manzano Base.... Dr. Bennewitz has been conducting independent research into Aerial Phenomena for the last 15 months. Dr. Bennewitz also produced several electronic recording tapes, allegedly showing high periods of electrical magnetism being emitted from Manzano/Coyote Canyon area. Dr. Bennewitz also produced several photographs of flying objects taken over the general Albuquerque area. He has several pieces of electronic surveillance equipment pointed at Manzano and is attempting to record high frequency electrical beam pulses. Dr. Bennewitz claims these Aerial Objects produce these pulses. ...After analyzing the data collected by Dr. Bennewitz, Mr MILLER related the evidence clearly shows that some type of unidentified aerial objects were caught on film; however, no conclusions could be made whether these objects pose a threat to Manzano/Coyote Canyon areas. [11]

When AFOSI took no action, Bennewitz approached the then New Mexico Senator, Harrison Schmitt, who demanded to know why Bennewitz's claims were not being investigated. Frustrated by the lack of official support for his discoveries, Bennewitz issued a detailed report titled Project Beta and continued to accumulate data on ET operations in the area. [12]

Based on his intercepted electronic communications, Bennewitz revealed in his Project Beta report the following about the size of the base and the ET population:

The total alien basing area apparently contains several cultures, (all under the designation 'unity') and is approx 3km wide by 8km long and is located in the middle of nowhere on the Jicarilla Indian Reservation west of Dulce, NM. Based on the number of ships presently in this area, the total alien population is estimated to be at least 2,000 and most likely more. [13]

Bennewitz's work had attracted much attention and soon led to a covert effort by AFOSI to discredit him. In a 1989 Mutual UFO Network conference, a prominent UFO specialist, William Moore, caused an uproar when he openly declared that in 1982 he had been co-opted into this effort, and began passing on information about Bennewitz's activities to AFOSI and played a role in feeding disinformation to Bennewitz. Moore described the events as follows:

... when I first ran into the disinformation operation... being run on Bennewitz... it seemed to me... I was in a rather unique position. There I was with my foot... in the door of a secret counterintelligence game that gave every appearance of being somehow directly connected to a high-level government UFO project, and, judging by the positions of the people I knew to be directly involved with it, definitely had something to do with national security! There was no way I was going to allow the opportunity to pass me by without learning at least something about what was going on. I would play the disinformation game, get my hands dirty just often enough to lead those directing the process into believing that I was doing exactly what they wanted me to do, and all the while continue to burrow my way into the matrix so as to learn as much as possible about who was directing it and why. [14]

The public declaration by Moore confirmed that Bennewitz had, at least partially, succeeded in electronic monitoring of ET craft in the area, communicating with ETs at the Dulce base, and monitoring ET control of abductees in the area. This might help explain why AFOSI began what emerged as an intense covert effort to discredit Bennewitz. The basic strategy in the campaign by AFOSI was to suggest that the most egregious aspects of Bennewitz's claims - the Dulce base as a site where humans were abducted for genetic experiments, placed in cold storage and even used as a food source for ETs - was disinformation rather than accurate reports of the nature of the ET presence in the Northern New Mexico area. Indeed Moore argued that by the time he met him in 1982, the bulk of Bennewitz's information was already disinformation fed by AFOSI. [15]

Many UFO researchers despaired of finding the truth of what was happening at Dulce due to the fog of disinformation rumored to be circulating around Bennewitz, and the various activities orchestrated by AFOSI and/or other intelligence services that targeted Bennewitz and his supporters. [16] The dominant view was that Bennewitz was definitely on to something but had succumbed to beliefs that discredited his early and most persuasive work. One UFO researcher claimed that the disinformation was passed on through the intercepted communications: "Where the truth began and ended in the information collected by Bennewitz is debatable but one thing is without doubt true - the content of the intercepted messages certainly caused Bennewitz to become a paranoid and deluded man who eventually suffered a colossal nervous breakdown in 1985." [17] The intensity of his investigations and the official response had a heavy personal toll on Bennewitz caused his nervous breakdown. He later withdrew entirely from any public discussion of the Dulce base and ended his involvement with UFO issues.

Despite his controversial withdrawal from the UFO scene, Bennewitz's credibility as an undisputed electronics genius was not at question, and the extensive database of films, photos and raw electronic communications data of UFO/ET phenomenon, was powerful evidence that something was occurring around the Archuletta Mesa. Aside from the raw physical evidence accumulated by Bennewitz, a number of whistleblowers have come forward to give further testimony and even physical evidence of an underground base at Dulce, and of ETs committing human rights violations on abducted civilians. Before analyzing whistleblower testimony concerning the Dulce underground base, I will point out the legal position of whistleblowers when disclosing classified information since this would help explain why comparatively few individuals have stepped forward to confirm the allegations of massive human rights abuses at Dulce and other joint government-ET underground bases.

Whistleblowers and National Security

'Whistleblowers' have been described as courageous employees who often with the zeal of a martyr disclose unethical or criminal government/corporate practices that involve great damage to the public interest. [18] Often the short-term result for whistleblowers is the loss of jobs, reputation, economic security, and even life. A whistleblower can be defined as any employee of any branch of government or corporation that publicly discloses unethical or corrupt practices by a government agency/corporation that violate the law and/or damage the public interest. There are an extensive series of state and federal whistleblower laws for those who come forward to disclose such practices and risk their own careers, reputations and physical safety. [19] When it comes to employment in government agencies/corporations that involve working in projects with national security implications, whistleblower protection laws have some important qualifications as evidenced by the Basic Federal Whistleblower Statute concerning National Security Whistleblowers (5 USC 2302). [20] The relevant section of this Statute [5 USC Sec. 2302. (8) (A)] concerns the prohibition of action taken against an employee (whistleblower) because of any disclosure of information that the employee believes is evidence of "a violation of any law, rule or regulation," or "an abuse of authority, or "substantial and specific danger to public health or safety." The relevant section then states the critical qualifying condition: "if such disclosure is not specifically prohibited by law and if such information is not specifically required by Executive order to be kept secret in the interest of national defense or the conduct of foreign affairs."

As evident in the qualifying statement, whistleblowers are not permitted to disclose information if such disclosure compromises national security. This means that if one is employed in a government agency and/or corporation working on a classified project with national security implications, such individuals do not receive protection under Federal Whistleblower Statutes for publicly disclosing classified information. Furthermore, if government/corporate employees sign contracts that permit severe penalties for disclosing classified information, such individuals essentially sign away their constitutional rights since they have no legal recourse to prevent the imposition of even the most draconian penalties. Consequently, if employees witness, for instance, egregious human rights abuses committed in the operation of classified projects, they have no legal protection if they choose to disclose this to the general public. One individual who apparently risked disclosing egregious human rights violations while working on a highly classified project is Thomas Castello.

Thomas Castello & the Dulce Papers

In 1987 an apparent whistleblower organized the release of 30 photos, video and a set of papers to UFO researchers that were apparently physical evidence of a joint US government/extraterrestrial base two miles beneath the Archuletta Mesa, near the town of Dulce, New Mexico. The collection came to be called the 'Dulce Papers' and provided graphic evidence of the operations of this secret underground facility and appeared to provide powerful support to Bennewitz's conclusions regarding activities at the underground base. [21] The Dulce Papers described genetic experimentation, development of human-extraterrestrial hybrids, use of mind control through advanced computers, cold storage of humans in liquid filled vats, and even the use of human body parts as a nutritional source for extraterrestrial (ET) races. The papers provided possible evidence that humans were used as little more than laboratory animals by ET races working directly with different US government agencies and US corporations fulfilling 'black budget' military contracts in a joint base. If the papers were genuine, experiments and projects were being conducted that involved human rights violations on a scale that exceeded even the darkest chapters of recent human history.

The individual responsible for assembling and releasing the Dulce Papers, Thomas Castello, claimed to have worked as a senior security officer at the base before 'quitting' the Dulce facility after a military confrontation that occurred in 1979 between elite US military personnel, base security guards, and resident extraterrestrials. The military confrontation he described has been dubbed the 'Dulce Wars' and a number of other 'whistleblowers' and UFO researchers have subsequently described similar incidents at Dulce or nearby that substantiate many of Castello's claims. [22] In the time since he claims he left his Dulce employers in 1979, and subsequent release of the Dulce Papers in 1986, Castello gave a number of interviews and corresponded with UFO researchers before eventually vanishing from the scene. The transcripts of these interviews and correspondence provide further 'whistleblower' testimony of events at the purported Dulce facility, and the secret 'war' that occurred there.

Thomas Castello claims to have served in the US Air force and specialized in military photography and video monitoring. He further claims to have served on a highly classified underground base near the Northern New Mexico town of Dulce. His background has been summarized as follows:

In 1961, Castello was a young sergeant stationed at Nellis Air Force Base near Las Vegas, Nevada. His job was as a military photographer with a top secret clearance. He later transferred to West Virginia where he trained in advanced intelligence photography. He worked inside an undisclosed underground installation, and due to the nature of his new assignment his clearance was upgraded to TS-IV. He remained with the Air Force as a photographer until 1971 at which time he was offered a job with RAND corporation as a Security Technician, and so he moved to California where RAND had a major facility and his security clearance was upgraded to ULTRA-3. ... In 1977 Thomas was transferred to Santa Fe, New Mexico where his pay was raised significantly and his security clearance was again upgraded... this time to ULTRA-7. His new job was as a photo security specialist in the Dulce installation, where his job specification was to maintain, align and calibrate video monitoring cameras throughout the underground complex and to escort visitors to their destinations. [23]

It is the extensive video monitoring that occurred at Dulce that apparently provided Castello the bird's eye information he needed to learn what was occurring at the base, and the human rights abuses that eventually led to his departure from the base and distribution of classified material. Castello's claims are outlined in two sources, first are the Dulce papers themselves that presumably involved classified material taken from the base; and second, the interviews/correspondence Castello had with a number of UFO researchers. Much of Castello's material has since been circulated on the Internet and has been incorporated in a book titled The Dulce Wars that was authored by a UFO researcher who uses the name 'Branton'. [24]

Officially confirming Castello's employment, military and educational background and therefore his status as a whistleblower has not been possible. This is possibly due to a practice that has been claimed to be standard for civilians who work under contract to corporations and/or military/intelligence agencies on classified projects involving ETs: the official removal of all public records of contracted employees as a security precaution in the event they intentionally or unintentionally publicly disclose what is occurring in such projects. For example, Dr Michael Wolf claims to have been a former scientist and policy maker on ET affairs that began to serve from 1979 on the coordinating policy group for ET affairs, the Special Studies Group (PI-40) in the National Security Council. [25] In a series of interviews with the prominent UFO researcher, Dr Richard Boylan, Wolf claimed that he was being directed by his superiors to participate in a controlled leak of information to the UFO community while providing a fall back of 'plausible deniability' for the government. [26] All public records of Wolf's advanced university degrees and contractual services to different military/intelligence/national security branches of government were eliminated making it very difficult if not impossible to confirm his background and substantiate the startling information he was releasing. He claimed that this removal of public records was 'standard practice' for all civilians employed by either corporations and/or the US military in clandestine projects involving ETs. [27] A further source confirming Wolf's description of the existence of such a 'standard practice' was Bob Lazar, a physicist who found that after leaving in 1988 the secret S-4 facility (Dreamland) in Nevada where his job was to reverse engineer the propulsion and power system of recovered ET craft, his birth certificate was no longer available at the hospital he was born at, along with the disappearance of his school, college and all employment records – he simply ceased to officially exist! [28]

It can now be suggested that a standard practice exists for civilians contracted to corporations and/or military/intelligence agencies whereby their employment and public records are removed as a security precaution against either public disclosure of ET related information as in the case of Bob Lazar, or to maintain a highly controlled leak of information as in the case of Dr Wolf. This means that confirming Castello's employment background and therefore his credibility, as a whistleblower is very difficult if possible at all. There are three possibilities for Castello's true identity and credibility as a whistleblower. The first is that he is who he claims to be, a whistleblower who worked at the base. The second is that he is using the name and identity of 'Thomas Castello' as a cover in order to reveal information on Dulce. In this case, he may be an 'insider' leaking information on abuses at the base who wishes to remain an anonymous whistleblower. The third, possibility is that Castello is a bogus identity created by an intelligence officer to disseminate disinformation that steers UFO researchers and the general public away from genuine military related projects in the area. A number of UFO researchers were apparently able to get in contact with Castello before his eventual 'disappearance' in the late 1980s and were able to get answers to a series of questions. [29] According to both Branton and William Hamilton, fellow UFO researchers had personally met with Castello and could vouch for his existence and credibility. [30] While the list of contacts and personal interviews with Castello are not extensive, it does appear that he exists while casting doubt on, without eliminating, the third possibility that his identity was concocted by intelligence officers. It is this uncertainty that led to most UFO researchers not taking seriously Castello's claims that supported much of what Bennewitz had been earlier arguing and was now associated with a disinformation campaign led by Air Force Intelligence (AFOSI). In a later section, other whistleblowers will be cited who confirm many aspects of both Bennewitz's and Castello's claims indicating that the third possibility can be dismissed as the least likely possibility concerning Castello's identity. Consequently, it is worth exploring in some depth what Castello claimed to have experienced in the Ducle underground base since he provides the most extensive testimony of what may have occurred there.

In the Dulce papers and his personal testimonies Castello claims the existence of a seven level underground facility that jointly houses humans and different extraterrestrial races in Dulce, New Mexico. Castello claims that the humans employed at the base comprised scientists, security personnel, and employees from various corporations who were servicing military contracts. [31] There were four extraterrestrial races he claimed worked at Dulce: the standard 'short' Grays' from Zeta Reticulum (approx 4ft in height); tall Grays from Rigel, Orion (7 ft); and Reptilian species either native to Earth or from the Draco star system in Orion (ranging from 6-8 ft). Castello claims that the earth based Reptilians, who he described as the 'working caste', were led by a winged Reptilian species he described as the Draco (ETs from Orion). [32] He said that the short grays (depicted in movies such as

Close Encounters of the Third Kind) are subservient to the Draco Reptilians. Castello says he was employed as a 'Senior Security Technician' at the Dulce facility and that his primary job function was to sort out any security issues between the resident ET races and the human employees at the base. He described some of his job functions and the ET hierarchy in response to a question by Branton about how often he communicated with the different ET species:

Since I was the Senior Security Technician at that base, I had to communicate with them on a daily basis. If there were any problems that involved security or video cameras, I was the one they called. It was the reptilian "working caste" that usually did the physical labor in the lower levels at Dulce. Decisions involving that caste were usually made by the white Draco. When human workers caused problems for the working caste, the reptoids went to the white Draconian 'boss', and the Draco called me. At times, it felt like it was a never ending problem. Several human workers resented the "no nonsense" or "get back to work" attitude the working caste lives by. When needed, intervention became a vital tool. The biggest problem were human workers who foolishly wandered around near the "OFF LIMITS" areas of the "Alien Section." I guess it's human nature to be curious and to wonder what is past the barriers. Too often someone found a way to bypass the barriers and nosed around. The camera's near the entrance usually stopped them before they got themselves in serious trouble. A few times I had to formerly request the return of a human worker. [33]

Castello claimed that the different projects at Dulce involved reverse engineering of ET technology, development of mind control methods; and genetic experiments involving cloning and creating human-ET hybrids. Similar projects have been conducted at Montauk, Long Island and Brookhaven laboratories [34] and been the subject of a number of other whistleblower testimonies. [35]

These projects were scattered among the seven levels of the Dulce underground base with the ETs occupying the deepest levels, five to seven. These lower levels were described by Castello as an extremely old series of natural caverns that had been used in the past by different ET races. In response to a question concerning the Caverns origin, he stated:

Nature started the caverns. The Draco [reptilian humanoids] used the caverns and tunnels for centuries. Later, through RAND Corporation plans, it was enlarged repeatedly. The original caverns included ice caves and sulfur springs that the 'aliens' found perfect for their needs. [36]

In describing the way command was shared at the joint base between the US government and the ET races, Castello said:

The worker caste [Reptilian] does the daily chores, mopping the latex floors, cleaning the cages, bringing food to the hungry people and other species. It is their job to formulate the proper mixture for the type one and type two beings that the Draco Race has created. The working caste work at the labs as well as at the computer banks. Basically speaking, the reptilian races are active at all levels of the Dulce Base. There are several different 'races' of aliens that work on the east section of level six.... That section is commonly called "the alien section." The Draco are the undisputed masters of the 5-6-7 levels. The humans are second in command of those levels. [37]

Castello says that he directly witnessed the products of the trans-species genetic experiments in the sixth level of the facility. Most disturbing was his discovery that humans were used as a kind of laboratory animal in the lowest level where they were placed in cold storage, used as test subjects in mind-control programs, and even used in genetic experiments. Castello wrote: "Level #7 is worse, row after row of thousands of humans and human mixtures in cold storage. Here too are embryo storage vats of Humanoids in various stages of development. 'I frequently encountered humans in cages, usually dazed or drugged, but sometimes they cried and begged for help.'" [38]

Castello claims he was told in his initial briefing that the humans suffered different forms of insanity and were being subjected to a range of high-risk medical procedures and mind control experiments designed to treat insanity. He claims that he and other human workers were exposed daily to signs that said: "this site does high risk advanced medical and drug testing to cure insanity, please, never speak to the inmates, it can destroy years of work." [39]

Castello argues that he performed his duties without any great problem until he began to suspect that rather than being insane, the humans were normal civilians who were simply abducted to be used as laboratory animals by the Grey and Reptilian ET races:

I'm sensible, when doctors say don't speak to them, who was I to destroy the delicate situation? But one man some how caught my eye. He repeatedly stated that he was George S---- and that he had been kidnapped and he was sure someone was searching for him. I don't know why he sticks in my mind, I found I was remembering his face, thinking he sure didn't look or sound insane, but many inmates said that. The next weekend I convinced a friend of mine, a cop, to run a check on the guy, saying I had a run in with him and was curious. I didn't mention the base at all. It was a sickening feeling when the computer confirmed that George S. was missing. [40]

It was the realization that the humans were ordinary civilians abducted from that led to Castello's decision to join a small number of other base personnel in helping free the trapped humans.

It was another security officer that came to me saying he and some lab workers wanted an off duty meeting at one of the tunnels [off the record]. Curiosity took over and I said OK. That night, about nine men showed up. They said they knew they were risking me turning them in but they wanted to show me some things they thought I should see. One by one they showed records that proved many inmates were missing people. There were newspaper clippings, and even photos that they had some how smuggled into the base. They hoped to smuggle them back out, without me turning them in to the honchos. I could see the fear in their faces as they spoke. One man stated he would rather lose his life by trying, than to lose his soul by not doing anything at all. It was that remark that turned the tide. I told them about George and the things I found out about him. After a few hours we pledged to attempt to expose the Dulce Base. [41]

Castello describes how the small band of human workers began to cooperate with some Reptilians from the worker caste who also had an interest in freeing the abducted humans in the deep levels. Eventually, Castello described how the an elite Delta force contingent attempted to destroy the 'resistance movement':

Ultimately, it ended when a military assault was initiated via the exit tunnels and they executed anybody on their list, human or reptilian. We fought back, but none of the working caste had weapons, nor did the human lab workers. Only the security force and a few computer workers had flash guns. It was a massacre. Every one was screaming and running for cover. The halls and tunnels were filled as full as possible. We believe it was the Delta Force [because of the uniforms and the method they used] that chose to hit at shift change, an effort that killed as many as named on their list. [42]

Castello quit the facility, he took along with him photos and a video recording eventually distributed to the general public as the Dulce Papers.

Due to the importance of Castello's claims and the evidence he provided that appears to support much of what Bennewitz had concluded from his extensive electronic monitoring and field research, it is necessary to analyze any further whistleblower testimonies that independently substantiate the Dulce underground base hypothesis.

Was a Treaty Signed Between US Government Representatives and ET races?

The first claim that needs analysis is Bennewitz's and Castello's contention that a joint government-ET bases exist in the first place. This would imply some sort of formal treaty or agreement between US government representatives and ET races. There is significant whistleblower testimony that a treaty was signed between the Eisenhower administration and Grays from Zeta Reticulum as early as 1954. According to Dr Wolf the Eisenhower administration entered into the treaty with the so-called Grey extraterrestrials from the fourth planet of the star system Zeta Reticulum, but this treaty was never ratified as Constitutionally required. [43] Alluding to the same treaty signed by the Eisenhower administration, Col Phillip Corso, a highly decorated officer that served in Eisenhower's National Security Council wrote: "We had negotiated a kind of surrender with them [ETs] as long as we couldn't fight them. They dictated the terms because they knew what we most feared was disclosure." [44] The secret Treaty signed in 1954 between the Eisenhower administration and an ET race has been disclosed by a number of other 'whistleblowers' claiming former access to secret documents disclosing the existence of such a treaty. [45] Phil Schneider, a former geological engineer that was employed by corporations contracted to build underground bases wrote:

Back in 1954, under the Eisenhower administration, the federal government decided to circumvent the Constitution of the United States and form a treaty with alien entities. It was called the 1954 Grenada Treaty, which basically made the agreement that the aliens involved could take a few cows and test their implanting techniques on a few human beings, but that they had to give details about the people involved. Slowly, the aliens altered the bargain until they decided they wouldn't abide by it at all. [46]

Missing several fingers to prove his case, Phil Schneider committed suicide after facing an alien force at Dulce in hand to hand combat.

The treaty has been argued to essentially lead to technology transfers between ET races and the US government in exchange for certain basing rights, and monitoring of ET abductions of US civilians. Col Phillip Corso believed that this treaty was essentially something that was imposed on the Eisenhower administration suggesting that the technology transfer would be exchange for the ET harvesting the diverse genetic material available in the US. This genetic diversity was something that made the US a much more attractive treaty signatory than the more racially homogenous major powers of Russia and China. It is likely that the administration reasoned that since the Grays had been abducting US civilians anyway, that the Treaty would provide them with a means of monitoring the abductions, and observing at close range what happened with the civilians who were part of the genetic experiments pursued by the Grays. The Grays were obliged to provide lists of abducted civilians, something that apparently did not occur and later became a source of friction between the Grays and US authorities.

The treaty with the Grays from Zeta Reticulum presumably led to the creation of secret joint bases whose functions most likely included: technology exchange; mind control experiments; monitoring genetic experiments of Grays; and collusion in the abduction of civilians for the various projects at these shared bases. The existence of both the Treaty and the joint base(s) with the Grays would have received the highest possible classification levels and would only have been known by a limited number of elected and appointed public officials.

Consequently, whistleblower testimony supporting the existence of a secret treaty negotiated by the Eisenhower administration for technology transfers with an ET race suggest the possible construction of underground facilities where this could be done without public, congressional or foreign national scrutiny. Having laid the possible 'legal' foundation for a joint US government-ET underground facility, I now move to analyzing evidence supporting the existence of such a base.

Based on evidence presented so far it may be concluded that three possibilities stand out as the most likely explanations for what was occurring at Dulce. First, a top secret joint ET-human facility exists at Dulce that is (or was) conducting projects that involve(d) the abduction of human subjects whose rights are (were) severely violated. Second, the Dulce base exists (or existed) but reports of horrific ET abuses of humans were part of a disinformation campaign designed to discredit Paul Bennewitz and any legitimate research into the ET activities and secret government projects being conducted at Dulce. A third possibility is that all the stories about Dulce are disinformation designed to deliberately steer serious investigation away from UFO's and to divide the UFO community. [47] Keeping these three possibilities in mind, I now examine whistleblower testimonies concerning an apparent military conflict that occurred at the Dulce base in order to determine which of these three possibilities is more accurate.

The Dulce War

The whistleblower testimonies supporting the existence of the Dulce base suggest that such a secret facility is indeed conducting a range of projects that focus on technology exchange, mind control, genetic experiments, and human rights abuse of abducted civilians. It is likely that one or more of these projects became an area of dispute between ET races and clandestine government organizations. This dispute led to military hostilities that became known as the 'Dulce War'. The precise cause of this confrontation remains unclear, however what does emerge from the various testimonies is that it did occur and involved significant number of fatalities involving US military personnel, Dulce security guards, and ET races.

According to Castello, the Dulce military conflict began as a result of the growth of a resistance movement between both security guards and sympathetic ETs that desired to help imprisoned humans in the ET sections of the base. Eventually 100 elite Delta force military personnel were sent to eradicate the resistance movement that began to threaten established security procedures at the joint base. This force suffered a number of fatalities and inflicted heavy casualties upon both resident ETs and base security personnel. The military confrontation at Dulce has been reported by other whistleblowers including Phil Schneider who worked as a geological engineer in the construction of the Dulce base, another underground base in the US, and other underground bases around the globe. Schneider gave the following details of his background and the existence of a military confrontation in 1995:

To give you an overview of basically what I am, I started off and went through engineering school. Half of my school was in that field, and I built up a reputation for being a geological engineer, as well as a structural engineer with both military and aerospace applications. I have helped build two main bases in the United States that have some significance as far as what is called the New World Order [a UN run world secretly controlled by 'tall Gray' ETs]. The first base is the one at Dulce, New Mexico. I was involved in 1979 in a firefight with alien humanoids, and I was one of the survivors. I'm probably the only talking survivor you will ever hear. Two other survivors are under close guard. I am the only one left that knows the detailed files of the entire operation. Sixty-six secret service agents, FBI, Black Berets and the like, died in that firefight. I was there. [48]

Schneider described the cause of the 1979 military confrontation as little more than an 'accident' that arose from drilling for a planned extension of the Dulce base:

I was involved in building an ADDITION to the deep underground military base at Dulce, which is probably the deepest base. It goes down seven levels and over 2.5 miles deep. At that particular time, we had drilled four distinct holes in the desert, and we were going to link them together and blow out large sections at a time. My job was to go down the holes and check the rock samples, and recommend the explosive to deal with the particular rock. As I was headed down there, we found ourselves amidst a large cavern that was full of outer-space aliens, otherwise known as large Grays. I shot two of them. At that time, there were 30 people down there. About 40 more came down after this started, and all of them got killed. We had surprised a whole underground base of existing aliens. Later, we found out that they had been living on [in] our planet for a long time... This could explain a lot of what is behind the theory of ancient astronauts. [49]

An important difference between Schneider's and Castello's versions is that Schneider did not refer to the underground base as a joint facility. He described it as a seven level US military facility that had 'accidentally' been built on top of an ancient ET base. He believed that his job was to simply extend the existing base rather than attacking ET races for an undisclosed purpose. The unlikelihood that the Dulce facility was 'accidentally' built on an ancient ET base suggests that Schneider was only partly informed of the true nature of his mission and what was occurring on the lower levels. The more likely scenario was that Schneider had to assist US military forces to access the innermost layers of the Dulce facility, level 7, that had been closed off and where the true cause of the dispute lay.

Sometime in 1993 Schneider quit working for his various corporate clients that serviced military contracts after becoming convinced of a plot by the tall Gray ETs to develop a New World Order dominated by the United Nations that they would be secretly controlling. He subsequently began a series of public lectures revealing the activities at the underground bases he helped construct and the role of extraterrestrial races in infiltrating national governments and being the true architects of a New World Order. Schneider gave a keynote lecture at a MUFON conference in May 1995, and was found dead in his apartment seven months later in January 1996. [50] Circumstances surrounding the death of Schneider and his autopsy report led many to declare that Schneider had been murdered for going public with his knowledge of ETs and the secret underground base. [51] Schneider's testimony, his clear knowledge of geological engineering, and mysterious death all support his central thesis that an underground base exists at Dulce, and a military confrontation between ETs and elite US military forces occurred at the lowest level of this underground facility.

Another 'whistleblower' that lends credence to the possibility that a firefight had occurred between US military forces and ETs in a secret underground base was Dr Michael Wolf. Wolf's book Catcher's of

Heaven described a firefight between ETs and elite US military forces that had occurred in 1975 at the Groom Lake, Nevada facility that may have been related to what occurred later at the nearby Dulce:

The Greys shared certain of their technological advances with military/intelligence scientists, apparently often while prisoner "guests" within secure underground military installations in Nevada and New Mexico. The extraterrestrials have given the U.S. government some of their antigravity craft and a huge amount of fuel (element 115). On May 1, 1975 during one such technology exchange in Nevada, a demonstration of a small ET antimatter reactor, the lead Grey asked the Colonel in charge of the Delta Forces guarding the ETs to remove all their rifles and bullets from the room, (so that they would not accidentally discharge during the energy emissions.) The guards refused, and in the ensuing commotion a guard opened fire on the Greys. One alien, two scientists and 41 military personnel were killed. One guard was left alive to attest that the ETs apparently used directed mental energy in self-defense to kill the other attacking Delta Forces. Dr. Wolf states that "this incident ended certain exchanges with (the Greys)." [52]

There are important parallels with the 'Dulce war' in the description of the 'Nevada' confrontation described by Wolf, with that described by Castello and Schneider. In both cases, a significant number of US military personnel are killed after a confrontation with ETs. These parallels suggest either that Wolf was narrating an entirely different conflict, or the same conflict but with some inaccuracies intended to hide the true nature and location of the conflict between the US military and ET races. Some notable differences in the accounts are that Wolfe said that the ETs were 'prisoner' guests rather than sharing joint base facilities with the US. It is unlikely that ETs as 'prisoner guests' would participate in the kind of significant technology exchange described by Wolf. It is likely that Wolf's reference to the ETs as 'prisoner guests' was intended to hide the true extent of the cooperation between US military and ET races in a shared base that might lead to a connection being made with Bennewitz claims regarding Dulce. This also casts doubt on whether the conflict did occur in Nevada in 1975 as Wolf writes, or whether he was alluding to the 1979 military conflict at Dulce, New Mexico. If the latter is the case, then Wolf was instructed by his superiors in the 'controlled release of information' to sow some inaccuracies (disinformation) into the information he was releasing that a firefight had indeed occurred at a shared Government-ET facility and the US had taken heavy casualties. Such a disinformation strategy would strengthen any fall back position of 'plausibility deniability' that the government could choose to take over the sensitive information released by Wolf. Wolf further disclosed in an interview that he had worked at the Dulce laboratory, thereby providing more confirmation for the existence of this secret underground base that is the key claim made by Bennewitz. [53]

Another whistleblower that revealed evidence of the existence of a joint government-ET base and the 'Dulce military conflict' is Bob Lazar. Lazar worked for a few months in 1988 at the S-4 Nevada facility on reverse-engineering the propulsion and power system of ET craft. In an interview he described his background as follows:

I have two masters degrees, one's in physics; one's in electronics. I wrote my thesis on MHD, which is magnetohydrodynamics. I worked at Los Alamos for a few years as a technician and then as a physicist in the Polarized Proton Section, dealing with the accelerator there. I was hired at S-4 as a senior staff physicist to work on gravitational propulsion systems and whatnot associated with those crafts. [54]

Lazar revealed that in his briefing prior to working on the ET craft he was required to read 200 pages of briefing documents in preparation for his job. [55] He recalled that the briefing document mentioned a battle between ETs and humans at a secret base in 1979. He said the conflict was caused by a security guard that tried to take a weapon in the ET area and resulted in fatal wounds to security personnel. Lazar's recollection of the briefing document he read in 1988 is very likely referring to the 1979 Dulce firefight.

In sum, the strongest evidence for Bennewitz's claims regarding the Dulce base come from: Thomas Castello's testimony of his employment and defection from the Dulce underground base after witnessing human rights abuses; testimony of Phil Schneider who was directly involved in the Dulce firefight; important parallels with Michael Wolf's revelation of a firefight that may have occurred four years earlier at another underground base in Nevada and his admission of having worked at Dulce; Bob Lazar's recollection of a written briefing disclosing a 1979 firefight between ETs and security personal at a secret base; and the reports of abductees who underwent hypnotic regression and whose testimonies are recorded in the book, The Dulce Wars. Furthermore, the disinformation campaign instigated against Bennewitz, and the mysterious death of Schneider after his going public on the existence of secret underground facilities, both lend circumstantial support to the view that there was sufficient basis to whistleblower claims concerning the existence of the Dulce underground facility, and possible gross human rights abuses occurring there.

I can now return to the three possibilities mentioned earlier concerning Bennewitz's major claims of the existence of the Dulce base, a military conflict having taken place, and extensive human rights having occurred (or continuing to occur) at the base. The first possibility was that the evidence substantiates Bennewitz's claims. The second possibility was that Bennewitz's claims concerning ET abuses against civilian abductees was disinformation intended to steer researchers away from the existence of the base and/or a military conflict having taken place there. The third possibility was that Bennewitz's claims were compromised by disinformation intended to steer UFO researchers away from genuine sightings of UFO's. In order to determine which possibility is most plausible, I will now consider some of the criticisms made of Bennewitz's and others claims surrounding the Dulce base:

Critique of the Dulce Underground Base Hypothesis

Ever since Bennewitz first began circulating his claims concerning the Dulce base in the early 1980s, and latter physical evidence and personal testimonies provided by Castello and others, there has predictably been intense criticism of the evidence supporting the Dulce base hypothesis. These criticisms fall into three categories. First are criticisms of physical evidence such as Bennewitz's intercepted electronic transmissions, communication transcripts, photos, video recordings, and the 'Dulce Papers' provided by Castello; and lack of physical evidence of an underground base in terms of entrances, air vents, etc. Second, are criticisms that focus on the credibility of Bennewitz, Castello and Schneider as reliable sources for the Dulce base hypothesis. Finally, there are criticisms that the whole Dulce underground base hypothesis is a clever disinformation strategy launched by intelligence services such as the Air Force Office of Special Intelligence (AFOSI) to divide the UFO community. I will examine each of these criticisms in turn.

As far as the Bennewitz evidence was concerned, his photographs and films from 1980 clearly demonstrated some anomalous phenomenon that was acknowledged even by Air Force Intelligence, but the difficultly lay in conclusively showing what these showed. [56] Nevertheless, many UFO researchers believed this was some of the strongest evidence yet discovered of UFO's captured on film. [57] Bennewitz electronic communications while again demonstrating something odd was occurring was subject to most controversy and was again not conclusive proof. As far as the physical evidence found in the Dulce Papers was concerned, most researchers simply didn't take these seriously and assumed they were part of the disinformation campaign against Bennewitz. The lack of conclusive proof by way of photos, videos and physical sights is reminiscent of the entire history of the UFO community's efforts to find sufficient evidence to persuade even the most skeptical of professionals. [58] This suggests that the validity of physical evidence surrounding Bennewitz electronic records of UFO activity and ET communication, and the Dulce Papers, will continue to be subject to debate. A clear conclusion over what the physical evidence provided for the existence of the Dulce base is therefore elusive.

Private investigators have explored the terrain where the underground base is allegedly located. The Archuletta Mesa is situated on Jicarilla Apache Indian reservation land. One investigator, Glen Campbell, found that there were no visible security restrictions on the land, no evidence of a military presence, and no concealed entrances, air vents, water intakes from the nearby Navaho river, etc., were found. He subsequently concluded that there was no physical evidence of an underground base. [59] Other field investigators, however, have found evidence of strange occurrences in the area lending support to the existence of a base. [60] For instance, Norio Harakaya visited Dulce with a Japanese film production crew in 1990 and concluded:

I've been to Dulce with the Nippon Television Network crew and interviewed many, many people over there and came back with the firm conviction that something was happening around 10 to 15 years ago over there, including nightly sightings of strange lights and appearances of military jeeps and trucks. [61]

Some of the criticisms raised by Campbell might be explained in a number of ways. Castello and Schneider, for example, both described an extensive underground infrastructure that used advanced technology such as a high-speed rail link. [62] This would make it possible for entrances to the Dulce base to be concealed in more secure areas. Also, air circulation and water could also be provided in other ways by those possessing the advanced technology to do so. This suggests that criticism of a lack of physical evidence on Jicarilla Apache land to support the idea of a secret underground base is not conclusive, and even conflicts with other testimonies of mysterious military troop movements and anomalous sightings in the area .

The covert disinformation campaign launched by AFOSI against Bennewitz suggests that the physical evidence he had of an underground base in the area, and the public support he attracted, were perceived to be a national security threat. This covert disinformation campaign that began in 1980 suggests that criticisms of the physical evidence provided by Bennewitz and Castello, are not conclusive and may themselves be part of an ongoing disinformation campaign. Consequently, criticism of the lack of physical evidence for the existence of an underground base in Dulce fails to dismiss the Dulce base hypothesis.

The second set of criticisms focus on the credibility of the whistleblowers/witnesses who provided evidence or testimony of the Dulce base. Establishing credibility in a field rife with disinformation, intimidation and official efforts to discredit expert witnesses and 'whistleblowers' requires some flexibility in analyzing whistleblower behavioral and/or personality characteristics. A 'nervous breakdown', 'refusal to give interviews', or use of 'cover identities', for instance, may be more of a result of covert intimidation than a sign of an individual who lacks credibility. Focusing on the mental or health problems encountered by whistleblowers/witnesses advocating the Dulce base hypothesis may amount to little more than veiled personal attacks against the credibility of the principle advocates of the hypothesis. For instance, in an online article that is critical of evidence for the Dulce base, the writer Roy Lawhon, glosses over the challenges faced in establishing the credibility of the three principle witnesses/whistleblowers advocating the Dulce Underground base hypothesis - Bennewitz, Castello and Schneider. Lawhon finishes his description of their respective claims with references to a range of personal problems or behaviors each exhibited in a way that appears to be little more than a veiled attack on their credibility. [63] For example, he refers to Bennewitz being "committed for a time to a mental hospital", and then becoming a "reclusive, refusing to talk about UFOs." [64] As mentioned earlier, Bennewitz became the subject of an intense disinformation campaign, public scrutiny, attacks on his credibility, and unusual activities being directed against him that finally led to him having a nervous breakdown. This doesn't affect the quality of his material nor his credibility, but only displays that in intense circumstances, many individuals succumb to the psychological pressure that has been directed against them.

Moving on to Castello, Lawhon concludes that Castello "has only provided stories, nothing solid, and has yet to come forward in person," and that there "is some doubt as to whether he actually exists." [65] While only a relatively few researchers can vouch for Castello's existence, there would be very good reason to believe that as a possible whistleblower revealing classified information, he would be subject to arrest or other official efforts to 'silence' him, if he emerged into the public. This may explain his mysterious movement while at the same time leaving open the possibility that he is part of a disinformation strategy. Therefore, while his testimony and the Dulce Papers on their own lack persuasiveness, they become significant as supporting evidence for Bennewitz's claims.

Finally, with regard to Schneider, Lawhon refers to unquoted sources that Schneider "had severe brain damage and was also a paranoid schizophrenic." [66] This would have to be the most unfair of the criticisms raised by Lawhon. Schneider spent nearly two years on the lecture circuit (1993-95) candidly revealing his activities while an employee for corporations that built the Dulce and other underground bases. There were ample opportunities for his integrity and mental resilience to be tested, and it appears that he did not disappoint his growing number of supporters. [67] He gave the appearance of a man who knew his life would soon end from either natural causes (he had terminal cancer) or from being murdered. His apparent 'suicide' had the tell tale signs of murder that was not seriously pursued by public authorities. [68] Schneider's testimony represents the most solid whistleblower disclosure available on the existence of the Dulce Base and of a firefight between ETs and elite US troops having occurred there in 1979. In conclusion, criticisms of the credibility of the principal advocates of the Dulce base hypothesis fail to be persuasive.

Finally, there are criticisms that focus on William Moore's 1989 declaration at a MUFON conference that he had been co-opted into a covert effort by AFOSI to feed disinformation to Bennewitz in order to discredit him. While furious that one UFO researcher would actively participate in a disinformation campaign against another researcher, many UFO researchers were quick to accept Moore's story that the most bizarre aspects of Bennewitz's claims, human rights abuses involving ET abductions, cold storage of humans and underground vats filled with cattle and human parts were disinformation. Bennewitz's claims had been gaining widespread support in the UFO community and being championed by controversial individuals such as John Lear, William Cooper and William Hamilton. Some well-established UFO researchers believed that Lear's and Hamilton's claims, reflecting Bennewitz's statements about the Dulce underground base, would damage legitimate UFO research. [69] When it was learned that John Lear had been invited to host the 1989 Mutual UFO Network (MUFON) conference, for instance, prominent MUFON members began to resign in protest. [70] Many UFO researchers did not believe that Bennewitz's electronic interceptions, interpretations of the data, and interviews with abductees, were sufficient proof of an underground ET base at Dulce. Bennewitz's claims of ETs committing gross human rights violations at the base were widely dismissed as little more than disinformation even by those who believed in his integrity and the quality of the hard evidence he had compiled. [71]

As far as the view that disinformation played a major role in Bennewitz developing his views concerning the base and human rights abuses, Bennewitz had already compiled an extensive database of information based on his two years of electronic surveillance prior to approaching AFOSI in 1980. Consequently, Bennewitz had already developed many of his views about Dulce before AFOSI began to feed him disinformation after Bennewitz's 1980 AFOSI interviews and subsequent meeting with Moore in 1982. It is likely that Bennewitz's observation of UFO/ET activity in the area, electronic monitoring of radio and video transmissions, and his electronic communications, leading up to and including the Dulce war, gave him an overall picture of what was occurring in the base. The more likely explanation is that US intelligence services were in damage control mode after Bennewitz's intercepts of electronic communications between ET ships and the Dulce base. The even more revealing evidence and testimony provided by Castello, and later by Schneider, became intertwined with disinformation that was actively being fed into the public debate surrounding the Dolce base hypothesis. Criticism that the most alarming aspects of the Dulce base hypothesis, ET human rights abuses, etc., were simply AFOSI disinformation, fails to take into account how disinformation is actively used as a standard tool by the intelligence community to create confusion and prevent discovery of what is precisely occurring. [72]

I now return to the three possibilities raised earlier concerning the Dulce underground base hypothesis: 1. the physical evidence, whistleblower claims and witness testimonies provide conclusive evidence of the Dulce base and extensive ET abuses of abducted civilians; 2. claims of the base are likely accurate but some disinformation has occurred as far as the more extreme stories of human rights abuses; and 3. the Dulce base hypothesis is disinformation. Based on the evidence presented thus far, and the lack of conclusive criticism of this evidence, the third possibility can be dismissed. This suggests the conclusion that a secret joint government-ET base did exist at Dulce, that military conflict did occur over issues that remain open to debate, but most likely involved perceptions of a treaty violation by one or both sides. Reports of gross human rights abuses against civilians abducted for various projects at the base while not at this point conclusive have sufficient evidentiary support to warrant further investigation on the part of responsible government authorities and human rights organizations. One further issue to be examined for understanding the human rights and political implications of the evidence presented thus far is to identify how Dulce and any similar bases are funded without legislative oversight.

Funding Dulce and other Joint Government/ET Underground Bases without US Congressional Oversight

According to Phil Schneider, funds used for the construction of underground bases in the US and elsewhere come from a 'black budget' - money that is not part of the normal Congressional appropriations and supplemental processes that fund government agencies in the US. In his 1995 lecture, Schneider declared:

The Black Budget is a secretive budget that garners 25% of the gross national product of the United States. The Black Budget currently consumes $1.25 trillion per year. At least this amount is used in black programs, like those concerned with deep underground military bases. Presently, there are 129 deep underground military bases in the United States. [73]

These bases according to Schneider are "connected by high-speed magneto-leviton trains that have speeds up to Mach 2". [74] Thomas Castello also described the high-speed underground rail system that connected Dulce to other bases in the US and the world: "[the] world wide network is called the "Sub-Global System." It has "check points" at each country entry. There ARE shuttle tubes that 'shoot' the trains at incredible speeds using a mag-lev and vacuum method. They travel at a speed that excels the speed of sound." [75] A researcher confirming some of Schneider's and Castello's claims of a vast underground infrastructure linked by high speed Maglev train system is Dr Richard Sauder who has investigated and identified secret underground bases in the US and around the globe. [76] If Schneider's description and budget estimates are correct, then a massive secret underground infrastructure exists that is funded in ways that escape Congressional oversight despite the underground infrastructure's vast size and consumption of economic resources. It is therefore worth investigating whether Schneider's estimate could be accurate, how Congress exercises oversight over classified programs in the US, and where a base such as Dulce fits into the overall picture of Congressional funding and oversight of clandestine military programs.

Confirmation of Schneider's surprisingly high estimate of the 'black budget' comes from an unlikely source. A former Assistant Secretary of Housing and Urban Development (HUD), Catherine Fitts, claims that a total of 3.3 trillion dollars was siphoned out of HUD and the Department of Defense (DoD) for the fiscal years 1998, 1999 and 2000. [77] Fitts bases her 2000 estimate on a report from David K. Steensma, Acting Assistant Inspector for auditing DoD who wrote in a 2002 report that "DoD processed $1.1 trillion in unsupported accounting entries to DoD Component financial data used to prepare departmental reports and DoD financial statements for FY 2000." [78] Reporting on the missing DoD funds in fiscal year 2000, investigative reporter Kelly O'Meara also supported Fitts finding:

[T]he deputy IG [Inspector General] at the Pentagon read an eight-page summary of DOD fiduciary failures. He admitted that $4.4 trillion in adjustments to the Pentagon's books had to be cooked to compile the required financial statements and that $1.1 trillion of that amount could not be supported by reliable information. In other words, at the end of the last full year on Bill Clinton's watch, more than $1 trillion was simply gone and no one can be sure of when, where or to whom the money went. [79]

If the 'black budget' is indeed as high as Fitts' and Schneider's estimates, then it is very likely that these are used to fund programs such as the Dulce base which would appear to fall into the category of a 'Special Access Program' (SAP). SAPs are programs that have additional security measures attached to them over and above the normal classificatory system (confidential, secret, top-secret) attached to most classified information and programs. [80] According to a 1997 Senate Commission Report, there were approximately 150 SAPs that operated with DoD approval. [81] These SAPs are divided into two classes 'acknowledged' and 'unacknowledged' as described in the Senate Report:

Publicly acknowledged programs are considered distinct from unacknowledged programs, with the latter colloquially referred to as "black" programs because their very existence and purpose are classified. Among black programs, further distinction is made for "waived" programs, considered to be so sensitive that they are exempt from standard reporting requirements to the Congress. The chairperson, ranking member, and, on occasion, other members and staff of relevant Congressional committees are notified only orally of the existence of these programs. [82]

Essentially, a waived unacknowledged SAP (deep black) is so sensitive that only eight members of Congress (the chairs and ranking members of the four defense committees divided between the House of Representatives and Senate) are notified of a waived SAP without being given any information about it. This would enable them to truthfully declare no knowledge of such a program if asked, thereby maintaining secrecy of this SAP. If unacknowledged SAPs are 'black programs', then 'waived' unacknowledged SAPs are 'deep black'. The Dulce base appears to be a candidate for one of these 'deep black' programs currently in operation in the US.

SAPs are funded in a manner that fulfills federal guidelines and subject to both Executive and Congressional oversight. In practice though, Congressional oversight in the case of waived acknowledged SAPs is nominal. President Clinton's Executive Order # 12958 issued on April 17, 1995, reformed how SAPs would in future be created and oversight established. The main components of the Executive Order was that only the Secretaries of State, Defense and Energy, and the Director of Central Intelligence (or their principal deputies) could create a SAP; these would be kept to an "absolute minimum"; and would be created when "the vulnerability of, or threat to, specific information is exceptional," and their secrecy cannot be protected by the normal classification system. [83] As far as oversight was concerned, the key clause in the Executive Order was an effort by the Clinton administration to coordinate oversight through a central executive office (Information Security Oversight Office) that would be responsible to the National Security Council (NSC) and annually report to the President:

(3) ... the Director of the Information Security Oversight Office shall be afforded access to these programs, in accordance with the security requirements of each program, in order to perform the functions assigned to the Information Security Oversight Office under this order. An agency head may limit access to a special access program to the Director and no more than one other employee of the Information Security Oversight Office; or, for special access programs that are extraordinarily sensitive and vulnerable, to the Director only. [84]

In practice, however, effective oversight of SAP's is performed by a DoD committee, the Special Access Program Oversight Committee (SAPOC), and a similar committee in the intelligence community, Controlled Access Program Oversight Committee (CAPOC) for its SAPs, rather than the Information Security Oversight Office. [85] It is SAPOC that has the authority for the "approval, termination, revalidation, restructuring procedures for DoD special access programs." [86] Essentially, there is very little authority that a US President can exercise over SAPs in the DoD and the intelligence community. [87] The oversight system that has evolved effectively excludes the President from having control over the DoD and intelligence committees that have real power over SAPs, but which in theory are subordinate to the President as 'Commander in Chief'. [88] It will be argued that those branches of the Executive Office that are under direct control of the President, as President Clinton discovered, have little power to influence or provide oversight of 'deep black programs'. [89] Those branches of the Executive Office that deal with ET affairs are embedded in the National Security Council, and are not under control of the President. [90] To distinguish between these as far as Executive Office oversight of deep black programs is concerned, I will refer to those executive offices under control of the President as 'Executive Office oversight', and those offices not under the President's control as 'Shadow Government' oversight.

The 'deep black' programs described by Schneider require funds well in excess to the federal funds officially allocated to SAPs. For example, in the 2001 financial year, somewhere between $10-12 billion dollars was budgeted for SAPs by all services in the DoD, well below the sums mentioned by Schneider and Fitts that were likely being spent on the 'deep black programs' that were not included in the list of SAPs submitted to Congress. [91] Even with the increase of the DoD budget to 380 billion dollars in 2003, the portion allocated to SAPs would rise only marginally thereby maintaining a large discrepancy between the actual cost of all 'deep black programs' and the budget allocated to them.

To fund 'deep black programs' that are directly connected with the ET presence without attracting Congressional and Executive Office oversight, clandestine organizations embedded in the military and intelligence branches of government have developed a complex financial system for circumventing the normal appropriations process and oversight requirements for the use of Federal funds. According to Kelly O'Meara, the use of a range of accounting mechanisms such as "unsupported entries," "material-control weakness," "adjusted records," "unmatched disbursements," "abnormal balances" and "unreconciled differences" the DoD effectively cannot account for up to a trillion dollars annually. [92] The huge unaccounted annual sum, well in excess of the DoD's official budget suggests that federal government departments are being used to siphon money without the US taxpayer, Congress and responsible federal authorities being aware of what is occurring. [93]

Rather than siphoned federal money going directly into the pockets or Swiss bank accounts of corrupt US politicians, a practice the leaders in many developing nations have developed to a fine art, the money goes directly into the 'black budget' which then funds 'deep black programs' in addition to the official list of SAPs that can be run without Congressional and Presidential oversight. These 'illegal' funds are channeled to clandestine organizations in the different branches of the US military and intelligence services to directly fund their pet 'black programs' for dealing with the ET presence. These funds are then used to award contracts to US corporations such as EG&G, Westinghouse, McDonnell Douglas, Morrison- Knudson, Wackenhut Security Systems, Boeing Aerospace, Lorimar Aerospace, Aerospacial in France, Mitsibishi Industries, Rider Trucks, Bechtel, Raytheon, DynCorp, Lockheed Martin, Hughes, Dryden, SAC, and others that provide the necessary services for ET related projects. [94] Retired DIA intelligence officer, John Maynard reports on the nature of the relationship between corporations and the DoD:

The Department of Defense has had an ongoing program since the mid-1950's, which provided contracts to U.S. Civilian Contractors/Organizations/Corporations that worked in the intelligence community. These projects came under very tight security and usually were very highly compartmentalized. What this means is that you have several concentric circles: the closer you are to the inner circle the more information you could find on the project. The further you get away from this inner circle, the less information is available. All this is established on a very strict need-to-know basis. Within these circles you could, if you looked hard enough, find contractors that worked on various parts of the project but really had no idea what the overall project was. This also happened with the military's interaction with the primary contractor. Also in this respect, each military branch had certain projects that came under the compartmentalization security measures. [95]

Corporations awarded military contracts generated from illegal 'black budget' funds, are not subject to Congressional or Executive

Office oversight, do not have to disclose to the general public the true nature of the activities they perform for their military employers, and force their employees to sign non-disclosure agreements with severe penalties. According to Bob Lazar his true employer while at the S-4 Nevada facility was the US Navy, but he had to sign a contract with the company EG&G which involved signing away his constitutional rights in the case of disclosure. [86] After his decision to quit his work at area S-4 Lazar disclosed that he received death threats.

An estimate of the number of 'deep black programs' funded by the 'black budget' can be gained by using estimates of the official funding for 'deep black programs', and then revising this up when funds available through the 'black budget' are used. According to Executive Order 12958 and recommendations from the 1997 Senate Commission Report, the number of deep black programs (unacknowledged waived Special Access Programs) is to be kept to an absolute minimum. This suggests that of the 150 SAPs identified by the Senate Commission in 1997, it can be estimated from proportionally breaking this down into 'acknowledged' and 'unacknowledged', and then breaking 'unacknowledged down into 'waived' and 'unwaived' SAPs, and then using an arbitrary figure of 50% to factor in the 'absolute minimum' requirement that is used for permitting waived SAPs, that somewhere in the range of 15-20 SAPs (approximately 10% of the total) are 'deep black'. Using the same process to break down the estimated annual budget for SAPs of 10-12 billion dollars, approximately 1.5 billion dollars are annually spent on 'deep black programs'. This means that approximately 1.5 billion dollars are spent on approximately 15-20 'deep black' programs whose existence is verbally reported to only eight Congressional committee chairs & ranking members who are not briefed on them.

The extraordinary security precautions surrounding 'deep black' programs has been historically acceptable to Congressional leaders based on their belief of the limited number and modest budgets allocated to these programs – $ 1.5 billion would be less than 0.5% of the total DoD budget for 2003 ($380 billion). If the estimates provided by Fitts, O'Meara, and Schneider are correct, then the true size of the budget for 'deep black programs' is almost three times the annual DoD budget! Comparing this astounding figure to the $1.5 billion estimate for 'deep black' programs supplied to Congressional leaders, this suggests that waived SAPs, together with unacknowledged SAPs, are really only a cover for an entirely different category of deep black programs – those that are directly related to the ET presence.

Using Fitts estimates as closer to the true size of the 'black budget' and the estimate for the waived SAPs budget ($1.5 billion), the total actual funding for this different category of 'deep black programs' can actually be multiplied by a factor of approximately 700. This might suggest that the number of 'deep black programs' could also be increased by this factor, however the extra funding might well be used to expand each program rather than add new programs. Consequently, if a factor of ten is used to account for an expansion of a 'deep black program' to get a closer approximation of the program's actual cost, then the true number of 'deep black programs' would be expanded by a factor of 70. If an estimate of the 'official' number of 'deep black programs' is 15-20, then the true number is somewhere in the range of 1,050 to 1,400. It can be therefore by concluded that over 1,000 'deep black programs' are funded by a 'black budget' estimated to be in the vicinity of 1.1 trillion dollars annually. Given that the Senate Commission reported the existence of approximately 150 SAPs in total, it can be further concluded that Congressional leaders and the President are not informed of the true number of deep black programs that exist, nor of the 'black budget' that funds more than 99% of these 'deep black' programs.

If the 'black budget' is what funds the Dulce underground base and the other approximately 99% of deep black programs that are not reported to Congress even in the perfunctory manner of 'waived unacknowledged SAPs', then it is clear there are two types of deep black programs. Those funded from the regular budget (waived unacknowledged SAPs) that are constitutionally legal, and those funded by the 'black budget' that are not part of the SAP oversight process at all, are outside of the normal constitutional process and are technically illegal. It can be concluded that the legal 'deep black programs' are merely a cover for the illegal 'deep black programs' that are specifically oriented towards responding to the ET presence. These cover programs are designed to steer Congressional and Executive Office officials away from the truth about the ET related 'deep black programs' that exist and which consume enormous resources from the US economy.

Consequently, approximately 15-20 (2%) of all deep black programs are legal with a known oversight process, while approximately 750 – 1000 (98%) are illegal and have a very different oversight process. It is possible that the DoD and Intelligence community committees (SAPOC & CAPOC) that have direct oversight of legal 'deep black programs' are aware of illegal 'deep black programs' but do not effectively have oversight of these. It is likely that the main responsibility of SAPOC & CAPOC is to ensure that legal 'deep black programs' and acknowledged 'black programs' whose details are supplied to Congressional committees and the Executive Office, are effective covers for the illegally funded deep black programs. Oversight of illegal deep black programs is most likely directly exercised by clandestine organizations embedded in the various military services, Intelligence branches, and the National Security Council responsible for managing ET affairs. [97] Clandestine organizations embedded within Executive Office agencies such as the National Security Council, Federal Emergency Management Agency, and Homeland Security, form the 'shadow government' responsible for coordinating military, intelligence and governmental activities that deal with ET affairs. [98]

In conclusion, the funding for the construction and running of joint government-ET underground bases at Dulce and elsewhere in the US comes from 'black budget' funds that are not subject to the normal oversight requirements associated with regular DoD and intelligence community SAPs. The US corporations awarded contracts for providing their services to the military and intelligence agencies are unregulated, and have been very 'successful' in enforcing secrecy upon their employees – a critical factor in receiving future military contracts! Effectively this means that clandestine organizations embedded in the military, intelligence community and National Security agencies, have found a way of circumventing Congressional and Executive Office oversight and approval for the true cost and number of illegal 'deep black programs'.

Table 1.
Summary of Funding and Oversight System
for Deep Black Programs

Program Classification	Oversight	Estimated Number	Funding Source	Estimated Annual Budget	ET Related
'Acknowledged' Special Access Program (SAP)	Congress*/SAPOC /CAPOC/Executive Office	75	Congress/DoD/ Intelligence Community	$5 - 6 billion	No
Unacknowledged SAP - Black	Congress*/SAPOC /CAPOC/Executive Office	55-60	Congress/DoD/ Intelligence Community	$3.5 - 4.5 billion	Cover
Waived Unacknowledged SAP - Deep Black	SAPOC/CAPOC	15-20	Congress/DoD/ Intelligence Community	$1.5 billion	Cover
Illegal – Deep Black	Shadow Government	1050-1400	Black Budget	$1.1 trillion	Yes

Acronyms

SAPOC – Special Access Program Oversight Committee, Department of Defense

CAPOC – Controlled Access Program Oversight Committee, CAPOC

*Congress Committees – House National Security Committee, the Senate Armed Services Committee, and the defense subcommittees of the House and Senate Appropriations committees.

ã Michael E. Salla, PhD. *The Dulce Report* (September, 2003)

Conclusion:
Political Implications of
Alleged Human Rights Abuses at Dulce

The whistleblower testimonies examined in this report persuasively point to the existence of the Dulce base as a former and/or current joint US government-ET underground facility built with 'black budget' funds that operated/operates without Congressional and Executive Office oversight. The testimonies further support the view that the 'Dulce war' did involve armed conflict between US military forces, Base Security Personnel, and resident ET races. While the precise cause of the military confrontation remains unclear, it does suggest that one or both sides were not keeping commitments specified in an undisclosed treaty. Given whistleblower testimony that one of these treaty commitments was ensuring that abducted civilians used in genetic experiments undertaken at the base would be fully accounted for, not harmed, and safely returned to civilian life, there is cause to believe gross human rights violations may have played a role in sparking the conflict. Similar human rights abuses may well be occurring in other possible joint government-ET bases in the US and other countries around the planet.

The immediate political fall out from the 'Dulce Wars' and alleged ET abuses of abducted civilians was very likely an indefinite delay in public disclosure of the ET presence. The release of the Steven Spielberg movie Close Encounters of the Third Kind in 1977 has been long speculated to have been part of an 'acclimation program' to prepare the general public for disclosure of the ET presence. [99] NASA sent a 20 page confidential letter to Spielberg outlining what should and shouldn't be in the movie prior to its release suggesting an unusual degree of official interest in how ETs and the government were depicted. [100] The 1979 'Dulce War' where the clandestine authorities in charge of ET affairs (the shadow government) ordered an attack on ET occupied levels of a joint underground base would surely have signaled a dramatic shift in attitudes towards the ET presence and an indefinite hold on full public disclosure.

There is sufficient evidence to justify further investigation into the accuracy of claims surrounding extensive human rights abuses at joint government-ET bases that exist(ed) at Dulce and elsewhere in the US. The most effective means of exploring alleged human rights abuses at Dulce would be for a prominent human rights non-government organization such as Amnesty International or Human Rights Watch to initiate an investigation of the claims surrounding such abuses. These organizations have extensive experience in performing accurate and confidential investigations in countries that have historically conducted gross human rights, and repressed those who have stepped forward to reveal such abuses. An investigation by a human rights NGO could provide the opportunity for whistleblowers to step forward and/or pass information concerning alleged human rights abuses at Dulce. This would provide a means of preserving confidentially and preventing criminal charges against whistleblowers for disclosing 'classified information'. In the case of criminal charges being brought against such whistleblowers by US federal agencies, or of their disappearance, such individuals could become the focus of 'emergency alerts' that human rights organizations have pioneered over the years to secure the release of those revealing 'human rights' abuses.

Another means of exploring alleged human rights abuses at Dulce would be for a Congressionally backed inquiry into allegations of such abuses and the full scope of activities at these underground facilities examined in terms of the degree to which they contributed to human rights abuses. Comprehensive congressional immunity and protection should be given to all government/military officials and employees of corporations willing to step forward to give information of human rights abuses of US citizens and other nationals in bases on US territory or around the globe. Due to high public interest in learning about such alleged abuses, the Congressional inquiry should be open with full media coverage. Where genuine national security considerations merit non-disclosure of such information, this should be put before the Congressional Inquiry for proper consideration and appropriate action.

The 'shadow government' in charge of managing ET affairs has been a factor, either mitigating or causal, in gross human rights abuses that occurred in secret bases under its control and/or shared with ET races. The role of the shadow government can be investigated and made accountable for human rights abuses through appropriate reforms in much the same way that many former autocratic states have had to reform their governments as a result of international scrutiny of human rights abuses. Due to the experience of human rights NGO's in conducting such investigations of autocratic regimes, this provides a highly desirable means of addressing the alleged abuses committed under the leadership of clandestine groups embedded in national security agencies that collectively constitute a 'shadow government'.

A congressionally backed inquiry into the financial mechanisms used for funding illegal 'deep black projects' is also required in order to fully account for all funds generated from the US economy, and to end the practice of funds being used for 'deep black programs' that operate without Congressional/Executive Office oversight, and even outside of the relevant oversight committees in the DoD and intelligence communities. The use of corporations for servicing military contracts funded by illegal revenue received by clandestine organizations in the US military and intelligence services needs to be ended.

In order to deal with the full extent of the alleged human rights abuses committed at joint government-ET bases by corporate employees/military personnel, a 'Truth Commission' should be convened for government/military officials and/or corporate employees who directly participated in experiments and projects that involved such violations; and/or in the suppression of such information through intimidation of witnesses and whistleblowers. Such a Truth Commission can be modeled on the South African example where a blanket amnesty was given to all public officials in the Apartheid era who participated in human rights abuses provided they fully disclose the nature of their activities, and that these abuses were politically motivated rather than personal. [101] The granting of amnesty for officials/employees stepping forward to admit their participation in projects that violated the basic human rights of US citizens and foreign nationals forcibly held in joint government-ET bases will be an important means for discovering the full extent of what has occurred during the operation of these bases.

In order to begin the process of promoting Congressional and/or Human Rights NGO action for dealing with the alleged human rights abuses committed at Dulce, former/current public officials or corporate employees who in their official capacities or employment have first hand knowledge of such abuses committed at Dulce and/or any other joint Government-ET facility are encouraged to step forward. There are a number of whistleblower legal services available that would be able to provide legal counsel for those interested in disclosing their activities without violating legal/contractual obligations. [102]

The political implications of the human rights abuses of what occurred at the Dulce underground base require immediate attention through credible human rights organizations investigating such allegations. Furthermore, congressionally sponsored inquiries are required on a number of key issues stemming from alleged abuses at Dulce: participating in treaties with ET races without congressional ratification; 'black budget' funding of illegal deep black programs that operate without Congressional or Executive Office oversight; military hostilities between US security agencies and ET races without the general public or Congress being informed of the causes and justifications of such actions; and accountability for human rights abuses committed at Dulce and possibly other underground bases in the US and elsewhere. Rather than what occurred at Dulce being limited solely to the US government, it is very likely that other major world governments have agreed to similar arrangements with ET races where the human rights of its citizens are traded for advanced ET technology. The full extent of what occurred at Dulce may be a watershed in human history. It could well be the first time in recorded history that humanity has to deal in a politically responsible way with the legacy of human rights abuses committed by another species upon members of the human race, and complicity by various military, intelligence and/or corporate personnel in not taking the appropriate actions to prevent such abuses.

ENDNOTES

[1] My most sincere thanks to H.M. who generously provided the hospitality, intellectual stimulation, thoughtful suggestions and research environment for completing this Report.

[2] Estimates of the size of the annual black budget go as high as 1.1 trillion dollars. For description of how money is annually siphoned from the US economy see Catherine Fitts, "The $64 Question: What's Up With the Black Budget? – The Real Deal," *Scoop: UQ Wire* (23 September, 2002). Available online at: **http://www.scoop.co.nz/mason/stories/HL0209/S00126.htm**

[3] See Branton, *The Dulce Wars: Underground Alien Bases and the Battle for Planet Earth* (Inner Light Publications, 1999); and Christa Tilton, *The Bennewitz Papers* (Inner Light Publications, 1994). Websites with articles and discussion on Dulce include: http://eaglenet.enochgraphics.com/dulce/ and http://groups.yahoo.com/group/Dulce_Base_Investigations

[4] An online overview of Bennewitz's research is by Chris Lambright, "Paul Bennewitz, electronic recordings, and films of "aerial objects'," (July 1, 1996) available online at: http://www.cufon.org/contributors/chrisl/PB/bennewit.htm

[5] For some of these images, see Chris Lambright, "Paul Bennewitz, electronic recordings, and films of "aerial objects'," (July 1, 1996) available online at http://www.cufon.org/contributors/chrisl/PB/bennewi2.htm

[6] Paul Bennewitz, Project Beta, available online at: http://www.paraarchives.com/documents/p/beta01.htm

[7] Dr Sprinkle is the Director the Academy of Close Clinical Encounters Therapists (ACCET), and is widely known expert in abductees. For online website to ACCET go to: http://drboylan.com/accetpg2.html

[8] See Branton, The Dulce Wars, chs. 21& 26. Available online at: http://eaglenet.enochgraphics.com/dulce/ . Bennewitz refers to the mother and her son in Project Beta, available online at: http://www.paraarchives.com/documents/p/beta01.htm

[9] See Chris Lambright, "Paul Bennewitz, electronic recordings, and films of "aerial objects'- Part 3" (June, 2003) available online at http://www.cufon.org/contributors/chrisl/PB/bennewi3.htm

[10] In Bennewitz's report, Project Beta, there are many references to how to militarily defense against ET ships suggesting that his communications revealed the hostile relationship that existed between the humans and the ETs. Bennewitz's report, Project Beta, is available online at: http://www.paraarchives.com/documents/p/beta01.htm

[11] Cited online on by World of the Strange, http://www.worldofthestrange.com/modules.php?name=Documents&op=ViewItems&vid=138

[12] Bennewitz's report, Project Beta, is available online at: http://www.paraarchives.com/documents/p/beta01.htm

[13] Bennewitz, Project Beta, prologue, available online at:
http://www.paraarchives.com/documents/p/beta01.htm

[14] For details on Moore's confession 1989, see
http://www.worldofthestrange.com/modules.php?name=Documents&op=ViewItems&vid=144

[15] For details on Moore's confession 1989, see
http://www.worldofthestrange.com/modules.php?name=Documents&op=ViewItems&vid=144

[16] See Chris Lambright, "Paul Bennewitz, electronic recordings, and films of "aerial objects', Part
3" (June, 2003) available online at http://www.cufon.org/contributors/chrisl/PB/bennewi3.htm

[17] "The Aviary," *Think-aboutit.com*, available online at: http://www.think-
aboutit.com/ufo/aviary.htm

[18] For discussion of the whistleblower phenomenon, see Myron Peretz Glazer and Penina Migdal
Glazer, *The Whistleblowers: Exposing Corruption in Government and Industry* (Basic Books, 1991);
and C. Fred Alford, *Whistleblowers: Broken Lives and Organizational Power* (Cornell University,
2002). For online information go to: http://www.whistleblowers.org/

[19] For detailed discussion of legal definitions and laws concerning whistleblowers, see Stephen
M. Kohn, *Concepts and Procedures in Whistleblower Law* (Quorum Books. Westport, Conn. 2000). For
online information go to: http://www.whistleblowers.org/

[20] A copy of this statute can be found online at
http://www.whistleblower.org/article.php?did=92&scid=96

[21] The Dulce papers including a video recording are available on a number of locations on the
internet. One site from which they can be downloaded is:
http://www.crowdedskies.com/pages/dulce.htm

[22] See Branton, *The Dulce Wars: Underground Alien Bases and the Battle for Planet Earth* (Inner
Light Publications, 1999). Available online at: http://eaglenet.enochgraphics.com/dulce/ & also at:
http://www.thewatcherfiles.com/dulce_book.htm

[23] The *Dulce Wars*, ch 21. Available online at
http://www.thewatcherfiles.com/dulce/chapter21.htm . See also William Hamilton, *Cosmic Top
Secret: America's Secret Ufo Program - New Evidence* (Inner Light Publications, 1990). An extract is
available online at: http://www.crowdedskies.com/files/down/cog.html

[24] Branton, *The Dulce Wars.*

[25] For discussion of PI 40 and other key ET management organizations, see Michael Salla,
"Political Management of the Extraterrestrial Presence – The Challenge to Democracy and Liberty in
America." *Exopolitics.Org*, July 4, 2003. Available online at: http://exopolitics.org/Study-Paper-
5.htm Also in Michael E. Salla, *Exopolitics: Political Implications of the Extraterrestrial Presence*
(forthcoming Dandelion Books, 2004).

[26] See Richard Boylan, "Quotations from Chairman Wolfe," http://drboylan.com/wolfqut2.html

[27] See Richard Boylan, "Quotations from Chairman Wolfe," http://drboylan.com/wolfqut2.html

[28] "Billy Goodman Interview with Bob Lazar: Partial transcript, *Billy Goodman Happening*
(December 20, 1989), available online at: http://www.swa-home.de/lazar3.htm See also "George
Knapp Interview with Bob Lazar,' *On the Record, KLAS-TV*, (December 9, 1989). Transcript available
online at: http://www.swa-home.de/lazar2.htm

[29] Interviews with Castello are published as chapters 11 & 27, in The *Dulce Wars*, Available online
at http://www.all-natural.com/dulce-11.html and
http://www.thewatcherfiles.com/dulce/chapter27.htm . See also William Hamilton *Cosmic Top
Secret.* An extract is available online at: http://www.crowdedskies.com/files/down/cog.html

[30] See Branton, The Dulce Wars, ch 27. Available online at
http://eaglenet.enochgraphics.com/dulce/ & http://www.thewatcherfiles.com/dulce/chapter27.htm
See also William Hamilton *Cosmic Top Secret*. An extract is available online at:
http://www.crowdedskies.com/files/down/cog.html

[31] For discussion of the evolution of the system whereby corporations played a primary role in
servicing military contracts vis-à-vis ET projects, see Michael Salla, Exopolitics: Political
Implications of the Extraterrestrial Presence (forthcoming Dandelion Press, 2004), ch 2. Published
also as Study Paper #5, www.exopolitics.org

[32] See Branton, Dulce, chapter 11, Available online at http://www.all-natural.com/dulce-11.html &
http://eaglenet.enochgraphics.com/dulce/

[33] Branton, Dulce, chapter 11, Available online at http://www.all-natural.com/dulce-11.html &
http://eaglenet.enochgraphics.com/dulce/

[34] For a detailed discussion of US government sponsored experiments in mind control, see Helmut
Lammer & Marion Lammer, *Milabs: Military Mind Control & Alien Abductions* (Illuminet Press, 1999).

[35] See Preston Nichols, *Montauk Project: Experiments in Time* (Sky Books, 1999); Al Bielak and
Brad Steiger, *The Philadelphia Experiment and Other UFO Conspiracies* (Innerlight Publications,
1991); Stewart Swerdlow, *Montauk: The Alien Connection* (Expansions Publishing Co. 2002); Wade
Gordon, *The Brookhaven Connection* (Sky Books, 2001). For an online interview with Al Bielak, go to
http://psychicspy.com/montauk1.html

[36] Branton, Dulce, chapter 11, Available online at http://www.all-natural.com/dulce-11.html &
http://eaglenet.enochgraphics.com/dulce/

[37] Branton, Dulce, chapter 11, Available online at http://www.all-natural.com/dulce-11.html &
http://eaglenet.enochgraphics.com/dulce/

[38] Branton, Dulce, chapter 11, Available online at http://www.all-natural.com/dulce-11.html &
http://eaglenet.enochgraphics.com/dulce/

[39] Branton, Dulce, chapter 11, Available online at http://www.all-natural.com/dulce-11.html &
http://eaglenet.enochgraphics.com/dulce/

[40] Branton, Dulce, chapter 11, Available online at http://www.all-natural.com/dulce-11.html &
http://eaglenet.enochgraphics.com/dulce/

[41] Branton, Dulce, chapter 11, Available online at http://www.all-natural.com/dulce-11.html &
http://eaglenet.enochgraphics.com/dulce/

[42] Branton, Dulce, chapter 11, Available online at http://www.all-natural.com/dulce-11.html &
http://eaglenet.enochgraphics.com/dulce/

[43] See Richard Boylan, "Official Within MJ-12 UFO-Secrecy Management Group Reveals Insider
Secrets," http://www.drboylan.com/wolfdoc2.html

[44] Phillip Corso, *The Day After Roswell* (Pocket Books, 1997) 292.

[45] See William Cooper, "Origin, Identity and Purpose of MJ-12,"
http://www.geocities.com/area51/shadowlands/6583/maji007.html ; See also Neruda Interview #1,
http://www.wingmakers.com ; Boylan gives a more extensive coverage of events surrounding the
Treaty signing in "Extraterrestrial Base On Earth, Sanctioned By Officials Since 1954,"
http://drboylan.com/basespst2.html

[46] Phil Schneider, MUFON Conference Presentation, 1995, available online at:
http://www.ufocoverup-conspiracy.com/20.htm

[47] An advocate of this view is William Cooper, *Behold a Pale Horse* (Light Technology Publishing,
1991) 222. For another critical review of evidence surrounding Dulce, see Loy Lawhon, "Dulce,"
About.com, available online at: http://ufos.about.com/library/weekly/aa112597.htm?terms=Dulce

[48] Schneider's 1995 lecture is available at a number of websites and is titled, "A Lecture by Phil Schneider – May, 1995" One site is
http://www.ufoarea.bravepages.com/conspiracy_schneider_lecture.html

[49] "A Lecture by Phil Schneider – May, 1995," available online at:
http://www.ufoarea.bravepages.com/conspiracy_schneider_lecture.html

[50] Schneider's 1995 lecture is available at a number of websites and is titled, "A Lecture by Phil Schneider – May, 1995" One site is
http://www.ufoarea.bravepages.com/conspiracy_schneider_lecture.html

[51] Cynthia Drayer, "The Death of Philip Schneider, January 17, 1996," available online at:
http://www.worldofthestrange.com/modules.php?name=Newsletters&op=ViewItems&vid=69 For discussion of Schneider's whistleblower testimony, see "Tribute to Phil Schneider," available online at: http://www.apfn.org/apfn/philip.htm

[52] Richard Boylan, "Official Within MJ-12 UFO-Secrecy Management Group Reveals Insider Secrets," http://drboylan.com/wolfdoc2.html

[53] Richard Boylan, "Quotations from Chairman Wolf," quoted online at:
http://www.drboylan.com/wolfqut2.html

[54] "Billy Goodman Interview with Bob Lazar: Partial transcript, *Billy Goodman Happening* (December 20, 1989), available online at: http://www.swa-home.de/lazar3.htm

[55] Jim Marrs, *Alien Agenda* (HarperPaperbacks, 1998) 270-71

[56] For discussion of Bennewitz's physical evidence, see Chris Lambright, "Paul Bennewitz, electronic recordings, and films of "aerial objects', Part 3" (June, 2003) available online at http://www.cufon.org/contributors/chrisl/PB/bennewi3.htm

[57] See Chris Lambright, "Paul Bennewitz, electronic recordings, and films of "aerial objects', Part 3" (June, 2003) available online at http://www.cufon.org/contributors/chrisl/PB/bennewi3.htm

[58] For history of efforts to provide conclusive evidence of the UFO history, see Richard Dolan, *UFOs and the National Security State*.

[59] For lack of physical geological features to support the existence of Dulce, see Glen Campbell, "A Field Trip to Dulce, New Mexico," available online at:
http://ufos.about.com/gi/dynamic/offsite.htm?site=http://www.ufomind.com/area51/list/1997/nov/a04%2D001.shtml . See also Roy Lawhon, "Dulce!," available online at:
http://ufos.about.com/library/weekly/aa112597.htm &

[60] See Hamilton, *Cosmic Top Secret: America's Secret Ufo Program*, an extract is available online at:
http://www.crowdedskies.com/files/down/cog.html

[61] See Branton, *Dulce Wars*, ch 5, available online at:
http://eaglenet.enochgraphics.com/dulce/G-HAYAKO.html

[62] For discussion of Maglev transportation and the global underground system, see Richard Sauder, *Underwater and Underground Bases* (Adventures Unlimited Press, 2001). Sauder has a website at: http://www.sauderzone.com

[63] Roy Lawhon, "Dulce!," available online at: http://ufos.about.com/library/weekly/aa112597.htm

[64] Roy Lawhon, "Dulce!," available online at: http://ufos.about.com/library/weekly/aa112597.htm

[65] Roy Lawhon, "Dulce!," available online at: http://ufos.about.com/library/weekly/aa112597.htm

[66] Roy Lawhon, "Dulce!," available online at: http://ufos.about.com/library/weekly/aa112597.htm

[67] See "Tribute to Phil Schneider," available online at: http://www.apfn.org/apfn/philip.htm

[68] For documents suggesting he was murdered, see "Tribute to Phil Schneider," available online at: http://www.apfn.org/apfn/philip.htm

[69] See Chris Lambright, "Paul Bennewitz, electronic recordings, and films of 'aerial objects', Part 3" (June, 2003) available online at http://www.cufon.org/contributors/chrisl/PB/bennewi3.htm

[70] See resignation letter of MUFON member of Richard Hall, Letter to Walter H. Andrus, Jr. (March 18, 1989). Cited online at: http://www.worldofthestrange.com/modules.php?name=Documents&op=ViewItems&vid=143

[71] See Chris Lambright, "Paul Bennewitz, electronic recordings, and films of 'aerial objects', Part 3" (June, 2003) available online at http://www.cufon.org/contributors/chrisl/PB/bennewi3.htm

[72] For an overview of the role of disinformation, see a report by a Senate Commission convened to discuss secrecy, *Report of the Commission on Protecting and Reducing Government Secrecy: 1997*. Available online at: http://www.access.gpo.gov/congress/commissions/secrecy/index.html

[73] See "A Lecture by Phil Schneider – May, 1995," available online at: http://www.ufoarea.bravepages.com/conspiracy_schneider_lecture.html . Later in the same interview, Schneider refers to 1.3 trillion every two years thereby creating some confusion over his true estimate.

[74] For Schneider's discussion of the MagLev underground rail system, see "A Lecture by Phil Schneider – May, 1995," available online at: http://www.ufoarea.bravepages.com/conspiracy_schneider_lecture.html. See also Branton, Dulce Wars, ch 11. Available online at http://www.all-natural.com/dulce-11.html ..

[75] Branton, Dulce, chapter 11, Available online at http://www.all-natural.com/dulce-11.html

[76] For a list of underground US military bases see Richard Sauder, *Underground Bases and Tunnels: What Is the Government Trying to Hide?* (Adventures Unlimited Press, 1996). For discussion of Maglev transportation and the global underground system, see Richard Sauder, *Underwater and Underground Bases* (Adventures Unlimited Press, 2001). Sauder has a website at: http://www.sauderzone.com

[77] Catherine Austin Fitts, "The $64 Question: What's Up With the Black Budget? – The Real Deal," *Scoop: UQ Wire* (23 September, 2002). Available online at: http://www.scoop.co.nz/mason/stories/HL0209/S00126.htm . Fitts has a website with a number of resources describing how more than a trillion dollars are annually unaccounted for in a number of government agencies.

[78] David K. Steensma,. "Agency Wide Financial Statements. The Department of Defence Audit Opinion." (February 26, 2002) The Report can be viewed online at: http://www.dodig.osd.mil/Audit/reports/fy02/02-055.pdf

[79] Kelly Patricia O'Meara, "Rumsfeld Inherits Financial Mess," *Insight on the News* (Aug. 10, 2001). Available online at:

http://www.insightmag.com/main.cfm?include=detail&storyid=139530 . Another media report on the 1.1 trillion missing dollars is Tom Abate, Military waste under fire $1 trillion missing – Bush plan targets Pentagon accounting, San Francisco Chronicle (May 18, 2003. Available online at: http://www.ratical.org/ratville/CAH/DODtrillions.html#p6

[80] For an overview of the classification system, see *Report of the Commission on Protecting and Reducing Government Secrecy: 1997*. Available online at: http://www.access.gpo.gov/congress/commissions/secrecy/index.html

[81] *Report of the Commission on Protecting and Reducing Government Secrecy: 1997*. Available online at: http://www.access.gpo.gov/congress/commissions/secrecy/index.html

[82] *Report of the Commission on Protecting and Reducing Government Secrecy, 26*. Available online at: http://www.access.gpo.gov/congress/commissions/secrecy/index.html

[83] Office of the Press Secretary, "White House Press Release: Classified National Security Information," *Executive Order #12958* (April 17, 1995) Section 4.4. Available online at: http://foia.state.gov/eo12958/part4.asp#rtt

[84] *Executive Order #12958* (April 17, 1995). Available online at: http://foia.state.gov/eo12958/part4.asp#rtt

[85] See, Deputy Secretary of Defense, "Special Access Program Oversight Committee," *Information Bulletin: November 1994.* Available online at: http://www.fas.org/sgp/othergov/sapoc.html . For the intelligence community oversight body, see Director of Central Intelligence, "Controlled Access Program Oversight Committee," *Directive 3: 29* (June 1995) http://www.fas.org/irp/offdocs/dcid3-29.html .

[86] *Report of the Commission on Protecting and Reducing Government Secrecy, 26.* Available online at: http://www.access.gpo.gov/congress/commissions/secrecy/index.html

[87] For discussion of the erosion of Executive oversight in ET/UFO issues, see Study Paper #4.

[88] See US Constitution, Section 2, article 2.

[89] See Michael Salla, "Political Management of the Extraterrestrial Presence – The Challenge to Democracy and Liberty in America." *Exopolitics.Org*, July 4, 2003. Available online at: http://exopolitics.org/Study-Paper-5.htm Also in Michael E. Salla, *Exopolitics: Political Implications of the Extraterrestrial Presence* (forthcoming Dandelion Books, 2004).

[90] See Michael Salla, "Political Management of the Extraterrestrial Presence – The Challenge to Democracy and Liberty in America." *Exopolitics.Org*, July 4, 2003. Available online at: http://exopolitics.org/Study-Paper-5.htm Also in Michael E. Salla, *Exopolitics: Political Implications of the Extraterrestrial Presence* (forthcoming Dandelion Books, 2004).

[91] This range is estimated from figures provided in the following article, Bill Sweetman, "In search of the Pentagon's billion dollar hidden budgets - how the US keeps its R&D spending under wraps," *Jane's*, 5/01/2000, available online at:http://www.janes.com/defence/news/jidr/jidr000105_01_n.shtml

[92] Kelly Patricia O'Meara, "Government Fails Fiscal-Fitness Test," *Insight on the News* (April 29, 2002). Available online at: http://www.insightmag.com/news/246188.html

[93] See Catherine Fitts, "The Missing Money: Why the Citizens of Tennessee Are Working Harder & Getting Less," Available online at: http://www.scoop.co.nz/mason/stories/HL0207/S00031.htm#a

[94] See Bill Sweetman, "In search of the Pentagon's billion dollar hidden budgets;" "A Lecture by Phil Schneider – May, 1995," available online at: http://www.ufoarea.bravepages.com/conspiracy_schneider_lecture.html ; & John Maynard, "From Disinformation to Disclosure," *Surfing the Apocalypse*, available online at: http://www.surfingtheapocalypse.com/maynard.html

[95] See interview with John Maynard, "From Disinformation to Disclosure," *Surfing the Apocalypse*, available online at: http://www.surfingtheapocalypse.com/maynard.html

[96] "George Knapp Interview with Bob Lazar,' *On the Record*, KLAS-TV, (December 9, 1989). Transcript available online at: http://www.swa-home.de/lazar2.htm

[97] An analysis of how ET affairs are politically managed in the US, see Study Paper #5.

[98] For discussion of the role played by the NSC, see Michael Salla, "Political Management of the Extraterrestrial Presence – The Challenge to Democracy and Liberty in America." *Exopolitics.Org*, July 4, 2003. Available online at: http://exopolitics.org/Study-Paper-5.htm Also in Michael E. Salla, *Exopolitics: Political Implications of the Extraterrestrial Presence* (forthcoming Dandelion Books, 2004).

[99] See "Disclosure Pattern – 1977," available online at: http://www.presidentialufo.8m.com/disclosure_1977.htm

[100] See Alex Ioshpe, Close Encounters of the Third Kind, available online at:
http://www.geocities.com/Hollywood/Studio/3469/making_enc.html

[101] See Dorothy Shea, *The South African Truth Commission: The Politics of Reconciliation* (United States Institute of Peace, 2000)

[102] Information on available legal services for whistleblowers can be found at www.whistleblower.org or at www.whistleblowers.com. For more information please contact the author. All communications will be treated as confidential. The author can be reached by email at: drsalla@exopolitics.org or by regular mail Dr Michael Salla, 1718 M St., NW., PMB #354, Washington DC 20036

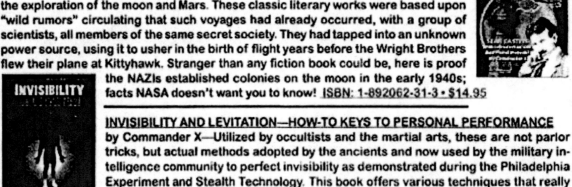

CPSIA information can be obtained at www.ICGtesting.com
Printed in the USA
BVOW06s1851031114

373486BV00009B/130/P